GW01458382

Helion & Company Limited
Unit 8 Amherst Business Centre
Budbrooke Road
Warwick
CV34 5WE
England
Tel. 01926 499 619
Email: info@helion.co.uk
Website: www.helion.co.uk
Twitter: @helionbooks
https://helionbooks.wordpress.com/

Published by Helion & Company 2026
Text © Gustavo Marón 2025
Illustrations © as credited
Colour profiles © Luca Canossa and Tom Cooper 2025
Maps drawn by b.b.h. illustrations © Helion & Company 2025

Front cover illustration by Renato Dalmaso © Helion & Company 2025

Designed and typeset by Mach 3 Solutions (www.mach3solutions.co.uk)
Cover design Paul Hewitt, Battlefield Design (www.battlefield-design.co.uk)

ISBN: 978-1-804519-35-6

British Library Cataloguing-in-Publication Data
A catalogue record for this book is available from the British Library

We always welcome receiving book proposals from prospective authors.

CONTENTS

Note: In order to simplify the use of this book, all names, locations and geographic designations are as provided in *The Times World Atlas*, or other traditionally accepted major sources of reference, as of the time of described events.

ABBREVIATIONS AND ACRONYMS

AC-327311	Argentine civil aircraft registration AC-327311 (as cited in the text).
ADC	Air Defense Command (US Air Force major command responsible for air defence).
AEDS	Atomic Energy Detection System (US global nuclear explosion detection network).
AFB	Air Force Base.
AFCRC	Air Force Cambridge Research Center (USAF research organisation).
AFCRL	Air Force Cambridge Research Laboratories (successor to AFCRC).
AFMSW-1	Air Force Materiel Special Weapons-1 (USAF special weapons support unit).
AFOAT	Air Force Office of Atomic Energy (USAF office overseeing atomic energy matters).
AFOAT-1	Air Force Office of Atomic Energy-1 (unit operating the early Atomic Energy Detection System).
AFSWP	Armed Forces Special Weapons Project (US joint nuclear weapons organisation).
AFTAC	Air Force Technical Applications Center (USAF Organisation for nuclear test monitoring).
AGN	Aerojet General Nucleonics (US nuclear engineering company).
AIR-2	AIR-2 Genie (US unguided nuclear air-to-air rocket).
AME	Angle/Automatic Measurement Equipment (specialised measurement kit referenced in the text; precise expansion context-specific).
AMQ-2	AN/AMQ-2 aerograph / meteorological recorder (airborne meteorological measuring equipment).
AMT	AN/AMT series radiosonde transmitter (airborne meteorological transmitting equipment).
AN	Army–Navy equipment designation prefix in US military nomenclature.
AN-CPN4	AN/CPN-4 ground-controlled approach radar facility.
APN	AN/APN-series airborne navigation or radar equipment (e.g., LORAN, radar altimeters).
AQUATONE	Project AQUATONE (CIA codename for development of the U-2 reconnaissance aircraft).
ARA	Armada de la República Argentina (Argentine Navy).
ARGUS	Operation ARGUS (1958 high-altitude nuclear test series in the South Atlantic).
ASHCAN	Project ASHCAN (Upper Atmosphere Monitoring Program sampling stratospheric nuclear debris from tests).
BAAA	Bureau of Aircraft Accidents Archives (online database of aviation accidents).
BALD	Operation BALD (codename referenced in the text; nuclear detection/intelligence project; precise details limited in open sources).
BAPI	BAPI – Argentine Navy identifier for Base Aeronaval Punta Indio.
BBC	British Broadcasting Corporation.
BLUENOSE	Project/Operation BLUENOSE (codename for high-latitude/meteorological or sampling operations; context-specific).
BRAVO	Castle BRAVO (US thermonuclear test, Bikini Atoll, 1 March 1954).
BROILER	Shot BROILER (Operation GREENHOUSE nuclear test).

BW	BW – commonly used for biological warfare; used contextually that way in the manuscript.
CASTLE	Operation CASTLE (US 1954 Pacific thermonuclear test series).
CIA	Central Intelligence Agency (United States).
CIA-USAF	CIA–USAF joint management/operations (e.g., AQUATONE/U-2 programs).
CL-282	Lockheed CL-282 (design study precursor to the U-2).
CNEA	Comisión Nacional de Energía Atómica (Argentina's National Atomic Energy Commission).
COZI	COZI – civil aircraft registration (e.g., G-COZI) cited illustratively.
CROWFLIGHT	Project CROWFLIGHT (AFTAC U-2 air sampling project measuring gases from foreign nuclear production).
CV-42	USS Franklin D. Roosevelt (CV-42), US Navy aircraft carrier.
DASA	Defense Atomic Support Agency (US Department of Defense nuclear support agency).
DC-3	Douglas DC-3 transport aircraft.
DC-4	Douglas DC-4 transport aircraft.
DNEA	Dirección Nacional de Energía Atómica (early Argentine atomic energy body, predecessor to CNEA).
FAI	Fédération Aéronautique Internationale (World Air Sports Federation).
FEAF	Far East Air Forces (USAF command in the Pacific).
FITZWILLIAM	Project FITZWILLIAM (USAF AFMSW-1 project related to nuclear detection activities).
GABRIEL	Project GABRIEL (US fallout hazard study that led to Project SUNSHINE).
GCA	Ground-Controlled Approach (radar guidance for aircraft landings).
GREENHOUSE	Operation GREENHOUSE (US Enewetak nuclear test series, 1951).
HALFMOON	Project HALFMOON (codename associated with early nuclear detection planning; context-specific).
HARDTACK	Operation HARDTACK (US Pacific nuclear test series, 1958).
HASP	High Altitude Sampling Program (HASP) – nuclear debris sampling project.
HU-16B	Grumman HU-16B Albatross amphibious aircraft.
IAGS	Inter-American Geodetic Survey.
ICBM	Intercontinental Ballistic Missile.
IM-99	IM-99 BOMARC (US long-range surface-to-air missile).
JP-4	JP-4 (NATO F-40) aviation turbine fuel.
JP-TS	JP-TS (high-temperature jet fuel specification).
JPL	Jet Propulsion Laboratory.
KC	KC – tanker aircraft prefix (e.g., KC-97, KC-135).
KC-125	KC-125 – proposed tanker designation mentioned in sources; not adopted operationally.
KC-135	Boeing KC-135 Stratotanker.
KC-135A	Boeing KC-135A Stratotanker variant.
KC-97	Boeing KC-97 Stratofreighter tanker.
KC-97G	KC-97G Stratofreighter tanker variant.
LANDSAT	LANDSAT (US Earth-observation satellite programme).
LASL	Los Alamos Scientific Laboratory.

LF-1A — LF-1A – aircraft designation (trainer/utility; see context in manuscript).

LLNL — Lawrence Livermore National Laboratory.

LM — Lockheed Missiles / Lockheed Martin (context-dependent).

LO — LO – "low observable" or local/line office; context-dependent.

LONG — LONG – longitude, as used in positional data.

LRD — LRD – long-range detection/detector (as used for nuclear monitoring).

MOGUL — Project MOGUL (US balloon project to detect Soviet nuclear tests).

MSQ-1A — AN/MSQ-1A radar bomb-scoring / guidance system.

NACA — National Advisory Committee for Aeronautics (predecessor to NASA).

NARA — National Archives and Records Administration (US).

NASA — National Aeronautics and Space Administration (US).

NATO — North Atlantic Treaty Organisation.

NW — NW – nuclear weapon(s), as commonly abbreviated.

OILSTONE — Project OILSTONE (USAF–CIA framework supporting AQUATONE/U-2 operations).

OL — OL – Operating Location (USAF term for detached unit sites).

PANAGRA — Pan American-Grace Airways (US airline in Latin America).

PGM — PGM – Precision Guided Munition / missile designation prefix (context-specific).

PGM-17 — PGM-17 Thor (US intermediate-range ballistic missile).

PLUMBBOB — Operation PLUMBBOB (US Nevada nuclear test series, 1957).

QB-17 — QB-17 (drone conversion of the Boeing B-17 Flying Fortress).

RAF — Royal Air Force (United Kingdom).

RAINBARREL — Project RAINBARREL (US programme monitoring fallout via rainwater sampling).

RAND — RAND Corporation (US research and analysis Organisation).

RAOB — Radiosonde Observation.

RAWIN — Radar wind (upper-air wind measurement using radar-tracked balloons).

RB — RB – reconnaissance bomber (US aircraft designation prefix).

RB-29 — RB-29 reconnaissance version of the Boeing B-29.

RB-29A — RB-29A reconnaissance version of the B-29.

RB-52B — RB-52B reconnaissance version of the B-52 Stratofortress.

RB-57 — RB-57 reconnaissance version of the B-57 Canberra.

RB-57D — RB-57D high-altitude reconnaissance version of the B-57.

RDS-1 — RDS-1 "First Lightning" – first Soviet atomic bomb test (1949).

REDWING — Operation REDWING (US Pacific nuclear test series, 1956).

RNA — Ribonucleic Acid.

RS-50 — RS-50 – rocket/system designation; details context-specific.

SA-16 — SA-16 Albatross (US designation for HU-16 amphibious aircraft).

SA-54 — SA-54 – surface-to-air system designation; context-specific.

SAC — Strategic Air Command (USAF major command).

SANDSTONE — Operation SANDSTONE (US Enewetak nuclear test series, 1948).

SC-54 — SC-54 – US Navy/USCG designation for C-54 transport.

SC-54D — SC-54D – variant of SC-54.

SCR — Signal Corps Radio (US Army communications equipment prefix).

SCR-718 — SCR-718 airborne radar altimeter/ navigation set.

SKYLAB — Skylab (US space station).

SM-65A — SM-65A Atlas (early Atlas ICBM variant).

SNAPPER — Operation SNAPPPER (US Nevada nuclear test series, 1952).

SS-3 — SS-3 "Shyster" (NATO designation for Soviet R-5M missile).

SSR — Secondary Surveillance Radar.

SUNSHINE — Project SUNSHINE (US study of global fallout and strontium-90 in humans).

TAC — Tactical Air Command (USAF major command).

TASS — TASS (Soviet Telegraph Agency).

TEAPOT — Operation TEAPOT (US Nevada nuclear test series, 1955).

TF-100 — TF-100 – two-seat trainer version of the F-100 Super Sabre.

TF-100C — TF-100C – trainer variant of the F-100C.

TR-737 — TR-737 – civil aircraft registration (as cited with Chuck Yeager in the text).

TUMBLER — Operation TUMBLER (nuclear tests, later incorporated in TUMBLER–SNAPPER).

UC-45 — UC-45 (military Beechcraft Model 18 liaison/ utility aircraft).

UC-45B — UC-45B variant of the UC-45.

UCRI — Unión Cívica Radical Intransigente (Intransigent Radical Civic Union, Argentine political party).

UPSHOT-KNOTHOLE — Operation UPSHOT–KNOTHOLE (US Nevada nuclear test series, 1953).

USAAF — United States Army Air Forces (pre-1947).

USAEC — United States Atomic Energy Commission.

USAF — United States Air Force.

USAF-CIA — USAF–CIA joint collaboration (e.g., AQUATONE/U-2).

USAFE — United States Air Forces in Europe.

USAFHRA — USAF Historical Research Agency.

USBM — United States Bureau of Mines.

USGS — United States Geological Survey.

USIS — United States Information Service.

USN — United States Navy.

USS — United States Ship (US Navy vessel prefix).

WADC — Wright Air Development Center (USAF R&D command at Wright-Patterson AFB).

WB — WB – weather reconnaissance aircraft prefix.

WB-29 — WB-29 weather reconnaissance version of the B-29.

WB-29A — WB-29A weather reconnaissance version of the B-29.

WRSP-1 — 1st Weather Reconnaissance Squadron, Provisional.

WU — Weather Unit (used in cover designations such as WU-2).

WU-2 — Weather U-2 (cover designation for U-2 aircraft).

WU-2A — Weather U-2A (cover designation for U-2A aircraft).

XF-104 — Lockheed XF-104 (F-104 Starfighter prototype).

INTRODUCTION

This book owes its title to the fact that it is indeed made of flashes. I am not only talking about the flashes caused by the nuclear explosions whose radioactive remains that were hunted by the United States' spy planes based in Argentina between 1958 and 1974, but rather the sporadic flashes of information that emerged during more than 20 years of investigation; the documents, photographs and testimonies that I was collecting on the air operations of the Cold War in Argentina. This book details both those operations and the context and circumstances that led to their being kept secret, even outside the knowledge of the political and military authorities of our country.

The purpose of this work is to tear the veil of silence and concealment that has wrapped US military activities in our country for decades to make known to the Argentine public aspects of our contemporary history unknown until today, specifically the years of the Cold War. This can serve to reflect on our recent past and, even more, on the safeguards that Argentina should assume in the future in the case of hosting bases or activities of military interest from other countries in its vast territory.

The facts and circumstances recounted in this work are practically contemporary with the creation of the United States Air Force (USAF) as an independent defence institution, which occurred in 1947. A few months later, in August 1948, the Air Force Office of Atomic Energy (AFOAT-1) was created in order to manage the so-called Atomic Energy Detection System (AEDS). The top-secret purpose of AFOAT-1 was to discover foreign atomic tests and detect other activities related to nuclear weapons, such as the collection of gases and radioactive microparticles that would make it possible to deduce the industrial capabilities, the technological level and the size of the arsenal of the countries concerned; initially the Soviet Union and, later, France and China.

AFOAT-1, later renamed Air Force Technical Applications Center (AFTAC), had an early triumph in discovering the first Soviet atomic test, conducted in secret on 29 August 1949 in the Semipalatinsk steppe, Kazakhstan SSR. The radioactive debris released into the atmosphere was detected by a specially modified Boeing WB-29 Superfortress flying, under weather investigation cover, between the US air bases at Misawa, Japan, and Eielson, Alaska. This allowed the Tracerlab Incorporated laboratory in Cambridge, Massachusetts to quickly confirm that the Soviet Union had achieved nuclear capability. Based on the advice of the newly created Central Intelligence Agency (CIA), on 23 September 1949, US President Harry S. Truman made the discovery public, which suddenly drew the veil of Soviet secrecy and forced his rival, Soviet Premier Josef Stalin, to acknowledge that his country had indeed carried out a successful first nuclear test.

Subsequently, this intelligence game was repeated countless times, providing accurate information to the highest executive levels of the US government, one more reason to keep secret the operations carried out by the meteorological planes that, it was publicly declared, were only conducting atmospheric research. The intelligence potential of AFOAT-1/AFTAC and its importance to the national security of the United States were such that both agencies always operated in absolute secrecy, to the point that their existence was not recognised until 1975, a year after the USAF stopped using its permanent base on Argentine territory.

Despite this official acknowledgment, much remains secret around AFOAT-1 and its successor, AFTAC, a shield to which USAF lawyers have contributed very efficiently, having refused to approve the declassification of their documents and even the preparation of an official history focused even on the first years of the unit's operation, those during which the first deployment of US spy planes to Argentina took place.

However, other United States federal agencies have released to the National Archives and Records Administration (NARA) documentation that alludes to, or is linked to, AFOAT-1/AFTAC, which made it possible to trace the first years of long-range nuclear detection, a ultra-secret activity carried out globally, including in Argentina, with an astonishing degree of precision. Although the discovery of these documents was important, they only represented flashes in the dark, isolated notes of a symphony that was masterfully performed for 15 years in our country without anyone being able to hear it.[1]

During their early years of existence, AFOAT-1 and AFTAC developed and deployed a variety of nuclear activity detection systems, including acoustic, seismic, and radiological sensors, to discover foreign tests and monitor nuclear industrial activities outside the United States, specifically the production of fissile materials such as plutonium and enriched uranium. For methodological reasons, in this work I will only deal with air detection operations carried out in and from air bases or Argentine airspace under various covers or screens (for example, meteorological research flights). It will be left to other researchers to address the acoustic, seismic and radiological detections carried out in secret from our national territory. It is noteworthy that espionage was not always carried out with spies, but with ultra-sensitive detection instruments.[2]

Needless to say, this investigation has been extremely difficult. By itself, the armed forces are discreet in terms of their activities, largely to prevent snooping by foreign intelligence services, so it was not expected that the USAF would be loquacious regarding its activities in our country, much less in the context of the Cold War between the United States and the Soviet Union; and even less so in a Latin American country that, by 1960, was already suspected signs of infiltration by left-wing subversive elements, that is, pro-Soviet communists.

To this secrecy, that I could describe as natural and typical of the military, it must be added that the different USAF units that operated permanently in Argentina were not acting in their own territory, so their level of closure was even greater. As if the above were not enough, the operations they were carrying out had been classified as Top Secret and Top Secret Umbra, so their officers took pains not to leave a single trace, indication or record behind. Such was the secrecy that not even the Argentine Air Force could know in depth what was happening at the Ezeiza and Mendoza airports, both under its jurisdiction. All the documents generated by the USAF during its passage through Argentina were classified as secret. On the covers or first pages of documents it was clarified:

> This material contains information that affects the national defense of the United States in the sense indicated in the Espionage Laws, Title 18, United States Code, Sections 793 and 794. The transmission or Disclosure of this information in any way to an unauthorised person is prohibited by law. Special handling of the document is required. Not revealable to foreigners. The information contained in this document will not be disclosed to foreigners or their representatives.[3]

The zeal around the secret missions carried out by the USAF in Argentina, and around the documents that recorded them, remains intact even today, more than 40 years after the definitive departure of the spy planes from our territory and more than 20 years after the end of the Cold War, when all terms of safeguarding, confidentiality or secrecy have expired. Perhaps an example will suffice to illustrate this to the reader. In conducting this investigation, I found dozens of documents neatly archived at the USAF Historical Research Agency (USAFHRA) located at Maxwell Air Force Base, Alabama. When requesting a copy of these documents, strangely I was informed that the query should be addressed to the Air Force Office of Public Affairs since the 'USAFHRA was not the appropriate agency to release these documents to the public'.

When asked why historical documents on file with the USAF's historical research agency were not able to be accessed, I was told that 'government documents are not automatically cleared for public release because they are not marked as classified'. I immediately transferred the request for access to information to the department indicated, which, of course, never responded. In practical terms, USAF historical documents are not released to the public (much less foreigners) if they were originally classified as secret.

Given the unprecedented and sensitive nature of the issues addressed in this book, I have taken care to cite all the bibliographical and documentary sources to which I have had access, so that other authors can exploit them in the course of future research. Much more remains to be discovered than what I have found, since this work has focused only on air operations. I leave to other researchers the land operations (mainly intelligence) and, above all, the naval activities deployed in Argentina by the superpowers that waged the Cold War.

I would never have been able to produce this work alone. I was able to do it thanks to the support and collaboration of many friends, historians, researchers, and photographers, to whom I owe a debt of gratitude that I hope to repay starting from this paragraph. Go,

then, our words of gratitude to those who did not hesitate to give us a hand throughout these hard years of research. They were, in strict alphabetical order: Carlos Abella, José Abelardo Agrusti, Eduardo Amores Oliver, Marcel Antonisse, Carlos Ay, Joe Bachrach, Atilio Baldini, Fernando Benedetto, Hugo Berreta, René-Paul Bonnet, Jean Henry Bouffard, Sergio Bontti, Linda Ríos Bromley, Tim Brown, Joe Bruch, Vladimiro Cettolo, Juan Carlos Cicalesi, Cristina Cosci, Alfonso Cuadrado Merino, Analía Cuozzo, Gustavo Roberto D'Antiochia, Loomis Dean, Alfred Eisenstaedt, Mercedes Esquivel de Cocca, Kurt Finger, Eduardo Oscar Fraire, Pablo Fraire, José Luis Giani, Lucas Giani, Dan Hagedorn, Francisco Halbritter, Paul-J. Han, Jacob Harris, Fernando Jara, Maurice Jarnoux, Russell Juzdan, Peter Kelly, Charles Kern, Jeff Kew, Robert Knudsen, Art LeBrun, Robert Leifer, Aníbal Leiva, Jorge Leonardi, Carlos Jesús Maita, Atilio Enzo Marino, John Martin, Marcelo Wilfredo Miranda, Pedro Notti, Jorge Félix Núñez Padín, Pablo Luciano Potenze, Clever Refosco, Marina Rieznik, Hugo Sabatini, Joseph T. Page, Miguel Alejandro Sánchez Peña, Robert A. Scholefield, Robert Sullivan, George Sutton, Hernán Tejeda, Emmanuel Tula , Marialis Valencia, Roy Wagner, Robin A. Walker, Larry Weiler and Christian Zambruno, author of the cover illustration and the profiles that make up the colour section.

Two people deserve a special mention, for the generosity of their contributions and the accompaniment produced in the most difficult moments of the investigation. They are Vladimiro Cettolo and Carlos Ay, old friends with whom I took different paths (they on the Military Aviation side, I on the Civil Aviation side), but who did not hesitate to selflessly offer me their support when our paths crossed again.

I dedicate this book to my wife, Carina Cocuelle, and to our daughter Mercedes Marón.

Gustavo Maron
Mendoza, Argentina, 31 January 2023

1

THE RARE GASES OF LUIS WALTER ÁLVAREZ (1945-1946)

Many of us children in the west grew up reading the fantastic adventures of Superman in comics, which we later saw turned into movies. The character, a fictional superhero appearing in DC Comics publications, had been created in 1933 by American writer Jerry Siegel and Canadian artist Joe Shuster. Superman was invincible, nothing could beat him, but he had a weak point: his extraordinary powers were compromised by kryptonite, a bright green rock from his home planet, Krypton. Kryptonite, of course, was a product of the imagination. But something was real about it because Jerry Siegel took his name from something that did exist, krypton, a real chemical element that was not solid, but gaseous, an odourless and tasteless gas with little reactivity, characterised by a spectrum of very bright green and red-orange. Krypton was not toxic or dangerous, nor did it interact with other elements, making it a noble or inert gas.

Krypton was also a very difficult gas to obtain, as reflected in its name, which came from the Greek adjective kryptos, which means hidden. It was discovered in 1898 by British chemists William Ramsay and Morris William Travers while they liquefied air and subjected it

to a process of fractional distillation to see what chemical elements were hidden inside. Almost by accident, they found krypton in the residue left by liquid air just above its boiling point. After repeating the process several times, they also found another strange gas, which for that very reason they named xenon, from the Greek xenos, which means strange. For these discoveries, William Ramsay received the Nobel Prize in Chemistry in 1904.

Krypton and xenon could have remained two more elements on the periodic table, noble and inert, had it not been for the fact that in 1943, in the midst of the Second World War, a brilliant 33-year-old experimental physicist, Luis Walter Álvarez, discovered that its radioactive isotopes krypton-85 and xenon-133 were produced in nuclear tests during the nuclear fission of uranium and plutonium. Consequently, its detection in the air could serve to show if and where the scientists of Nazi Germany were producing atomic weapons, information of great importance for the United States government, which, at that time, was determined to win in the European and Asia-Pacific theatres.

Álvarez's discovery was not accidental, but the consequence of the investigations he was carrying out at the University of Chicago within the team led by Enrico Fermi (Nobel Prize in Physics in 1938), who, at the same time, was an integral part of a major scientific and technological effort, the Manhattan Project led by Julius Robert Oppenheimer with the purpose of building the world's first atomic bomb, a devastating weapon that was expected to end the war with Germany, Japan or both at the same time. The military chief of the Manhattan Project, General Leslie Groves, asked Alvarez to think about how the United States could find out if the Germans were operating nuclear reactors and, if so, where those reactors were so that they could destroy them and take Germany out of the nuclear race. Luis Álvarez suggested that an airplane could carry a filter system that would allow the detection of the radioactive gases that the German reactors must be producing, particularly the isotopes xenon-133 and krypton-85. If there was no isotope record, that would mean the reactors did not exist. If there were records, not only was the relevant industrial capacity of the enemy confirmed, but the place where that technology was being developed could be easily inferred.

Based on Alvarez's deductions and calculations, several specially equipped US military aircraft flew over Germany in 1943 and 1944. To everyone's surprise, the onboard recorders detected no radioactive xenon, leading to the conclusion that Nazi scientists had not built still a reactor capable of producing fissile material to achieve an atomic chain reaction. This information was vital to the Manhattan Project, as it allowed the conclusion that Germany, its most technologically advanced competitor, was out of the race. For Álvarez, the discovery added to the long list of technological advances that he had developed in previous years and gave him notable prestige within the group of scientists of which he was a part. For that reason, he was one of the few chosen to work directly on the first test atomic bomb that was already being secretly built at the Los Alamos Atomic Physics Laboratory in New Mexico.

Isologo of the Manhattan Project, the secret programme carried out by the United States government to build the super bomb that ended the Second World War. (USAEC)

Álvarez arrived at Los Alamos in the spring of 1944, much later than his other contemporaries, but he soon proved to be one of the most flexible and brilliant minds at the service of the Allied nuclear project. By then, work on the uranium bomb was well advanced, so he was assigned to design the plutonium bomb. Álvarez soon 'ised that the technique used to unleash the fission chain reaction

of uranium atoms, consisting of violently joining two subcritical masses using a kind of gun, would not work with a plutonium rod. The high level of spontaneous background neutrons would cause fission as soon as the two parts approached each other, so the heat and expansion would force the system to separate before enough energy had been released to generate an explosion, so the bomb would not be effective. For this reason, he decided to use a sphere of plutonium and compress it with explosives to make it into a much smaller and denser nucleus, which represented quite a technical challenge at the time.

To create the symmetrical implosion that would bring the core of plutonium to the required density, 32 explosive charges had to be detonated simultaneously around the central sphere. Using conventional explosive techniques, the required simultaneous explosion was impossible. Álvarez then proposed to his graduate student, Lawrence H. Johnston, that he use a large capacitor to deliver a high-voltage charge directly to each explosive lens, replacing the caps with a bridge of wire detonators. In the tests, the explosive wire detonated the thirty-two charges in a few tenths of a microsecond, which meant a practically simultaneous explosion, essential so that in the real bomb the centre of plutonium was compressed to the point of splitting its atoms, unleashing the chain reaction that would release atomic energy.

The precision mechanism devised by Álvarez was successfully used in the first real nuclear bomb, the Gadget device, which was detonated on 16 July 1945 in the desert at Alamogordo New Mexico. The explosion made it possible to confirm that the United States had achieved a real atomic weapon and that it could be mass-produced. It is not surprising, therefore, that the young physicist was appointed to the rank of lieutenant colonel in the US army and that, with such military rank, he was assigned to Tinian Island, in the middle of the Pacific Ocean, together with the select group of technicians who would prepare the bombs that would be used in the first nuclear attacks against Japan.

The city of Hiroshima was chosen as the primary target for the first atomic bombing mission, scheduled for 6 August 1945, with Kokura and Nagasaki as alternate targets. The aircraft chosen to transport the uranium bomb was the Boeing B-29 named *Enola Gay*, followed by six other B-29s named *Straight Flush* (weather reconnaissance over Hiroshima), *Jabit III* (weather reconnaissance over Kokura), *Full House* (weather reconnaissance over Nagasaki), *The Great Artiste* (instrumental measurement of the explosion), *Necessary Evil* (impact observation and photography) and *Top Secret* (photography). Such was the importance of Luis Álvarez, that he joined the crew of *The Great Artiste* to parachute a set of calibrated transmitter microphones that he himself had developed to measure the force of the shock wave of the atomic explosion, in order to allow the calculation of the total energy released.

At 8:09 a.m. Hiroshima local time, Álvarez could see from one of the windows of his plane how the hatches of the *Enola Gay*'s ventral bay opened. Six minutes later, he watched as the uranium bomb, codenamed *Little Boy*, detached from the bomber and fell toward its target. Less than a minute later, when it was 580 metres above the centre of Hiroshima, the bomb's altimetric trigger was activated and a flash of light brighter than the Sun illuminated the planes flying higher in formation. Minutes later, and more than 18 kilometres from the target, the shock wave hit and shook the B-29s hard.

Luis Álvarez, who had launched the measuring instruments at about the same time that he saw the bomb drop, could hardly believe what was happening below. As soon as the blast wave hit the ground, it literally "swept away" an area of 12 square kilometres. The power

The American physicist Luis Walter Álvarez at the age of 32, as he looked on his access credential to the Los Alamos Laboratory, New Mexico, the nerve centre of the Manhattan Project. (USAEC)

later (precisely from Álvarez's instrumentation) the Hiroshima explosion was considered very inefficient, with only 1.7% of the bomb's nucleus fissuring, which had released a blast equivalent to barely 16 kilotons, but enough to make 69% of Hiroshima's buildings disappear in a second and immediately kill some 80,000 people, 30% of the city's total population.

Upon returning to the Tinian base, all the crews participating in the observation were elated by the result of the mission, but Luis Álvarez was deeply dismayed as he knew that the hell that had broken loose was only the beginning. Indeed, a second nuclear bomb, with a plutonium heart, was already ready on Tinian, and no less than six more were being built in Los Alamos. Each of these bombs meant a Japanese city wiped off the map and the attacks would follow one after the other, at an increasing rate, until Japan surrendered.

Aware of the machinery of destruction that had been set in motion, and that he himself had contributed to creating, Álvarez decided to do something to prevent the apocalypse from continuing in Japan. Contrary to all the rules of secrecy he had sworn to uphold, he and other members of the Tinian base science team decided to write notes addressed to Professor Ryokichi Sagane, a renowned nuclear physicist at the University of Tokyo who had studied with three of them at the University of California at Berkeley. In the notes, which were to be dropped in the various measurement parachutes over the next city to be attacked, Álvarez and his friends urged Sagane to inform the Japanese public about the danger of nuclear weapons. It was a desperate appeal to a fellow scientist, an act of humanism in the midst of the worst barbarism humanity had experienced to date.

of the detonation generated a pressure wave of such force that it collapsed houses and uprooted trees. As this occurred, the heat from the explosion rose and created a suction effect, which produced a reverse hurricane force wind that converged from all sides towards the epicentre of the detonation. The column of dirt, smoke, and debris that rose from the heat soon reached its point of maximum ascent and, when it came to a stop, took on the characteristic mushroom shape that witnesses had already seen weeks before when the Gadget device detonated. in the New Mexico desert. As could be calculated

On 9 August 1945, three days after the devastating attack on Hiroshima, a new formation of B-29s took off from their base on Tinian. This time the bomb, a plutonium device named *Fat Man*, was loaded into the hold of the plane named *Bockscar* to be launched in the city of Nagasaki. Now, the *Enola Gay* would fulfil the role of meteorological reconnaissance over the alternative target (Kokura), the *Laggin' Dragon* would do the same over Nagasaki and its twins

The Boeing B-29-45-MO Stratofortress registration 44-86292 named *Enola Gay* lands on the runway of Tinian Island on 6 August 1945, after dropping the nuclear bomb that devastated Hiroshima. The power of the explosion was recorded by Luis Walter Álvarez from *The Great Artiste*. (USAAF)

Three Douglas A-26 Invader planes of the 429 Group of the IX Air Force equipped with a detector device manufactured by General Electric were used in the fall of 1944 to trace over Germany the xenon-133 isotope discovered by Luis Walter Álvarez as an indicator of the reactors in which Germany could be manufacturing enriched uranium or plutonium. (USAAF)

Big Stink and *Full House* would take photographic records of the explosion. The B-29 called *The Great Artiste*, the only scientific support aircraft, would reproduce his routine with the launch of the measurement equipment by parachute.

At 10:53 a.m. Nagasaki time, *Bockscar* opened its doors and minutes later the *Fat Man* bomb fell into the void. At 11:00 a.m. sharp, from his own plane, Luis Álvarez launched the parachutes with instruments, next to which he had attached the notes addressed to Professor Sagane. The nuclear explosion that followed released a blast of 21 kilotons, 40,000 people died instantly, and 65% of the city of Nagasaki disappeared in a second. As the mushroom cloud rose, several kilometres away instrument parachutes launched from *The Great Artiste* fell gently to earth. Several of them were found and turned over to the Japanese authorities. Professor Ryokichi Sagane only came across the notes a month later, but the message of the two nuclear attacks had taken effect: on 15 August 1945, Japanese radios broadcast a recorded message from Emperor Hirohito announcing Japan's capitulation. The official surrender document was signed on 2 September 1945 on the deck of the American battleship USS *Missouri*, anchored in Tokyo Bay.

Although the Second World War had ended, the same did not happen with the investigation of the use of nuclear weapons by the United States, nor with the talented scientific career of Luis Walter Álvarez. In fact, one of his most brilliant discoveries, the application of krypton-85 to deduce the power of a detonated atomic bomb, would play an important role during the ensuing period of tension. And it is that, in this way, the United States could know what was the real evolution of the nuclear arsenal of its rival superpower, the Soviet Union, during all the years of the so-called Cold War, which was nothing more than a very long hot peace among those who had been allies to defeat Germany and Japan.

The United States emerged from the Second World War as the most powerful nation in the world, despite the fact that its efforts to win the war had cost it a whopping 330 billion dollars. This allowed its president, Harry Truman, to say on 1 September 1945, that his country had achieved 'the greatest strength and the greatest power that man has ever achieved'. It was no exaggeration. During the war

years, the United States had doubled its national income, its wealth, and its industrial production. Steel production, a key indicator of American industrial strength, in 1944 reached a level more than four times that of the pre-war years. This in itself meant a lot, but it was even more when one considers that war damage and capital shortages had paralysed the steel industries of Britain, the Soviet Union, and the countries of western Europe, while virtually wiping out those of Germany and Japan.

To maintain its leading position, the United States needed to increase, rather than simply conserve, its existing resources in industrial plants, land, monetary reserves, energy, raw materials, and scientific talent. The results of a comprehensive assessment of US mineral resources, begun in 1944 by the US Geological Survey (USGS) and by the US Mines Bureau (USBM), indicated a generally favourable outlook for minerals, but available stocks for several strategic products were deficient in quantity or grade.

Consequently, the two agencies recommended a dynamic research and exploration programme to meet the current and future needs of the country. To this end, the USBM and the USGS significantly expanded their funds, personnel, technological resources, and operations. In the immediate post-Second World War period, the USGS staff nearly doubled, from 1,472 to more than 2,490 scientists, engineers, and support technicians, the vast majority of whom were very young.

In this context, on 6 September 1945, just four days after the Japanese Empire formally surrendered, President Truman sent Congress a 21-point message seeking to activate the post-war economy, including the development and conservation of natural resources and the establishment of a single federal agency to direct and finance scientific research. For the future of the United States, the discovery, use and conservation of natural resources was strategic, especially new sources of oil and new uranium deposits, wherever they were located in the world.

Simultaneously, the US government established an agency for the civilian and military research of atomic energy, and for the international projection of the resulting know-how. In terms of foreign relations, President Truman embraced the idea of international agreements, seeking, if possible, the renunciation of the use and development of the atomic bomb and promised to start talks to achieve that goal, first with representatives of the British and Canadian governments and, later, with those of other nations. In all cases it was assumed that the United States would have an effective monopoly on nuclear technology for at least 15 years (that is, until 1960) since the uranium deposits known and controlled by the Soviet Union were insignificant to allow the manufacture of atomic bombs. Several British experts, however, predicted that the American monopoly would only last for five years, that is, until 1950 at the latest.

In this context, Truman proposed to the United States Congress to create an Atomic Energy Commission (the future US Atomic Energy Commission, USAEC) made up of members appointed by the president himself, the objective of which would be to control all nuclear reserves and plants, acquire minerals from which atomic energy was derived and carry out all research, experimentation and operations for the development and use of atomic energy for industrial, medical, military and scientific purposes. The Atomic Energy Development and Control Bill had a foreign policy provision, since the United States would not recognise any foreign government imposed by force, but it would not unleash nuclear hell on it either. In this way, the US atomic bombs would remain an instrument of peace, in what one might term a kind of "trust for all humanity."

The Bill further provided for the promotion of private research the control and dissemination of knowledge, scientific development, the conduct of federal research and development programmes, and continued government control in nuclear production and administration. The Bill gave the future Commission authority to conduct or contract exploration and acquire basic materials anywhere in the world. The measure encouraged research on nuclear processes, atomic energy theory and production, utilisation of fissile materials, and health protection during study and production. It also specified the control of fissile materials and their traceability from origin, and authorised the military applications of atomic products.

After considerable debate in June and July 1946, Congress passed Truman's proposed Bill and the President signed it on 1 August 1946. The separate Atomic Energy Act reserved for the United States 'all uranium, thorium and all other materials determined and peculiarly essential to the production of fissile material contained, in whatever concentration, in deposits on public lands.' The new law transferred full control of all records, materials, facilities, production, research, and information from the War Department to the new USAEC. Additional responsibilities for the USAEC included prospecting for new sources of fissile material on US soil or abroad, building more bombs, conducting research and development, information control, monitoring international agreements, and establishment of regulations for nuclear safety and health.[1]

President Harry S. Truman signs the Atomic Energy Act on 1 August 1946, creating the US Atomic Energy Commission. Behind the president, from left to right, Senators Tom Connally, Eugene D. Millikin, Edwin C. Johnson, Thomas C. Hart, Brien McMahon, Warren R. Austin, and Richard B. Russell. (NARA)

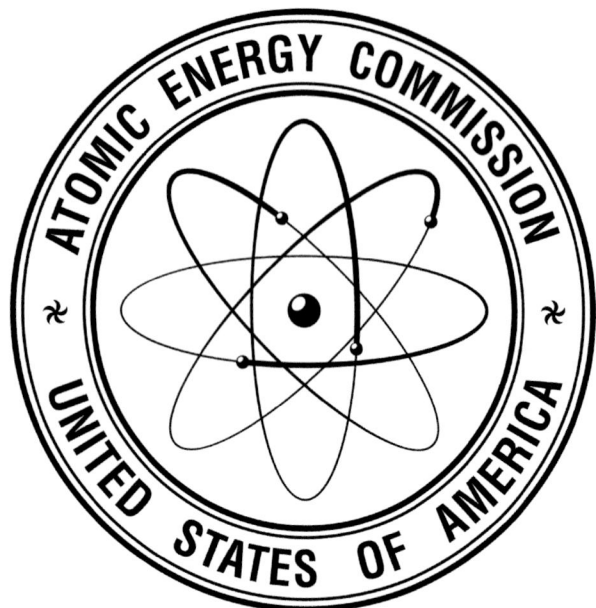

The logo of the Atomic Energy Commission, the highest US nuclear authority, which took charge of civil and military research and development of atomic energy. One of its first efforts was to detect uranium deposits around the world. (USAEC)

By virtue of the Atomic Energy Act, the emergency purchase of war material or strategic raw materials abroad was authorised, for which the survey of existing uranium deposits outside the territory of the United States was essential. Consequently, the Mines Bureau and the Geological Survey expanded their exploration programmes for the detection of strategic minerals (especially radioactive ones), word processing, and mapping, both in the United States and abroad.[2]

To this purpose, the Geological Survey formed its Divisions of Airborne Geology, Non-Metal Deposits, Geology, and Geography for the purpose of mapping and surveying radioactive minerals in the United States and abroad using airborne magnetometers. In this way, it was intended to study and inventory the mineral resources of Argentina, Bolivia, Brazil, Chile, Cuba, Mexico and Panama, just to mention the Latin American countries reached by the programme. All these works had to be carried out in coordination with the United States Department of State, which would provide diplomatic cover for search activities abroad, which would not always be known or approved by the governments of the countries overflown. The topographers of the Geological Survey were not only to geolocate deposits or reservoirs of strategic materials, especially uranium, but in parallel they were to complete maps and charts for the United States Department of War.[3, 4]

Geodesists of the Inter American Geodetic Survey, the organisation created on 15 April 1946 to map the territory of the countries of the Caribbean, Central America and South America, under the dependence of the Caribbean Defense Command. One of its tasks was to detect uranium deposits for the US Geodetic Survey. (IAGS)

The Douglas C-53D Skytrooper registration N19924 of the US Geodetic Survey extends a uranium magnetic detector during a radioactive prospecting mission in the Painted Desert. Arizona, in 1949. USAAF military aircraft serving the USGS secretly conducted identical surveys in the Latin American countries over which they operated. (USGS)

To carry out these activities, on 28 January 1946, the Geological Survey established the so-called Foreign Section, a division of its Geological Branch aimed at surveying mineral resources located outside the territory of the United States, particularly those which were radioactive. Since its creation in 1938, the Geological Survey had the power to work in other nations in the Americas, but never before with the deliberate purpose of obtaining information for the United States military-industrial system. With the help of the Department of State, cooperative research programmes were soon designed to be carried out during the fiscal year 1946-47 in Brazil, Cuba, Mexico and Peru.[5]

For those American countries not interested in signing what the US described as "collaboration agreements" (whether that collaboration was genuine or not) for the survey of their own resources, such as Argentina, covert geological survey operations and mapping of top-priority deposits were planned. Heavy mineral deposits in Mexico and Peru, tin deposits in Bolivia and manganese in Cuba, as well as various metallic minerals in Chile were studied collaboratively. Through a non-collaborative way, an attempt was made to trace and calculate the uranium deposits in Argentina, since it was known since December 1945 that the British and the Swedes controlled the highest quality mineral, while the Soviet Union and

The Beechcraft UC-45 Expeditor of the Air Attaché (Military Attaché) of the Embassy of the United States in Argentina. It was one of three aircraft of its type used for the aerial search for the missing Douglas C-47B over Corrientes. (Atilio Marino via Vladimiro Cettolo)

Boeing B-17F Flying Fortress used to repatriate the remains of the 14 occupants of the Douglas C-47B crashed in Corrientes. El Palomar Military Air Base, 12 December 1945. (Atilio Marino via Vladimiro Cettolo)

Argentina possessed 65 percent of the lower quality ore, which could be enriched in industrial processes.[6]

It is worth asking why Argentina was not willing to sign collaboration agreements with the United States for the exploration of its own natural resources, since both countries exhibited a very long tradition of common political, economic and diplomatic relations, to the point that the government Washington had been the first to recognise Argentine independence when it was proclaimed in 1816. From then, and for the next 130 years, the United States and Argentina developed with innumerable points in common that ended up making them very similar countries in many aspects, beginning with European immigration, the high income of its citizens, the strength of their currencies, the high reserves of their central banks and the respect that each generated in their respective areas of geopolitical influence. But all that changed abruptly during the Second World War as the United States did not look favourably on Argentina's neutrality in the conflict, which they considered helpful to the interests of the Axis powers made up of Germany, Italy and Japan.

This is how things were when, on 1 November 1946, the mining businessmen José Cabera Álvarez and Demetrio Ortega announced the discovery of a uranium deposit in the Province of Mendoza. It was a mineralised run of some 1,800 metres in length oriented in a north-south direction, located on land close to the San Isidro ranch, Las Heras department. The deposit was immediately named President Perón in honour of the new Argentine president inaugurated on 4 June 1946, but shortly after it was renamed Soberanía in a clear reference to the self-determination that Argentina would achieve in terms of atomic energy if it decided to exploit the deposit. valuable mineral resource. The discovery was confirmed by technicians from the Department of Mines, Geology and Hydrogeology of the Government of Mendoza and received abundant press coverage, not only because it was the first uranium deposit detected in Argentina, but also because after the explosions in Hiroshima and Nagasaki, it was public knowledge that uranium was the raw material for the construction of atomic bombs, which gave Argentina an unexpected geopolitical projection.[7, 8]

Uranio Argentino para la Paz

escribe el doctor MICHAEL M. NATURAVITA

The discovery of uranium in Mendoza opened enormous possibilities for the peaceful development of nuclear energy in Argentina. The news spread around the world just as the United States was launching its secret global prospecting campaign for radioactive resources. (Mendoza Antigua)

Unable to survey the newly discovered uranium deposit by land, the United States decided to do it by air and in the most veiled way possible, one that would not arouse any suspicion. To this end, the US government decided to use its human and organisational resources already present in Argentina, specifically the permanent Air Mission that had operated in Buenos Aires since 1940 under the auspices of the Department of State.

The presence of a large group of officers from the US Army Air Forces (USAAF) in Buenos Aires, Córdoba and Mendoza had been a consequence of the Military Aviation Mission Agreement, signed between the Argentine and US governments on 29 June 1940. This agreement, at the same time, was the continuation of an agreement of instruction for military pilots signed between the same parties on 12 September 1939 for the purpose of providing technical, operational, and tactical training and training to Argentine aviators who used US-manufactured aircraft, particularly Curtiss Hawk

75-O fighter planes, Martin 139WAA horizontal bombers, Northrop 8A-2 dive bombers and Douglas C-47 Skytrain transport planes, the most modern machines in the inventory of the then Argentine Army Aviation Command.[9, 10]

Precisely for this reason the 1940 agreement, which had led to the formation of the permanent mission of the US military aviation in Argentina, had been repeatedly renewed upon expiration, always through the exchange of diplomatic notes between both governments. The first renewal occurred after the exchange of notes between 23 May and 3 June 1941 (effective as of 29 June 1941). The second renewal took place through a second exchange of diplomatic notes on 23 June and 2 September 1943 (in force from the latter date), which extended and amended the original 1940 text. The links and commitments were inherited by the Argentine Air Force when it became a defence institution entirely independent from the Army on 1 January 1945 by mandate of Decree No. 288/45.[11, 12, 13]

The US Air Mission had its own aircraft that at the same time fulfilled transport functions for the US Ambassador in Buenos Aires and all the diplomatic officials assigned to his Embassy, as well as other ambassadors and members of the consular corps of other friendly countries, who were transported in and out of the country as a courtesy. These planes, like the others assigned to the rest of the US embassies located in the different capitals of the Latin American countries, were attached to the Caribbean Air Command of the United States Army Air Forces based in Panama and received regular maintenance in the workshops of the Howard Field and Albrook Field air bases, located in the Panama Canal Zone. In general, they were Douglas C-47 Skytrain transport planes in passenger configuration, with distinctive markings belonging to the air mission of the country in question, but other planes were also used, for example Douglas C-54 long-distance freighters, Skymaster or Boeing B-17 Flying Fortress bombers devoid of weapons given their diplomatic role.

The permanent operation of US military aircraft in Argentine territory was what allowed the Washington government to plan and execute its secret geological survey missions without raising any suspicion in the host country. To do this, it was enough to plan the operation over particular areas of Argentine territory, present an excuse or reasonable argument to the local government for the overflight over that place and, finally, transport on board the technical personnel of the Atomic Energy Commission or the Geological Survey with the photographic or measuring instruments that the circumstances required.

It is impossible to know how many secret flights to survey mineral deposits were carried out in this way, precisely because they were carried out with the utmost discretion to avoid diplomatic incidents or complaints that would have hurt Argentina's foreign relations with the United States. However, two of these clandestine missions have been confirmed, which came to light precisely because they resulted in separate accidents.

The first occurred on 3 December 1945, when the Douglas C-47B-5-DK Skytrain registration 43-48602, serial number 14418/25863, disappeared over Argentine territory en route from Asunción del Paraguay to Montevideo, Uruguay, during a strong summer thunderstorm. The aircraft belonged to the 311th Photo and Charting Wing (311th Reconnaissance Wing) of the 7 Geodetic Control Squadron based at Buckley Field, Colorado.

The C-47 crew consisted of First Lieutenants Orville A. Michelsen (pilot) and Earl S. King Jr (co-pilot), Sergeants James R. Roberson and Clarence J. Setko (mechanical technicians) and Corporal Charles W. Brown. As passengers were the lawyer J. Corden Delworth, legal attaché of the US embassy in Asunción, and the spare crews of the planes of the 7 Geodetical Control Squadron stationed in Montevideo and Buenos Aires that were to provide services for the Geological Survey in Uruguay and Argentina. These spare crews consisted of First Lieutenants William B. Nunemaker, Reuben Klein, Zane W. Gilcher, and Chester F. Lowe, Air Technical Sergeant Richard W. Schweitzer, Corporals Frank G. Dubinskas and David S. Kellogg, and Private First-Class Theodore H. Leopold.[14, 15]

The disappearance of the plane was reported by the Pan American Airways company, with whose radio stations it was communicating until it lost contact, which immediately triggered a large search operation that comprised two Piper J-3 Cubs from the Aero Club Posadas, two Beechcraft C-45 Expeditor of the Paraguayan Air Force, the Beechcraft UC-45B registration numbers 85-135 and 41-087 of the US Embassy in Uruguay (piloted by First Lieutenants Gordon Whelpley and Skofen), the Douglas C-47 of the US Air Mission in Buenos Aires and two other US planes of the Caribbean Air Command from Santiago de Chile.[16]

On 7 December 1945 at 10:30 a.m., while flying at the controls of the Glenn Martin 139 bomber, registration 514 of the Argentine Air Force, Lieutenant Saúl Oteiza spotted the remains of the lost US plane from the air, which appeared scattered throughout the Iberá lagoon, in the province of Corrientes, from which they protruded due to the shallow depth of the water. Oteiza reported the position of the discovery by radio (28° 43 South Latitude and 28° 43' West

The Douglas C-54 Skymaster registration 42-72552, serial number 10657, photographed on the platform of the IV Air Brigade of the Argentine Air Force on 12 November 1946, during its unexpected stopover in Mendoza. (Atilio Baldini)

Longitude) and from that moment on the difficult task of recovering the bodies began. The place was infested with mosquitoes, the heat was stifling, and the mud of the estuary made walking difficult. Since the plane had broken up in flight, the corpses were scattered and in an advanced state of putrefaction.[17]

The recovery task was in the charge of Colonel Stanley J. Donovan and Major Carlton Ashley, air attachés to the US embassies in Buenos Aires and Montevideo, who were accompanied by lawyers Robert Shaw, James Joyce and James Boyd, legal attachés to those embassies. Their transfer to the estuaries was carried out in horse-drawn carts, since it was impossible to do so on foot. The entire operation received the support of the officers, NCOs, and soldiers of the 12th Cavalry Regiment of the Argentine Army, commanded by Lieutenant Colonel Ignacio Verdura, as well as the Douglas C-47 of the US Air Mission in Buenos Aires, which dropped parachute supplies onto rescuers. Since it was impossible to move the bodies to the mainland, they were collected on one of the plane's wings, doused with petrol, and cremated on site on 10 December 1945. The ashes were then placed in small urns and thus prepared for shipment to the United States.[18]

On 12 December 1945, the bodies arrived at the Santo Tomé airfield, Corrientes, where they were loaded onto the US C-47. As Colonel Donovan would recall, 'one of the most moving scenes was seeing poor people walking barefoot on the dirt road, carrying flower arrangements to the airport on the morning of departure'. The C-47 took off for Buenos Aires under the command of the head of the US Air Mission in Argentina, Colonel Kenneth Cavenah, escorted by Lieutenant Oteiza's Glenn Martin 139 and Colonel Donovan's Beechcraft C-45. The formation flew over the site of the accident twice, onto which it threw flowers as a last tribute, and then went to the El Palomar Military Air Base, in Buenos Aires, where the Commander of the Argentine Air Force, Commodore Pedro Castex Lainford, was waiting for them along with a large group of Argentine officials and US diplomats. The bodies were immediately transferred to a Boeing B-17 Flying Fortress, which departed at 2:15 p.m. bound for the United States after a stopover to refuel at Albrook Field, Panama Canal Zone.[19]

On 13 December 1945, one day after the repatriation of the remains of the C-47 crash victims, Brigadier General A.R. Harris, Military Attaché at the United States Embassy in Buenos Aires, issued Special Order 16, by which he formed an investigative board that was to investigate what happened to the C-47. Colonel Stanley J. Donovan (president), Colonel Kenneth A. Cavenah (intelligence officer) and Major Samuel J. Easley (registrar) were appointed to serve on it. The investigation was carried out in the strictest secrecy given the reserved activities that the Geological Survey was carrying out at that time in Argentina, Uruguay, Paraguay and Chile. It soon became clear that the destruction of the plane and the loss of all lives had been due to poor flight planning, as the pilot had taken off with an excess weight of 3,000 pounds and without proper weather analysis despite the forecasts available from Pan American Airways stations in Asunción del Paraguay, Buenos Aires and Rio de Janeiro; as well as the hourly reports of the National Meteorological Services of Argentina and Paraguay. This inadequate analysis of the weather reports meant that the storm front could not be anticipated by the crew and, when severe turbulence began, the excess weight caused the aircraft to break apart in mid-air.[20, 21]

As tragic and spectacular as it was, the Corrientes C-47 accident did not reveal the activities of the Geological Survey in Argentina. The matter was handled from the outset by US military intelligence, for which reason the functionaries and officials in Buenos Aires did not mention the 311th Photo and Charting Wing or the 7 Geodetic Control Squadron at all, nor did they mention the functions fulfilled by the pilots in command or the passengers, who were mostly also crew members of planes at the service of the same mapping and geodetic control squadron.[22]

The second accident that compromised a plane at the service of the Geological Survey in Argentina occurred on Tuesday, 12 November 1946 in the afternoon, just 10 days after the announcement of the discovery of the first Argentine uranium deposit in the Mendoza mountain, when a four-engine Douglas C-54 Skymaster of the United States Army Air Force attached to the United States Embassy in Santiago de Chile hit El Pelado hill, in the Mendoza foothills, 48 kilometres northwest of the capital city of the province.

The plane had taken off at 2:30 p.m. on 12 November 1946 from the Presidente Rivadavia de Morón Airport bound for Santiago de Chile, but for reasons that were never clarified, it interrupted the flight near Mendoza and landed at the El Plumerillo Airport. at five in the afternoon. The arrival of the US plane in Mendoza did not raise any suspicions among the local aeronautical authorities,

The mysterious Skymaster that landed in Mendoza had been manufactured in 1944 at the Douglas Aircraft Company plant in Chicago, Illinois, under contract W535-AC-327311 signed in 1942 between the company and the USAAF. (Atilio Baldini)

despite the fact that the unexpected stopover had been made without reporting any mechanical failure and in optimal weather conditions. In addition, the Skymaster did not need to refuel to cover the Buenos Aires-Santiago de Chile route, since it had a range of 6,300 kilometres, more than enough to link both capitals in direct flight.[23]

At 5:45 p.m., three quarters of an hour after landing in Mendoza, the USAAF Skymaster revved up its engines on the El Plumerillo runway and took off for Santiago de Chile. But she did not arrive at her destination, not at the scheduled time, and not ever. Forty minutes after take-off, almost at the time she was supposed to be landing in Chile, she crashed into a pass on Cerro El Pelado, Las Heras, 13 kilometres from Casa de Piedra. Although there were no witnesses to the catastrophe, the final position of the plane revealed that the accident had been spectacular. The Skymaster crashed down the south wall of Cerro Pelado, losing a wing on impact and immediately catching fire. Except for the navigator, all the occupants suffered injuries of varying degrees.

Flying in the Skymaster were Lieutenant Thomas Ott (pilot), Captain Thomas Sabianski (co-pilot), Lieutenant Edward Palton McDermott (second pilot), Lieutenant Frank A. Edwards (navigator), and Sergeants Dal E. Clark and Henry Brown (mechanics), Arthur Martin (radio operator) and John Allen Spencer (flight manager). The only passenger on the aircraft was Lieutenant Frederick Doyle, who was seriously injured. All the members of the crew were attached to the US Mission in Panama and, according to what was indicated to the press, 'were engaged in a mission to deliver equipment to all the embassies of the United States in South America'.[24]

The news of the accident reached Mendoza early on the morning of 13 November through a telephone call from the foreman of the wire guard station that the All American Cable company had in the town of Casa de Piedra and that administered the telegraph service through the Andes Mountain range. The report was immediately transmitted to the El Plumerillo Military Air Base, from where the plane had departed, where it was presumed to have been damaged or lost since it had not arrived at its destination the day before.[25, 26]

For everyone involved in the rescue effort, the crash of the American plane made no sense. The aircraft was practically new, all the crew were Second World War veterans and the pilot had participated in the recent airlift to Berlin, in truly critical conditions. In addition, the course followed after take-off seemed wrong at first sight, since the plane had unnecessarily headed to the north west, when it should have headed to the west. For the rest, the height of El Pelado hill (3,452 metres above sea level) should not have represented any difficulty for the freighter, which was flying empty and could reach 3,000 metres in just 15 minutes. The plane had been flying so low that when impact was imminent, several of the crew decided to dive mid-air, confident that they had a better chance of surviving a low altitude fall than the plane crashing into the ground.

Although all the crew members of the Douglas C-54 survived, those who jumped from the plane in mid-air suffered more serious injuries, while the occupants of the flight deck were virtually uninjured. Lieutenant Thomas Ott suffered a broken nose and bruises; Captain Thomas Sabianski suffered skull contusions, fractures, and various abrasions; Lieutenant Edward Palton McDermott suffered a six-inch injury to the right temporal region and collapse, fracture, and multiple contusions; Lieutenant Frank A. Edwards suffered minor injuries; Sergeant Dal E. Clark suffered multiple fractures of the malleolus, left fibula, scaphoid, rib, multiple contusions and bruises; Sergeant Henry Brown suffered contusion of the spine in the lower back, a crush fracture of the first lumbar vertebra, a fracture of the second lumbar vertebra, and a fracture of the transverse process of the third lumbar vertebra; Sergeant Arthur Martin suffered blunt force wounds to the right browbone, second-degree burns, contusions to the thorax, and multiple abrasions; and Sergeant John Allen Spencer suffered a stab wound to his left hand and injuries.

The remains of the C-54 Skymaster that fell on El Pelado hill, Mendoza, on 12 November 1946. The structure of the plane withstood the impact, but not the flames of the fire that broke out afterwards. (Atilio Baldini)

A good part of the crew of the C-54 threw themselves from the plane in mid-flight before the impact was imminent. They were the most injured; those who remained on board suffered bruises and minor injuries. The most seriously injured were transferred to Mendoza on stretchers on horseback. Pictured is Frederick J. Doyle, geodesist for the Inter American Geodetic Survey. After his recovery, he had a brilliant professional career as a surveyor. (John Martin via Mendoza Police)

Immediately after the rescue of the survivors, inevitable questions arose: why had the plane landed in Mendoza, if it had not even been refuelled? Why did it take off in a deliberately incorrect direction? Why was it flying low over the Mendoza foothills, beginning with the overflight of the El Challao area? Why did it take so long to reach its crossover level? Why did it seem to fly in circles over the foothills and not over the plain, which is much safer for gaining altitude?

Neither the pilot of the plane, nor the USAAF, nor the US Mission in Chile nor its counterpart in Argentina gave any answer to these questions. According to what the plane's co-pilot, Lieutenant Frank A. Edwards, told the press, the entire crew was stationed in the Panama Canal Zone and had been sent to Buenos Aires along the Pacific coast with a shipment of spare parts for Panama Canal planes. Once the delivery took place, the C-54 simply returned to Santiago de Chile, where it provided services for the US Air Mission in that country. According to this version, the plane had crashed by pure chance while its pilot was trying to gain altitude for the Andean crossing, when he was circling over the foothills. The argument was coherent, but it left most of the obscure points of the event pending explanation.[27]

The first information to uncover the truth of what happened was provided by Dr Horacio Moretti, a doctor at the Mendoza Military Hospital, one of the professionals who came to the aid of the US crew, entering the foothills on mule back. According to Moretti, one of the American officers, although wounded and on a stretcher, clung tenaciously to a case that contained a complex apparatus for measuring radiation, probably a Geiger counter.

This allowed the aeronautical historian Atilio Baldini to deduce that what the Skymaster was actually doing was a mining exploration flight in search of uranium and other radioactive metals. That is why it had made the unnecessary stopover in Mendoza, that is why it had headed west and not east to reach the crossing level. That is why it was flying in circles at low altitude and that is why it took the same time until the moment of the collision that the normal flight to Santiago de Chile would have taken.

Now, apart from Dr Moretti's reference, no trace of special equipment or instruments was found among the wreckage of the plane, because it was completely burned. In particular, the fire incinerated the cabin, the passenger compartment and the cargo hold, that is, the places where the radioactive measuring instruments could have been placed. The combustion of fuel reached such a high temperature that it melted the duralumin of the linings and frames,

which ended up dripping in incandescent threads down the slopes of the hill.[28]

However, subsequent investigations confirm that, at the time of its accident, the USAAF C-54 was carrying out a secret operation to survey radioactive minerals in the Mendoza foothills, specifically uranium from the Presidente Perón deposit (later Soberania), whose discovery had been widely publicised just 10 days before.

Furthermore, Lieutenant Frederick Joseph Doyle, the passenger carried by the C-54, was a specialist from the Inter-American Geodetic Survey (IAGS), the geodetic survey unit of the United States Department of War in charge of mapping the territory of the countries of the Caribbean, Central America and South America, with or without the knowledge or consent of their respective governments. The IAGS had been formed on 15 April 1946 and placed under the US Caribbean Defense Command. It was based in Fort Clayton, Panama, which is consistent with the press reports of the accident that occurred in Mendoza seven months later, which consistently indicated that the entire crew of the C-54 'was stationed in the Panama Canal Zone'.[29]

Frederick Joseph Doyle was barely 26 years old when he ended up in an accident in the Mendoza foothills, but he had real field experience gathering surface information and mapping. He had begun his career as a surveyor during the Second World War, assigned to the Guam Air Force Base, where he helped prepare the damage assessment and target approach charts for the B-29 bombers stationed there. In 1946, when the IAGS was formed, he was reassigned to Panama as one of the best specialists in the field.[30]

It is obvious that the Geodetic Survey and the Atomic Energy Commission relied on the IAGS regarding the detection in the field of Latin American deposits, particularly those of uranium and other radioactive minerals, since the so-called collaborative topography work of this organisation gave them the perfect coverage for it. Indeed, the IAGS had been created specifically to help Latin American countries draw up geographic maps of their vast internal regions, either because the existing ones were not accurate or because maps were simply lacking. To this end, a complete school of surveying, cartography, and map reproduction was formed at Fort Clayton, which was made available to military officers and civilian agents from most of the countries of Latin America and the Caribbean. As an American surveyor of the time would recall, it was not just goodwill:

We learned the hard way during the Second World War that many Latin American countries were at best reluctant allies and at worst active sympathizers with the Nazi regime. By the end of the Second World War, the political systems in these countries ranged from unstable democracies to hardline dictatorships. The United States government became concerned about the effects of political unrest and communist influence in the region, and instituted a series of programs designed to bring Latin America firmly under American influence and foster democratic principles and improve economic conditions. The IAGS was just one of many programs created as part of this effort. An extremely important benefit that the IAGS provided to the United States was that we were able to get US personnel on the ground in these countries to make detailed assessments of local conditions and we obtained maps that were created to US standards for vast areas of the Americas. Central and South.[31]

As if the claimed mapping capabilities were not enough, it turns out that the technique of aerial surveying of radioactive minerals using airborne instruments was already known to the US Geological Survey in 1946, whether it was carried out with magnetometers or with radioactivity meters. The first public record document noting the feasibility of aerial surveying dated from 1944, and the matter was first discussed in detail at a joint meeting held in Washington DC in January 1946 between representatives of the United States, UK and Canada. No experimental work had yet been done and the discussion turned to theoretical considerations regarding the types of instruments and aircraft that could be used. Although the signal strength received by an aircraft flying 150 metres above the surface was expected to be only 1/10,000 of the signal strength received by a prospector five feet above the ground, it was thought that from the air outcrops could be easily detected over areas large enough to be geo-referenced.[32, 33]

Aerial prospecting was reduced, then, to the improvement of airborne measurement equipment and the only way to do it was to start flying to develop the instruments and methods that would make uranium detection from the air more precise. The new technology was taking its first steps and for this reason it was not yet very precise, but it made it possible to detect deposits, locate them on a map and calculate their potential with reasonable accuracy, which was particularly useful for obtaining information on those places to which local governments would never grant access due to the sensitive nature of the material being surveyed, as was the case with the uranium discovered in Mendoza.[34, 35]

It will never be known what type of instrument Frederick Doyle cared for with such zeal during his long journey on a stretcher on the back of a mule, down the slope of Cerro El Pelado, while he was rescued by Argentinean baqueanos and doctors on 13 November 1946. It could have been a radioactivity meter, a complex mapping device or any other advanced technological device the secret nature of which justified the young man not leaving it, even when he was bruised and badly injured, with his left femur broken. Whatever the purpose of that instrument may have been, the truth is that it was handed over to US officials who met in Mendoza the next day to learn about the circumstances of the accident and salvage everything that could be recovered from the remains. Those officials were Colonel Stanley J. Donovan (assistant to General Charles H. Caldwell, Air Attaché of the United States Embassy in Buenos Aires), Colonel Kenneth Cavenah (head of the US military mission in Argentina)

and Colonel Cooper (Aeronautical Attaché and head of the US mission in Chile).[36, 37, 38, 39]

As soon as he was medically stabilised, Frederick J. Doyle was sent to Santiago de Chile on a Pan American-Grace Airways (PANAGRA) Douglas DC-3 and from there to the United States on a Pan American World Airways Douglas DC-4. He remained hospitalised for 18 months, which may give an idea of the seriousness of the injuries he had suffered. When he recovered, he entered Syracuse University, New York State, where he studied analytical photogrammetry with Professor Earl Church, an American pioneer in the field. He graduated with honours in civil engineering in 1951. Immediately after graduating, and thanks to a scholarship from the Fulbright Foundation, he studied for a year at the International Training Centre for Aerial Survey in Delft, the Netherlands, where he specialised in aerial photogrammetry.[40]

In 1952 Doyle joined the USAF Wright-Patterson Air Force Base Reconnaissance Laboratory and in 1954 was appointed associate professor in the newly created Department of Geodetic Sciences at the Ohio State University. In 1960 he became chief scientist for the Raytheon Autometric Company, a company responsible for developing spy satellites, for which he helped to develop sensors and optical systems. In 1967 he returned to the Geological Survey, where he served as director of spaceborne and airborne sensors for mapping the entire United States. With this experience, in 1969 he was summoned to serve in the Apollo Orbital Science Photographic Team, the team in charge of developing, planning and directing the mapping of the lunar surface during the Apollo 13 to 17 missions. After this, he was principal investigator in the mapping missions from the Skylab space station and in the LANDSAT mapping satellite programme. Doyle's career did not end there, as he directed the photographic projects for the Mariner and Viking missions to the Mars, Venus and Mercury. He finished his career working on the wide-angle camera attached to the Space Shuttle Challenger, which was launched in October 1984. After a long and fruitful life, Frederick J. Doyle passed away from a heart attack at age 97, on 17 April 2013, at his home in McLean, Virginia.

The other great protagonist of this chapter, Luis Walter Álvarez, died of oesophageal cancer on 1 September 1988, at the age of 77. He was one of the greatest scientists and inventors of his time, not only for his participation in the creation of the atomic bomb or the discovery of krypton and xenon, around which US nuclear intelligence would revolve in the Cold War, but for being the father of several of the technical and scientific advances that shaped modern science. To give an idea of this, it is enough to indicate that in 1945 he won the Collier Trophy for the invention of the GCA (Ground Control Approach) radar for landing approach control, and in 1947 he won the Presidential Medal for Merit for the design and construction of the linear accelerator. In 1961 he received the Einstein Medal for his contribution to the physical sciences, in 1964 he received the National Medal of Science for his contribution to high-energy physics, in 1968 he received the Nobel Prize in Physics for his discovery of resonance states in particle physics using the hydrogen bubble chamber he had invented, and in 1987 the Enrico Fermi Award for his career achievements. But his legacy did not end there, in 1965 he proposed the survey of the Egyptian pyramids using the tomography technique to discover secret chambers and in 1980 he postulated the theory of the mass extinction of dinosaurs due to the impact of an asteroid from outer space.[41, 42]

2

AN AIR FORCE OF SCIENTISTS (1947-1948)

By the end of the Second World War, the US Army Air Forces (USAAF) had more than 64,000 aircraft of all types in its inventory and about 2,200,000 personnel in service. Nearly 10 percent of these staff were permanent military personnel and it was expected that they would continue to be linked to the service in the post-war period. But the remaining 90 percent was made up of civilian personnel militarised for the conflict who had to return to their activities as soon as they were demobilised. To the surprise of everyone, the demobilisation process was rapid and also profound.

To verify this, it is enough to indicate that towards the end of April 1946 the USAAF had nearly 500,000 personnel. A year later, that number had dropped to 303,000, as the postwar American economy was reviving with the huge numbers of skilled labour now returning to their pre-war job activities. By 1947, the total USAAF airborne personnel numbered 24,000, including pilots and other aircrew, a stark contrast to the 413,000 men they had enlisted just two years earlier. Maintenance personnel, the core of any military service, were also cut by around 90 percent.[1]

With fewer planes to fly and fewer maintenance personnel, operational efficiency suffered greatly. During the war years, the general availability of combat aircraft had been close to 50 percent, meaning that for every two aircraft in inventory one was airworthy

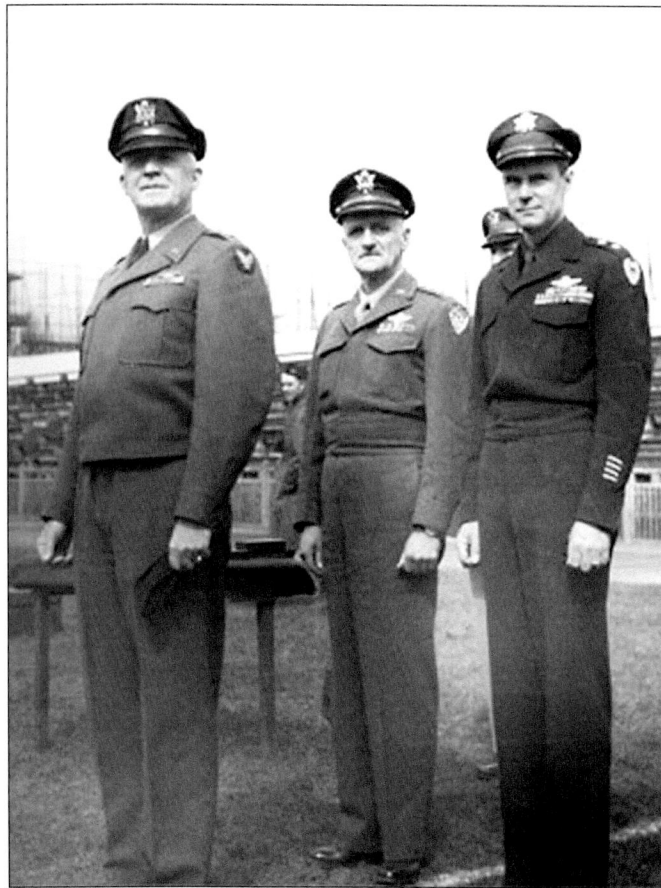

Generals Henry Harley Arnold and Carl Spaatz, and Lieutenant General Hoyt S Vandenberg, the fathers of US Air Force independence, pose during a military parade in Luxembourg City on 7 April 1945,. (USAAF)

and the other was under technical overhaul. By 1946, the availability rate was reduced to less than one operational aircraft for every five in inventory, since there were no longer technical personnel in a position to maintain the operational dispatch rate. The mighty USAAF, the air force that had dominated the skies over Germany and Japan with more than 218 groups of fighter aircraft, had been reduced by December 1946 to just two groups that had survived severe postwar cutbacks.[2]

This contraction was not a path towards disappearance, but towards a deep technological and organisational restructuring. At the end of the Second World War, the USAAF's highest-ranking officer, five-star general Henry 'Hap' Arnold, anticipated that the air force of the future should not be built around pilots, but scientists, as it would be the mastery of science and technology which would offer superiority in aerial combat to come. For this reason, in 1945, Arnold initiated Project RAND, an acronym for Research and Development, through which he summoned a select group of experts to design the bases of what should be a new air force.

Among these masterminds was Professor Theodore von Kármán, an Hungarian-American aeronautical engineer who had escaped Nazism and who by 1945 had founded the Jet Propulsion Laboratory (JPL) in Pasadena, California, with the aim of exploring jet engines, rockets and high-speed aerodynamics. In August of that year, with the two nuclear bombs already dropped on Japan, von Kármán and his group of scientists produced a secret report comparing the levels reached during the war by the USAAF and the German Luftwaffe. Assigned to develop a long-term research plan, he also prepared a second report, entitled Toward New Horizons, which was soon expanded by a companion volume entitled Science: the key to Air Supremacy. In these reports, he proposed that science was the key to future air supremacy, which was the major impetus for basic scientific research within the US Air Force.

Von Kármán's voluminous secret reports, as dense as they were accurate, constituted one more argument in favour of the need to create a US Air Force on an equal footing with the navy and the army. The origins of the idea could be traced back to 1916, but it had always been resisted because it meant reducing the budget of the two pre-existing armed forces. However, by the end of the Second World War the vision was different since air power had developed to such an extent that its entity was undeniable. It was also undeniable that the USAAF was, from every point of view, an institution that operated with its own logic, which is why the army supported its independence. In contrast, the navy opposed it. Thus, the independence plan presented to the United States Congress in March 1944 went nowhere due to the strong naval lobby.

The next step on the hard road towards independence was taken by the Joint Chiefs Staff, which appointed a committee of senior army and navy officers to evaluate three variants in the general organisation of post-war US national defence. The final recommendation, dated March 1945, favoured a single Department of Defense subdivided into three equalised services: army, navy, and air force. The committee also suggested that action be taken quickly, as the exceptional legal status granted to the USAAF during the war,

The Hungarian-American professor Theodore von Kármán, a scientist emigrated to the United States, postulated that the future USAF should be "an air force of scientists", since he predicted that the key to air supremacy would derive from mastery of applied science and technique. (JPL)

which gave it relative operational autonomy, was about to expire, thus returning it to being an organisation totally dependent on the army as soon as peace was restored.[3]

The USAAF independence project began to be discussed in April 1945 by different commissions of the United States Congress. The hearings constituted a veritable parade of witnesses, who spoke both for and against. At the very moment when the debate was heating up, the Second World War came to an end and, immediately, the post-war climate began without anyone knowing what to do with the problem under treatment. Then President Harry S. Truman decided to intervene. In a message sent to Congress on 19 December 1945, he called for new legislation to establish a single Department of Defense within which the air force would be on an equal footing with the army and the navy. Truman synthesised several suggestions made in earlier reports and thereby overcame prevailing antagonisms.

Despite this, the first attempt to treat Truman's bill failed as the navy resisted the change. The formidable power of naval influence was fully exercised over the legislators of the Democratic and Republican parties. The main argument of the naval officers, serving and retired, was that the creation of an independent air force would relegate the US Navy, which would no longer be considered the first line of defence of the United States. In this context, Truman summoned the Secretaries of the Army and the Navy to resolve their differences, but the rift was so deep that they could not agree.

Then the president imposed a compromise solution on both parties and ordered them to work on a new consensus project. In January 1947, when Congress began its legislative period, a final version of the draft of what ended up being the National Security Act of 1947, which entered into force on 26 July of that year, was already ready. Through it, a single Department of Defense and three military

The independence of the US Air Force was strongly resisted by the navy. The three main opponents were Admiral Ernest J. King, Secretary of the Navy James Forrestal, and Admiral Chester W. Nimitz, all three captured in this photo taken on 21 November 1945 at the Department of the Navy. (USN)

departments (army, navy and air force) were established under civilian control. Simultaneously with the United States Air Force (USAF) the National Security Council, the Central Intelligence Agency and the National Security Resource Board were created.[4]

The functions and roles of the three services were detailed in Executive Order 9877. Under its terms, the newly created independent air force was to organise, train, and equip for a variety of different operations; it was to develop weapons, tactics, techniques, equipment, and combat elements, and organise missions and detachments for the foreign service. The new air force was further to provide means to coordinate United States air defence and assist the Army and Navy in their missions.[5]

It took time to organise the USAF to be fully autonomous, as hundreds of designations and transfers to the new regime had to take place. Consequently, although the National Security Act came into effect at the end of July 1947, it was not until 18 September 1947, that businessman William Stuart Symington III took office as the first Secretary of the Air Force. The date would then be considered the official USAF birthday.

Under the United States Constitution, it was up to Congress to authorise the size and general organisational structure of the military services, as well as the allocation and authorisation of their budgets. The existing legislation was applicable to the army and the navy, but not to the new air force, which barely started with the necessary funds to organise its headquarters and its commands. This initial lack of resources was key, since it made it possible to conceive a relatively small and agile administrative structure (compared to what happened in times of war).

The architect of the nascent USAF was General Carl Spaatz, who had replaced General Henry Arnold on 15 February 1946. Spaatz reorganised his service into 70 combat groups and 22 specialised squadrons, plus a support force. He created three functional and specific combat commands: the Strategic Air Command (SAC), the Tactical Air Command (TAC) and the Air Defense Command (ADC), all born on 21 March 1946. Five support commands and five for operations abroad, including Europe (USAFE) and Far East (FEAF, Far East Air Force), were also established. Commands abroad were operational and did not have combat aircraft in their inventory.

The USAF was given an organisation analogous to that of a private company, so its organisational charts looked like those of any large corporation. The Commander-in-Chief, who also had several staff officers, had four deputy chiefs (of operations, materiel, personnel, and administration, the last also in charge of finances). The directors of plans and operations, training and intelligence reported to the chief of operations. The chief of staff reported to the guided missile group and the air communications group. The directorates of research and development, acquisitions and industrial planning, supplies and services, and air facilities reported to the chief of materiel, with only one staff officer in charge of the special weapons group.[6]

From a technological point of view, the nascent USAF rested on two fundamental pillars: new bombers that were capable of delivering nuclear bombs to increasingly distant targets and new high-speed fighters that could provide effective air defence against long-range enemy bombers. Already in 1947 it was known that these bombers would be Soviet, since the Cold War between the United States and the Soviet Union had begun, but it was not known exactly

United States Chief Justice Frederick Moore Vinson swears in Stuart Symington as Secretary of the Air Force, in Washington, on 18 September 1947. The inauguration marked the beginning of the USAF as an institution independent of the army and navy. (USAF)

The USAF absorbed into its inventory the fleet of Boeing B-29 Superfortress nuclear bombers (left) and soon funded the development of the larger Convair B-36 Peacemaker (right). The size between one model and the other can be seen in this photo taken in 1948 at Carswell AFB, Fort Worth, Texas. (USAF)

when the rival would reach nuclear capacity. The Manhattan Project scientists speculated that it would not be before 1960, while their British counterparts claimed that it would be before 1950. In any case, it was to be expected that the American nuclear monopoly would come to an end at some point, at which time the Soviet threat would have to be faced.

Knowing when the Soviets would have their first atomic weapon became a top priority for American intelligence services, as well as for the British, due to the collaboration agreement on the exchange of sensitive information that they had secretly concluded on 5 March 1946. By virtue of this agreement, the parties agreed to exchange information obtained from the interception of foreign communications, documents that were acquired by espionage, analysis of data traffic, the results of the cryptanalysis of decrypted information and any other source of information that could be sensitive to their national interests.[7]

However, even with the guarantees provided by the intelligence sharing agreement, it was clear to the Americans that the traditional espionage network, made up of cryptanalysts and infiltrators, had to be complemented with new and better instruments that would make it possible to know precisely when the Soviet Union would reach nuclear capacity and, if possible, determine its industrial capacities for the manufacture of atomic bombs. Traditional espionage, carried out by spies, had been replaced by a new espionage carried out by scientists operating complex instruments.

The plan to establish a Long Range Detection (LRD) mechanism was devised during the early part of March 1947, but the decision to assign responsibility to the air force was not implemented until 16 September 1947 (two days before the creation of the USAF as an independent service), when General Dwight D. Eisenhower, then Chief of Staff of the United States Army, entrusted the task to General Spaatz. The LRD, then, was born simultaneously with the USAF, not only because it was an integral part of it but because it represented an essential activity that helped to give it meaning and reason for being.

The formation of the LRD task force was delayed for several months due to the organisational complications generated by the independence of the USAF, but towards the end of 1947 a small number of professionals had already been identified to be assigned to an office under the supervisory control of Major General William Ellsworth Kepner. On 14 December 1947, Major General Albert F. Hegenberger was appointed head of the Long Range Detection Division, Special Weapons Group with powers to experiment with all those technologies that would support the proposed objective of learning about Soviet activities and tests. This included the capture of radioactive particles and tracer gases in the atmosphere, the capture of seismic movements that denote nuclear tests, the detection of the electromagnetic pulses typical of a nuclear explosion, and even the determination of their occurrence by acoustic sensors.

The main promoter of these activities turned out to be Dr Julius Robert Oppenheimer, the father of the atomic bomb, who had been the director of the nuclear laboratory in Los Alamos, New Mexico, during the Manhattan Project. On 1 January 1947, when the US Atomic Energy Commission (USAEC) became the civilian agency dedicated to the control of nuclear research and its associated military affairs, Oppenheimer was appointed chairman of its General Advisory Committee, from where he gave his opinion and decided on a long series of issues related to civil and military aspects of nuclear energy, including the financing of projects, the construction of laboratories, state sponsorship of basic science and international politics.[8]

Oppenheimer was one of the first to warn of the arms race that was coming between the United States and the Soviet Union, which is why he encouraged the implementation of a long-distance detection system that would make it possible to know, with an acceptable degree of precision, the level of Soviet technological development. As a leading member of the Manhattan Project, he knew of Luis Walter Álvarez's studies of xenon-133 and krypton-85, and the possibility of detecting both radioactive isotopes in air by specially modified aircraft. The

As soon as serial production of the Convair B-36 Peacemaker as a long-range nuclear bomber had been secured, the USAF set about developing a high-speed successor, the Boeing B-47 Stratojet, which could be used as a photo-reconnaissance platform or as a nuclear bomber, since the speed and the service ceiling that its six turbines ensured made it suitable for both. (USAF)

detection of these tracers in the atmosphere could make it possible to know if the Soviets had secretly carried out a nuclear explosion, as well as the power achieved and the number of atomic weapons available in their arsenal. Oppenheimer's validation of a long-range detection system allowed the first monitoring network to have 22 ground stations plus a small fleet of Boeing B-29 Superfortress bombers modified to capture radioactive waste, which were conveniently operated by the US Air Weather Service, under the cover of innocuous aerial platforms for collecting meteorological information.[9]

On 16 January 1948, the Long Range Detection Division received the code designation AFMSW-1 (Air Force Materiel Special Weapon-1) and was housed in the North Interior Building located at the corner of 18th Street and F Street, NW, Washington DC. But the level of secrecy was such that its offices did not formally exist, so that address could not be indicated anywhere. Consequently, communications and correspondence were outsourced to and from other air force units. As of 1 April 1948, the unit was organised as the 51st Air Force Base Unit, but retained the code designation AFMSW-1 and was made up of two squadrons: one for administration and one for flying duties. The initial work team consisted of about 10 people, which by March 1948 had jumped to 131 (including 22 officers, 45 civilians, and 63 pilots) as the unit set out to carry out its first long-term activity: distant sensing, collection of radioactive waste and the calibration of all its measuring instruments from real nuclear explosions.

To this end, AFMSW-1 organised Operation FITZWILLIAM, the objective of which was to monitor three US atomic tests in order to obtain the largest volume of scientific information and the largest number of tests of all available methods and equipment for the long-range detection of nuclear explosions. Tracking stations had to pinpoint the exact location of the explosions by combining sonic, subsonic and seismic methods, while scouting planes had to obtain radioactive samples at different distances from the location chosen for the detonations. Subsequent radiochemical analyses were to determine accurately the power and composition of the nuclear bombs tested.[10]

The three planned nuclear explosions were carried out between April and May 1948 within the framework of Operation SANDSTONE, conducted by the USAEC with the logistical support of the US armed forces. The tests took place on the Enjebi, Aomon and Runit islands, part of the Eniwetok Atoll of the Marshall Archipelago, in the Pacific Ocean. The first detonation, codenamed X-Ray, took place on 14 April 1948 and created an explosion equivalent to 37 kilotons, more than twice the yield of the Hiroshima atomic bomb. The second test, Yoke, occurred on 30 April 1948, and achieved 49 kilotons. The last test, Zebra, was carried out on 14 May 1948 and achieved 18 kilotons (practically the same yield as the first bomb dropped three years before on Japan). The three tests were successfully detected by the AFMSW-1 sensor network, which made it possible to confirm the validity of its concept, calibrate its systems and adjust the sensitivity of its instruments in order to be able to detect equivalent nuclear tests in the distant territory of the Soviet Union.[11]

On 28 August 1948 AFMSW-1 and 51st AFB were renamed the Air Force Office of Atomic Energy-1 (AFOAT-1) and 1009th Special Weapons Squadron respectively. The main objective of AFOAT-1 continued to be to detect atomic bomb detonations abroad, anticipating that the Soviet Union was already secretly developing weapons of this type as was indicated by intelligence shared with the British.

Drawing on the experience gained in Operation FITZWILLIAM, AFOAT-1 organised the Atomic Energy Detection System (AEDS), a complex expanded network of ground and airborne sensors intended to detect Soviet atomic tests and other related nuclear activities taking place in outside of the US. The B-29 "meteorological" planes of the Air Weather Service joined a vast network of radioactive fallout measurement ground stations administered by the US Navy (Project RAINBARREL) and a veritable constellation of polyethylene stratospheric balloons equipped with acoustic sensors released in secret by the air force (Project MOGUL).[12, 13]

The AFOAT-1 unit did not work alone but was part of the nascent intelligence complex of the United States, also made up of the Central Intelligence Agency (CIA), formed by the same national defence law that had made the USAF independent of the army. CIA agents, scattered throughout Europe, also fed on information obtained by their counterparts from the Secret Intelligence Service (commonly known as MI6), the British foreign intelligence organisation. Beginning with the collaboration agreement of 1946 (which had its roots in the close

The long-distance nuclear detection network launched in 1947 used various devices to spy on the Soviet Union, including helium-filled polyethylene balloons equipped with acoustic sensors. (USAF)

The X-Ray nuclear test explosion, 14 April 1948, as part of Operation SANDSTONE, was used to calibrate airborne sensors and particle collectors that would later be used on the edges of the Soviet Union. (USAEC)

cooperation reached between the British and the Americans during the Second World War), each nation shared information, particularly on those aspects that were sensitive to the interests of both parties, such as the atomic development of the Soviet Union.

The climate of mutual suspicion between the United States and United Kingdom (on the one hand) and the Soviet Union (on the other) was already tangible in 1947. The fears were not only military but also political, because no one was unaware of the formidable expansion that communism had experienced in Europe and Asia, which had always been accompanied by a symmetrical territorial

occupation. As a philosophical and economic concept, Soviet communism was antagonistic on almost all issues to western capitalism. The difference was most evident in sensitive aspects of the individual, such as religion (communism was atheistic and anti-clerical) and private property (communism favoured collectivism). All these differences put to work simultaneously generated a conceptual gulf between the recent allies in the war against Nazi-fascism and Japanese imperialism. But the issue was not merely rhetorical, because the ideological expansion of communism ended up meaning the physical expansion of the Soviet Union, which threatened the postwar geopolitical interests of the United States and of the United Kingdom. The warlike confrontation between the two blocs seemed imminent, so each one prepared for a Third World War that seemed inevitable.

In 1948 the USAF used B-29 bombers modified to the WB-29 "weather" version to capture the radioactive debris released by the nuclear tests that were carried out that year in the Pacific, including registration 44-62214 at Eielson AFB, Alaska. (USAF)

Filter removal process of a QB-17 drone used on 14 May 1948 to fly into the mushroom cloud of the Zebra nuclear explosion. The analysis of filters and samples made it possible to confirm the long-distance nuclear detection method by capturing radioactive isotopes of xenon-133 and krypton-85 that Luis Walter Álvarez had postulated. (USAEC)

The presence of large US aircraft was frequent at the El Palomar Military Air Base, as is the case of this Douglas C-54 Skymaster of the Air Transport Command photographed in 1947, shortly after the creation of the USAF. (Atilio Marino via Vladimiro Cettolo)

The Douglas C-47B Skytrain serial 35284/15836 registration 44-76252 (painted 476252) was the first aircraft of the United States Air Mission to be used in Argentina after the creation of the USAF in 1947. Note the American and Argentina painted on the left side next to the cockpit. (Atilio Marino via Vladimiro Cettolo)

3

SUPERFORTRESSES OVER HUEMUL (1949-1952)

The US intelligence unit AFOAT-1 had an early triumph in discovering the first Soviet atomic test, carried out in secret on 29 August 1949 on the Semipalatinsk steppe, Kazakhstan SSR. The detonation was detected by acoustic, seismic and electromagnetic sensors, but it was the aerial capture of radioactive particles, carried out with planes and stratospheric balloons, which made it possible to confirm without any doubt of the presence of a nuclear explosion.

The first radioactive debris released into the atmosphere by the Soviet nuclear bomb was detected by a specially modified Air Weather Service Boeing WB-29 Superfortress flying, under weather research cover, between the US air bases at Misawa (Japan) and Eielson (Alaska). This allowed the Tracerlab Inc laboratory in Cambridge, Massachusetts, to quickly confirm that the Soviets had achieved the scientific and industrial capacity necessary to produce an atomic bomb almost in the time estimated by British intelligence and 11 years before the forecast by the US secret services. As a consequence of this finding, on 23 September 1949, President Harry S. Truman forced Soviet leader Josef Stalin to admit that his country had indeed carried out its first successful nuclear test.

The success of AFOAT-1 not only validated the money invested by the US government in its scientific air force but also guaranteed a virtually unlimited budget for long-distance detection air operations. With this endorsement, the USAF progressively expanded the acoustic, electromagnetic, radiological, and seismic network over which it would monitor foreign atomic activities.[1]

From the detection of radioactive particles carried out in 1948 in the Enewetak atoll during Operation SANDSTONE and in 1949 during the Soviet explosion in Semipalatinsk, by 1950 AFOAT-1 was already clear that the mass of plutonium produced in a natural uranium pile was proportional to the amount of krypton-85 produced in the same pile by fission of uranium-235. And it is that, in the uranium dissolution process to produce plutonium,

The first Soviet nuclear explosion took place on 29 August 1949 on the Semipalatinsk steppe, Kazakhstan. The RDS-1 bomb, codenamed Joe-1, was a copy of Little Boy, built from Manhattan Project blueprints obtained by espionage. (TASS)

the chemically inert gas krypton was released into the atmosphere with the rest of the dissolution gases in an amount proportional to the number of grammes of plutonium recovered. Therefore, measuring the total mass of the radioactive isotope krypton-85 in the atmosphere made it possible to measure the total amount of plutonium processed. The subject was extremely sensitive, because through laboratory processes the nuclear capabilities of the Soviets could be accurately determined, for which reason the US detection resources had to be kept under the utmost secrecy. Consequently, all AFOAT-1 documents, instructions and operations related to particle capture were classified as Top Secret.

For its long-range radioactive tracking missions, AFOAT-1 used modified bombers, such as this Boeing WB-29 of the USAF 53rd Strategic Reconnaissance Squadron (registration 42-65281), originally built as a B-29-25-MO. Note the absence of weapons on its tail turret, the sampling device at the rear of the fuselage, and the ventral weather radar hemisphere. (USAF)

The wrecks of the Douglas C-47B-50-DK Skytrain of the USAF that crashed in La Poma, Salta, on 17 February 1949. The plane was military but the documentation presented to the air traffic services referred to it as civilian and carrier of a commercial registration that, in reality, corresponded to another aircraft. (BAAA)

The scientists gathered at AFOAT-1 knew that the Earth's atmosphere did not contain krypton-85 before 1944, when the gas began to be released by virtue of the industrial processes that would lead to the construction of the first American nuclear weapons. They also knew that the United Kingdom had not released krypton-85 until 1951 and that the mass of krypton-85 released into the atmosphere by the operations of the Hanford Site (Benton, Washington State) and Chalk River (Canada) power plants could be calculated from 1945 to 1951, so all the rest would inevitably have to be of foreign production. To determine the amount of krypton-85 resulting from Soviet plutonium production, one only needed to subtract the amount produced by the United States,

the United Kingdom, and Canada from the measured total. Thus, the Soviet Union and any other country that might aspire to join the nuclear club in the future had to continue to be monitored. Under this paradigm, at the beginning of 1951 the AFOAT-1 unit organised a programme of continuous monitoring of krypton-85 outside the United States under the code name of Operation BLUENOSE.[2, 3, 4]

In this context, and unexpectedly, on 24 March 1951, President Juan Domingo Perón called a press conference at the Casa Rosada during which he stated that: 'on 16 February 1951, at the Huemul Island Atomic Energy Pilot Plant (…) thermonuclear experiments were carried out under control conditions on a technical scale.'

General (US Army) Matthew Bunker Ridgway, commander of all US forces in the Caribbean, on his arrival at Morón Airport, along with his wife, on 7 July 1949. He is accompanied by Argentine Army Generals Víctor Majó, Carlos von der Becke and Franklin Lucero. Ridgway had a lucid performance in the Second World War and the Korean War. The plane is a Boeing B-17 modified to executive transport. (AGN via Lucas Giani)

The Hanford Site, Washington nuclear plant, along the Columbia River, was the United States' primary facility for processing uranium and producing plutonium. On 2 and 3 December 1949, iodine-131 and xenon-133 was intentionally released so that they could be detected by AFOAT-1 intelligence planes, which had been calibrated to pick up these radioisotopes. (USAEC)

Immediately after the announcement, in the White Room of the Government House, the Austrian scientist Ronald Richter received the title of doctor honoris causa from the University of Buenos Aires and, later, the Peronist Loyalty Medal, which the president himself imposed on him. The president's wife, María Eva Duarte de Perón, absolute symbol of the ruling political power, ministers, some provincial governors, members of the legislative branch, generals, admirals and brigadiers representing the three armed forces participated in the event. The president's speech was broadcast on Radio Nacional and the entire event was extensively covered in the press.[5]

One day after Perón's announcement, on 25 March, Professor Richter, head of the Huemul atomic project, gave a press conference to some 20 journalists summoned to the presidential residence of the Unzué Palace, where he elaborated on technical aspects regarding what had been announced the day before by Perón. Richter was accompanied by Colonel Enrique P. González and his son (who acted as interpreter), the Secretary of Information Raúl Alejandro Apold, Colonel Nicolás Plantamura and other officials, which gave the meeting the importance of a true state event.

Richter's presentation lasted three hours, an awful lot of time for meetings of this nature, even considering that the questions and answers had to be translated from German to Spanish. Richter showed a knack for describing the intricate problems of nuclear research in terms understandable to the uninitiated, a knack he had used almost two years earlier in front of Perón, when he had expounded his ideas on nuclear fusion. He described in some detail how energy could be obtained by fissioning nuclei of uranium-235 or plutonium-239, or by fusing light elements such as hydrogen and lithium.[6]

At one point, Richter got onto the business of building nuclear bombs, a topic of eminent military interest. He said that 'the path chosen by the United States to obtain the first hydrogen bomb from tritium was wrong' and, speaking about the secrets of the hydrogen bomb, indicated that 'this we could verify at any time, but we do not because we respect the secrets of our friends'. Going even further, Richter stated that:

We worked, for example, with deuterium or lithium hydride but during the work a lot was learned, and this in turn is related to the hydrogen bomb. Perhaps it is interesting to state, referring now to the studies carried out on Huemul Island, that during thermonuclear reactions we have reached enormous gas velocities. In subsequent publications we will show that speeds of up to 3,200 kilometres per second have been reached, which is equivalent, more or less, to a thousand times more than the speeds of the gases of the explosives and fuels used in rockets. These results were obtained without difficulty. (…) For the first time it has been possible to produce a thermonuclear explosion inside a reactor. In Argentina it is possible to produce atomic bombs, but, according to what I know, the president is opposed to that. (…) The hydrogen bomb would only have disadvantages for us. We know the processes that lead to obtaining the hydrogen bomb and we know that they are enormously expensive. If we wanted to make hydrogen bombs we would have to proceed to invest the same amount of capital, as has been done in other countries, but we want to avoid that.[7]

In the first part of the interview, Richter devoted himself to providing a summary of the state of atomic research using uranium worldwide. In the second, he referred to Argentine research methods to generate atomic energy without uranium. Questioned by journalists regarding Argentina's ability to produce an atomic bomb, Richter stated that: 'Argentina can now manufacture the atomic bomb. However, President Perón has no intention of ordering the manufacture of this military device.'[8]

The Argentine Air Force was structured with British planes, German instructors and a US organisation. The photo illustrates the visit of Major Alexander Prokofiev de Seversky to the Tandil Air Base on 17 May 1949. He was one of the main promoters of the integrated air power doctrine and was one of the fathers of the Strategic Air Command of the USAF. He is accompanied by Commodore Eduardo Pacífico Correa, Lieutenant Alberto Gerardo Biedma, Captain Demóstenes Ramos, Commander Roberto José Renauld, Commodore Virgilio del Bosco and Commander Esteban Oscar Facio. (AGN via Lucas Giani)

Perón and Richter's announcements shocked the international scientific community as it seemed that Argentina, a distant country untouched by the Second World War, had joined the extremely select club of nuclear powers in record time. The matter was discussed in the Bulletin of the Atomic Scientists, where it was noted that the Austrian scientist's announcement had not revealed details of the operating system of his purported thermonuclear reactor. It was also pointed out that Richter had alluded to three key advances during the experimentation, but that he had not elaborated on any of them during the press conference. Finally, although Richter had announced the method for measuring the temperature inside his reactor, the temperature itself had not been measured. The US Atomic Energy Commission's comment on the statements made in Buenos Aires was simply that 'the Argentine government announced more than a year ago that it planned to engage in nuclear research'. The matter began to generate scepticism and there were not a few who affirmed that Argentina had aired the hypothesis of building

The first nuclear reactor proposed by Dr. Ronald Richter, cylindrical in shape, consumed 1,400 cubic metres of concrete, equivalent to almost 20,000 bags of cement. The structure had no iron. This is how it was seen by Juan Domingo Perón and his wife Eva Duarte during a visit to Huemul Island on 8 April 1950. Before it entered service, Richter ordered its demolition. (dr. Paul-J. Hahn)

an atomic bomb only for the lanterns of the bipolar world to turn towards Perón.[9, 10]

After thoroughly reviewing the matter, American physicists completely rejected Perón's and Richter's announcements. One of them, George Gamow, said that the whole thing 'seemed to be 95% pure propaganda, 4¾% thermonuclear reactions on a very small scale, and the remaining ¼% probably something better.' George Thomson, who at the time headed the United Kingdom Atomic Energy Commission, suggested that what Perón and Richter said was simply exaggerated. This opinion was replicated by Mark Oliphant in Australia and by Werner Heisenberg and Otto Hahn in Germany. Perhaps the most scathing criticism came from Manfred von Ardenne, a German physicist then working on the Soviet Union's atomic programme, who advised that Richter's claims should be ignored, pointing out that he had worked with him during the war and therefore he knew he was prone to mistaking fantasy for reality.[11]

Austrian physicist Hans Thirring, director of the Institute for Theoretical Physics in Vienna and a well-known author on nuclear issues, wrote to a journalist that 'if Richter had really achieved the path to controlled nuclear fusion, the Nobel prize would be too small for him.' Precisely for this reason, Thirring decided to investigate Richter's scientific and academic background, particularly his work prior to his settlement in Argentina. He discovered that Richter had studied at the University of Prague in the 1930s with Heinrich Rausch von Traubenberg (who described him as a peculiar eccentric), but he also found that von Traubenberg had died in 1944. On the other hand, Richter's thesis had never been published and the University of Prague had been destroyed during the war. To make matters worse, Thirring did not find a single scientific publication by Richter on nuclear or thermonuclear issues, that is, on what he claimed to be an expert in.

Against this background, in May 1951 Thirring published a short article in the United Nations World magazine entitled 'Is Perón's atomic bomb a scam?' in which he affirmed:

there is a 50 percent probability that Perón would have been the victim of a fantasist who, at the same time, would have succumbed to his own illusions; 40 percent that Perón had been the victim of a fraudster; 9 percent that Perón, with the help of Richter, was trying to fool the world; and, finally, the rest, that is, 1 percent, that what Richter maintained was true.

In other words: 'there is a 99 to 1 chance that the explosion in Argentina occurred only in [Richter's] imagination or that it was a hoax.' So sure was Thirring of what he was saying that he invited Richter to refute his statements.[12]

Richter's response appeared in the July 1951 issue of the United Nations World, where he gave no explanation of his findings, experiments, or discoveries, though he did say: 'in our pilot plant we probably have more knowledge of the kinetics of the thermonuclear reaction than the United States and Great Britain at the present time. [...] We successfully tested our thermonuclear reactor for the first time on a technical scale.' In the same letter, Richter dismissed Thirring as 'a typical textbook professor with a strong scientific inferiority complex, probably fuelled by political hatred'.[13]

Dr. Ronald Richter in his laboratory on Huemul Island, where he claimed to have accomplished thermonuclear experiments under control conditions on a technical scale on 16 February, 1951. (Dr. Paul-J. Hahn)

Richter's response to Thirring's severe questioning was so vague and insubstantial that it led many to suspect that the alleged thermonuclear fusion achieved on Huemul Island was actually a lie. One of the most lapidary comments came from the Brazilian press: 'Perón discovered atomic energy as Stalin invented the telephone'.[14,15]

However, not all opinions were contrary or sceptical about what could be happening in secret in Argentina. In his press conference on 25 March 1951, Ronald Richter had repeatedly spoken out about the hydrogen bomb, a top-secret weapon whose principle of operation had been proposed by Edward Teller and Stanislaw Ulam only a few weeks earlier, on 9 March.[16]

Furthermore, to the surprise of everyone, Richter was talking about thermonuclear bombs before the first of these devices had even been detonated. The controversy surrounding the existence of controlled thermonuclear reactions in the Huemul Island reactor persisted when on 8 May 1951, a few weeks after Richter's announcement, the first test of the concept took place on the Enewetak Atoll in the Pacific Ocean. The experiment, named George, was carried out as part of Operation GREENHOUSE and was considered small-scale as it achieved a blast of just 225 kilotons, but it raised scientists' expectations to near certainty that the Teller-Ulam concept would work. The final test came a few months later, on 1 November 1952, when the Teller-Ulam configuration was tested for the first time on a full scale in the Ivy Mike explosion, also carried out at Enewetak Atoll. The explosion had a yield of 10.4 megatons, that is, 450 times more greater than that of the atomic bomb dropped on Nagasaki during the Second World War.[17,18]

So, already in March 1951 there were reasons to be concerned about what Argentina could be secretly doing in nuclear matters. The suspicion that Perón could be looking for a nuclear bomb had already been installed in 1947 by William Mizelle, correspondent for the New Republic newspaper, based on several suggestive facts, especially the invitation addressed by the Argentine government to the world-famous physicist German Werner Heisenberg and other European physicists (Richard Gans, Giancarlo Vallauri and Léon Brillouin), as well as the discovery of the important Soberanía uranium deposit in Mendoza. The way in which Perón handled the

Austrian physicist Ronald Richter and Argentine President Juan Domingo Perón pose in the White Room of Government House on 24 March 1951. They could not understand each other, because the former did not speak Spanish and the latter did not speak German. For Washington analysts, what they announced together was worrying because it could unbalance the world geopolitical map. (Guido Ghiretti)

nuclear issue also generated suspicions, since the laboratories and facilities on Huemul Island were built in the utmost secrecy, in a totally isolated place, and surrounded by military security. On the other hand, the National Atomic Energy Commission (CNEA),

The George nuclear test, carried out on 9 May 1951 in the Enewetak Atoll as part of Operation GREENHOUSE, was a scientific experiment aimed at testing the feasibility of a thermonuclear bomb by atomic fusion as proposed by Edward Teller and Stanislaw Ulam. At that precise moment, Ronald Richter declared that Argentina had managed to release the same thermonuclear energy in a controlled manner in a reactor. (National Nuclear Security Administration)

created on 31 May 1950 by Decree No. 10,936/50, had been placed under the direction of a military man (Colonel Enrique P. González), who was also designated head of the National Directorate of Atomic Energy (DNEA), which was to provide assistance and logistical support to the project.[19, 20]

For the British scientists, who in March 1951 were secretly working on the concept of fusion by confinement of plasma in a magnetic field, the possibility that Ronald Richter had achieved very small-scale reactions could not be ruled out, nor could the possibility of replicating the experiment at higher levels once all its operating principles are known. For his part, the American physicist Ernest Orlando Lawrence, winner of the Nobel Prize in Physics in 1939, an eminent member of the Manhattan Project and one of the promoters of the hydrogen bomb, was not at all contemptuous of the atomic announcement made in Argentina. In his own words: 'there's a tendency to laugh it off like a lot of hot air or something. Well, maybe, but we don't know everything, and we should do everything we can to find out'.[21]

This constituted a direct appeal to action for the Atomic Energy Commission and also for AFOAT-1, which was the only organisation with the technical capacity to determine whether Argentina was processing materials for the construction of a conventional fission atomic bomb, the first step for the construction of the most powerful thermonuclear bomb. As if this were not enough, Richter had stated that he could check the secrets of the hydrogen bomb at any time, but that he had not done so at the Huemul Island Atomic Power Pilot Plant "because we respect the secrets of our friends." To which "friends" was the Austrian scientist referring? American scientists? To his government? To Soviet scientists? To the Soviet Union? British scientists? Who were the "friends" who could be collaborating with Argentina in the development of this technology? The expression had a profound implication considering that one of the pillars of the foreign policy of the Argentine Republic, postulated by the ruling Peronism, was the so-called Third Position, which consisted of maintaining a total equidistance with respect to the bipolarity born in the Cold War between the United States, the Soviet Union and their respective allied countries.

Cover of the Clarín newspaper of 25 March 1951. Following Perón's statements and the newsletter prepared by the President's Press Secretary, Raúl Apold, the newspaper speaks of the "liberation of atomic energy". US intelligence was immediately put on alert due to the military implications that this could have. (Clarín)

The American physicist Ernest Orlando Lawrence (8 August 1901 –27 August 1958), one of the brightest brains behind the hydrogen bomb. When Argentina announced that it was handling atomic energy, Lawrence recommended doing everything possible to find out, which was a direct call to action for AFOAT-1. (US Department of Energy)

Richter's statements caused deep concern in the American, British and Soviet intelligence services, each one suspicious of the contacts that Argentina could have with its rival. But only one country, the United States, had the instrumental capacity to detect long-distance traces of krypton-85, xenon-133 and other gases that would make it possible to infer the true state of progress of the Argentine atomic programme. Consequently, AFOAT-1 was activated to prepare for a series of secret aerial photography and radioactive isotope sampling missions over Huemul Island. The agency had the necessary resources to carry them out, specifically Boeing WB-29 aircraft from the Air Weather Service, which it was enough to present to the Argentine authorities, arguing any weather excuse or any weather screen. Once in Buenos Aires, these planes could easily reach Huemul Island and return; or continue in a triangular trajectory to Santiago de Chile or Mendoza, as necessary. Indeed, the B-29 Superfortress had a radius of action of 9,000 kilometres, although the WB-29 version enjoyed greater range since it did not have to carry the weight of the bombs or the guided machine gun turrets.[22]

As if the above were not enough, it turns out that since October 1950 the ultra-secret AFOAT-1 agency had one of its detachments, Unit 108 (also known as Special Weather Unit 108) at the El Tepual airport in the city of Puerto Montt, Chile, whose concrete runway supported the operation of a Boeing B-29. The airport was located at 41° 26' 19" south latitude, 73° 05' 38" west longitude, practically at the same latitude as Huemul Island (41° 06' 23" south–71° 23' 42'' west), from which they were barely 147 kilometres away in a straight line, an insignificant journey for a long-range reconnaissance plane like the B-29. These planes could also operate from Santiago

de Chile, where AFOAT-1 had another secret detachment, Unit 123, also active from 1951.[23]

Both Special Weather Units, the one in Puerto Montt and the one in Santiago, were under USAF control, which is to say that they had all the logistical and intelligence support necessary to operate. It was enough to draw up an innocuous international flight plan from Buenos Aires to Puerto Montt (even from Montevideo to Puerto Montt) to fly over Huemul Island, take pictures of its sensitive facilities, capture samples of radioactivity in the air, and then land innocently at its destination, where film rolls and particulate filters could be removed or recharged. Spy overflights could also be carried out in the opposite direction, starting from Santiago de Chile or Puerto Montt, although nothing prevented round-trip flights from and arriving at the same aerodrome located in Chilean territory. It goes without saying that Unit 108 of AFOAT-1 had full institutional coverage to operate secretly, since by 1950 a permanent Military Mission was operating in Chile in the United States with personnel who had diplomatic immunity and their own aircraft.[24, 25]

AFOAT-1 moved fast. On 21 September 1950, a USAF Boeing B-29 Superfortress arrived at the Morón Mixed Airport (civilian and military) which, according to the press, was arriving 'on a good-neighborly mission across the American Continent and will remain in our country until tomorrow'. The plane was received by the Commander of Transportation of the Argentine Air Force, Brigadier Eduardo T. Chueca, by the head of the I Air Brigade, Commodore Jorge Aníbal Rodríguez. and by the head of the United States Air Mission in Argentina, Colonel Robert B. Knapp. The 14 crew members of the B-29 were declared official guests of the Ministry of Aeronautics and housed at the Morón Military Air Base. They were Captain Orvand Fraker (Commander), Captains Bearde and Cassetti, Lieutenants Hondrek, Emde and Mass, Sergeants G Moss, S Moss, Mottola, Lefabe and Murray and Corporals Bensol, Bery and Wisse.[26, 27]

The journalistic coverage carried out by a chronicler from the newspaper La Nación, although very opaque, shed light on the strange visitor, since the report stated that the plane bore the name of *Miss Manuki II* and that it had the number 461947 painted on the tail. The chronicler was informed that the plane belonged to the Seventh Reconnaissance Group of the USAF, based at the Barksdale base. But it turns out that the 7th Photographic Reconnaissance Group did not exist, since it had been officially dissolved on 6 March 1947, long before the creation of the USAF, so that, by September 1950, it did not even appear on paper.[28] Nor was the B-29 really a B-29. Its registration number 461947, recorded by the La Nación chronicler, allows us to infer that it was the Boeing F-13A-55BN serial number 11424 built in 1944 at the Boeing plant in Renton, Washington State. The *Miss Manuki II* was, then, an RB-29, a spy plane that 'due to its reconnaissance and information functions is almost completely devoid of defense weapons', as noted by the La Nación chronicler.[29]

The strategic reconnaissance configuration of the B-29 was developed jointly by the Boeing and Fairchild companies. It consisted of the removal of the combat stations and the installation of six cameras in the rear pressurised compartment of the fuselage, behind the central fire control station. The cameras were arranged in three separate mounts. The first featured a single Fairchild K-18 vertical camera for general photo-reconnaissance work, but K-17, K-19 and K-22 cameras could also be installed there. The second setup consisted of two K-22 short-angle photo-interpretation cameras, which could accurately photograph a three-mile (4.82-kilometre) wide band of surface. The third installation consisted of three K-17B

In March 1951, when Perón and Richter announced that atomic energy had been produced on Huemul Island, the Argentine Air Force had 30 AVRO Lincoln long-range bombers, with a radius of action of 3,500 kilometres. The US intelligence services concluded that the country was secretly working on a nuclear bomb, since it already had the capacity to transport it by air. (Guido Ghiretti)

cameras, the central one pointed vertically and the other two tilted outward, their overlapping spotlights allowing coverage 30 miles (48.28 kilometres) wide.[30]

The chronicler of the newspaper La Nación that covered the arrival of *Miss Manuki II* indicated that the plane was based in Barksdale, which is not a minor fact. Barksdale AFB, near Bossier City, Louisiana, was the seat of the 91st Strategic Reconnaissance Wing, a USAF Strategic Reconnaissance Wing equipped precisely with Boeing RB-29. The purpose of the unit was to provide global intelligence with an emphasis on aerial photography and photo-surveying for mapping. The fact that one of their planes was sent to Argentina in September 1950 could only be due to a really relevant reason, since by then the United States was already engaged in the Korean War, which had begun on 25 June 1950. The long-distance reconnaissance planes of the 91st had already begun to deploy to Johnson Air Base in Iruma, Japan, from where they would fly throughout the war to provide reconnaissance on the movements of North Korean forces. It is, therefore, noteworthy that, in the middle of that conflict, the USAF diverted such a specific intelligence tool to move it to the antipodean Argentina.

Above: Three women from Salta pose in front of the USAF C-47 that crashed in Rosario de la Frontera on 19 August 1950. The plane belonged to the USAF and was based at Albrook AFB, Panama Canal Zone. (Carlos Jesús Maita via Esteban Lerín)

Left: On 19 August 1950, the Douglas C-47B-1-DK Skytrain serial 14091/25536 registration 43-48275 crashed at the Rosario de la Frontera aerodrome, 180 kilometres south of Salta. Note the titles on its fuselage, alluding to the US Air Mission in Buenos Aires. (Carlos Jesús Maita via Esteban Lerín)

A Boeing WB-29 of the USAF 55th Weather Reconnaissance Squadron is decontaminated for radiation at Indian Springs AFB on 20 April 1952, after being flown into the mushroom atomic bombs tested at the Nevada Test Site during Operation TUMBLER-SNAPPER. Note the weather radar hemisphere on its belly and the air sampling device emerging from the rear of the fuselage. (USAF)

As if this were not enough, it transpired that the *Miss Manuki II* arrived in Argentina with a remarkably large crew. Indeed, the F-13/RB-29 crew normally consisted of six or seven people: commander/pilot, flight engineer, navigator, radio operator, photo-navigator, a cameraman and, in some cases, a radar operator. The *Miss Manuki II* landed in Morón with twice as many crew members, which may indicate that its occupants would be very busy in a very short period of time, probably due to the continuous replacement of rolls and packages of photographic film that they were interested in obtaining. It is not clear where the plane was flying from, but since it was on a so-called good neighbour mission across the South American continent it is obvious that it must have flown to or from Chile, which means that it could have diverted to photograph the facilities of Huemul Island from high altitude. It would not have been detected because, by 1950, the Argentine Air Force did not have any air traffic or air defence radar installed in its territory. The first, an SCR 588-B, would just start operating in Merlo, Province of Buenos Aires, on 12 December 1952.[31]

Miss Manuki II was not the only intelligence aircraft deployed by the USAF to Argentina, presumably to spy on the degree of progress of the ultra-secret constructions on Huemul Island. It is possible that AFOAT-1 had several others, particularly those with the capacity to detect radioactive particles, and this hypothesis is confirmed from a photograph preserved in the General Archive of the Nation, where a second B-29 can be seen in Argentina, in this case a WB-29 of the Air Weather Service parked in front of the passenger terminal of the Morón Mixed Airport. It is a different plane from the *Miss Manuki II*, not only because its name does not appear painted on the nose, but also because the photo shows seven crew members in flight uniform in contrast to the 14 of the RB-29 reported by the newspaper La Nación

A USAF Boeing F-13/RB-29 warms up its engines on the apron of the Presidente Rivadavia Airport in Morón in 1952. Following Perón and Richter's announcements, several secret AFOAT-1 spy missions took place over the Huemul Island in an attempt to obtain data on the Argentine atomic project. (Juan Carlos Cicalesi via Vladimiro Cettolo)

In the photo kept by the General Archive of the Nation, the crew of the second B-29 detected in Buenos Aires can be seen together with two officers from the Argentine Air Force and six members of the USAF Air Mission in Argentina. The plane was clearly a scientific research plane, lacking the machine gun turret located on the top of the fuselage, it had a bulging weather radar on its belly, and it displayed a strange measuring instrument on the right side of the fuselage, just behind the cockpit. The photo reveals a final number "0" on the right cover of the nose wheel, which allows us to infer that the registration number of the photographed aircraft could have been 44-87440, corresponding to the Boeing WB-29 (B-29-90-BW) serial number 12543, then serving in the 57th Strategic Reconnaissance Squadron, 1500th Air Base Group, based at Hickam AFB, Hawaii.

The 57th Strategic Reconnaissance Squadron was in charge of conducting long-range weather flights over the Arctic and along the northern periphery of the Soviet Union to detect radioactive debris. To this end, their WB-29s were equipped with sensors that allowed them to detect particles and gases, and thus later determine in the laboratory the type and power of the detonated nuclear device or the production of the overflown nuclear power plant, just what AFOAT intended to do with the nuclear reactor that Argentina was building on Huemul Island. Although the Boeing RB-29 and WB-29 already had radioactive detection equipment since 1947, as of 24 October 1950, a highly classified measurement device called AME (Atmospheric Measurement Equipment) was installed, which suggests that the photo of the WB-29 of the Air Weather Service captured in Morón was taken after that date.[32] Thus, while the public missions of the WB-29 were meteorological reconnaissance, their real and covert missions consisted of atmospheric sampling in search of debris from atomic explosions or gases resulting from the atomic fission process in nuclear reactors. Each radioactive spy plane was equipped with air sampling ducts, called Bug Scoops or Crackerboxes by their crews. The first sampling ducts were placed under the wings, then under the fuselage and finally in the place of the B-29's aft upper machine gun turret, which was removed on the WB-29s. The ducts had paper or cloth filters inside that collected the radioactive particles that entered under pressure in accordance with the horizontal speed of the aircraft. The filters were changed at regular intervals throughout the mission, which required a particular effort from the crew since the process was manual. They were then analysed on land for the information they had recorded.[33]

Outwardly the WB-29s were identical to the B-29s, except for the removal of the machine gun turrets and the addition of a radar for weather and surface tracking. The interior had been modified to serve the new covert purpose, to which end all weapons circuitry and offensive capabilities had been removed from the plane. The radar operator's position was moved to the forward cabin, where he shared a table on the left side with the navigator. The position of the radio operator, in turn, moved from the right rear corner of the forward compartment to the rear pressurised compartment.

Special weather equipment installed aboard WB-29s, and manned by the weather observer, included a MIL-313 psychrometer that used wet and dry bulb thermometers to measure water vapour in the air, an ID/AMQ-2 airbrush to determine the relative humidity of the environment, an SCR-718 radio-altimeter, an AN/APN radar altimeter, and several AN/AMT extensible or ejectable radiosonde units that were deployed from the aircraft or were dropped in small parachutes, and that, in both cases, they radioed their temperature, humidity, and pressure readings. However, the most characteristic and specific modification of the WB-29 was the Bug Scoop for radioactive tracking, whose operation was quite complicated. Although each segment of the planned trajectory had precise points where the filters had to be changed, the general rule was to replace them at every change of heading or altitude, or every two hours. Each filter change required the complete depressurization of the aircraft and the use of oxygen masks by the entire crew. The plane was then re-pressurised and remained so until the full cycle began in an hour and a half.

The WB-29 had a crew of eight: the weather observer, the two pilots, the flight engineer, the navigator and the radar observer were located in the forward compartment. In the aft compartment were the descending radiosonde operator and team leader, each seated by the left and right circular observation windows. Also in the rear compartment were the radio operator and the radio-sounding operator, who transcribed the meteorological data received from the radiosondes.[34]

It is impossible to know precisely how many photographic or radioactive reconnaissance operations were carried out over Argentine territory by the Boeing RB-29 and WB-29 of the USAF and the Air Weather Service or how many planes were involved in these secret activities. However, there are some indications that allow us to infer that, at a certain moment, they were warned by the authorities of the Argentine Air Force or by the State Information Coordination Secretariat (CIDE) which, since its creation in 1946, unified the reports of the intelligence agencies of the Armed Forces.

The first indication that Argentine intelligence was aware of the strange "meteorological" flights carried out by the RB/WB-29 over our territory is the decision adopted by the national government at the beginning of 1951, according to which it was decided to put an end to the permanent mission of the USAF in Argentina. The measure

A USAF Boeing WB-29 refuelled at an air base in the Pacific before the start of a mission to collect radioactive samples in 1951. The AFOAT-1 Agency's long-distance nuclear detection network even reached Argentina. (USAF)

From 1940, the US Air Mission moved with absolute freedom in Argentina with planes that also carried out diplomatic missions, such as this Douglas C-47 Skytrain photographed at the Pigüé aerodrome, Buenos Aires, on 30 July 1950. An operation of aerial photography or atmospheric sampling over Huemul Island did not represent a major challenge for the USAF. (Jose Abelardo Agrusti)

was implemented through an exchange of diplomatic notes dated 2 March 1951 and 27 March 1951 in Washington, by virtue of which the United States and Argentina agreed to extend until 29 June 1951 the Military Aviation Mission Agreement signed on 29 June 1940.[35]

But when 29 June 1951 arrived, USAF officers continued working in Buenos Aires, so on 12 October 1951, the Argentine Embassy in Washington officially informed the US Department of State that the Argentine government had decided to dispense with the Military Aviation Mission, an elegant way of expressing that the permanent officers of the USAF could no longer continue working in Argentine territory, where they could not continue to operate their planes, except for prior authorisation considered on a case-by-case basis.[36]

As the US mission continued to function in fact, on 17 December 1951, the Department of State received a ratifying note of the decision of the Argentine government, dated in Buenos Aires on 12 December 1951, which put an end to the US Air Mission after 12 years of uninterrupted military activity.[37, 38]

It is obvious to say that a decision of this nature, communicated to the US government on three different occasions during the same year, not only demonstrated the determination of the Argentine government to withdraw all USAF officers from the country, but also allows one to assume the existence of a serious reason (or at least serious suspicions) as the basis for the measure, even if such reasons were not made explicit in order to maintain diplomatic relations in the face of the world's greatest military superpower.

The second indication that the Argentine government suspected that the Americans were carrying out intelligence with airplanes on its territory in general, and on Huemul Island in particular, is the

fact that the decision to put an end to the Military Aviation Mission was taken on 2 March 1951, almost a year after the visit to Argentina of the USAF commander in the Caribbean, General Rosenbaum Beam, coordinator of the US air missions in Latin America. The fact is not minor considering that his presence was linked, precisely, to consolidating the permanence of the USAF mission in Argentina.

Furthermore, on 16 March 1950, a few days after General Beam's visit, the USAF Chief of Staff, General Hoyt Sanford Vandenberg, together with General Robert LeGrow Walsh, had arrived in Buenos Aires aboard a Lockheed Constellation. During their two-day stay, the US officers were received by the highest aeronautical and defence authorities of Argentina, including the Minister of Aeronautics (Brigadier César Ojeda), the Minister of Foreign Affairs and Worship (Dr. Jesús Hipólito Paz) , the Minister of National Defence (General José Humberto Sosa Molina), the Minister of the Army (General Franklin Lucero) and the head of the Argentine Air Force (Brigadier General Oscar Muratorio).[39]

In addition to the above, on 2 May 1950, two months after General Vandenberg's visit, General Robert LeGrow Walsh visited Argentina again, arriving in an executive Boeing B-17 to meet with the President Peron. What could have happened in Argentina so that, barely a year after so many signs of consideration and respect for the highest authorities of the USAF, the government decided to order the departure of the US air mission?[40, 41, 42]

The third indication that the Argentine government was suspicious of the intelligence flights carried out over Huemul Island is that, after the departure of the US air mission, the Ministry of Aeronautics and the Argentine Air Force ordered that no foreign

Brigadier General Robert D. Knapp Jr (USAF Air Mission Chief) and General Bruce Hovey (Air Attaché to the United States Embassy in Buenos Aires) pose in 1952 with distinguished members of the Salta community. In the background is the Douglas C-47 Skytrain of the US Air Mission in Argentina. (Carlos Jesús Maita via Esteban Lerín)

military aircraft could fly in Argentine airspace unless it did so with an Argentine pilot in its crew, the only way to confirm, through effective control of their trajectories and points flown over, that their operation was innocuous to Argentine national strategic interests.[43]

The fourth indication that allows us to infer the suspicions of the Argentine government towards US intelligence is an aviation accident with tragic consequences. On 18 February 1949, Brigadier General B.H. Covey, military attaché at the US embassy in Buenos Aires, informed the Argentine Air Force that the previous day a Douglas C-47 Skytrain plane had disappeared in northern Argentina. The plane had lost radio contact on the way between the Chilean city of Antofagasta and the city of Salta. A search and rescue operation was immediately organised involving Argentine and Chilean aircraft, and two Boeing B-17 Flying Fortress bombers that departed from Antofagasta. The wreck of the lost plane were located about 150 kilometres west of the city of Salta, four kilometres from Cerro Incamayo, near a place called La Poma, department of San Antonio de los Cobres.[44, 45]

The remains of the C-47 were spotted from the air by Colonel Robert B. Knapp, head of the USAF Air Mission in Argentina, from another North American C-47 assigned to his embassy. The lost plane had been destroyed by the impact and its three crew members and five passengers were dead. The deceased were Colonel Gerald Evan Williams, Pilot in Command and Air Attaché of the United States Embassy in Buenos Aires, co-pilot Captain Charley Mayo, Chief Petty Officers Robert Frazier, Uriah Horst, Hugh Millis, Linwood Stanton, Petty Officer Augusto Canestrari and the pilot's wife, Marjorie V. Williams. The crashed aircraft was the Douglas C-47B-50-DK serial number 17141/34408 US registration 45-1138. However, it was flying under a civil flight plan and during the entire journey he had been communicating with air traffic services using the commercial registration NC1138, corresponding to another plane, the Travel Air B serial 205. By this simple device, the USAF could pass off a military flight as civilian and, in this way, move with much more discretion through Argentine airspace.[46, 47]

The fifth indication that supports the suspicions of the Argentine government towards US intelligence is the hasty sanction of Law No. 13,985 on the repression of espionage, sabotage and treason, proposed by the National Executive Power on 25 August 1950 and sanctioned in record time on 29 September 1950. In the legislation, raised by President Perón himself, an attempt was made to punish with a prison term of one to 10 years to anyone who 'procures, seeks,

reveals, sends or takes advantage of news, documents, information or objects, of a political, social, military or economic order that must remain secret based on the security of the defense or the foreign relations of the Nation'. The sentence rose to 15 years if the crimes were committed by the spy 'using his employment, function, status

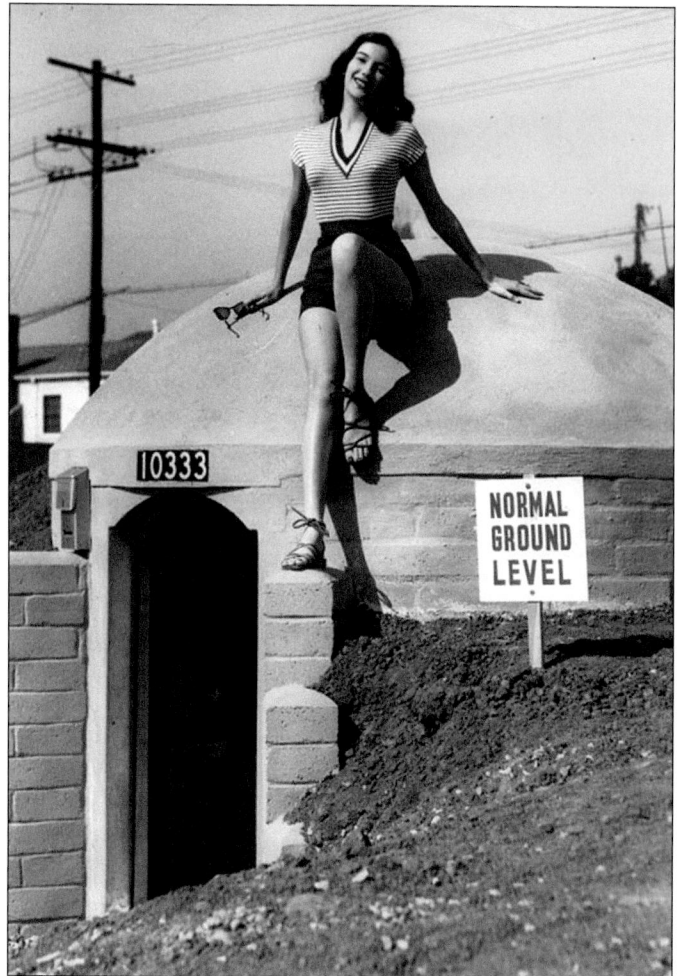

The announcement of the "Argentine atomic bomb" came just at the moment when the US population was experiencing its first nuclear hysteria. In the photo, taken in a San Francisco neighbourhood on 26 February 1951, model Mary Lou Minor is promoting a garden fallout shelter that could be used as a guest house. It was made of reinforced concrete, weighed 12.5 tons and had capacity for six people. (Los Angeles Public Library)

The electronic intelligence and reconnaissance versions of the B-29 bomber were unarmed and therefore overlooked as "harmless". In the photo, an RB-29A-70-BN, very similar in its configuration to the RB-29 named *Miss Manuki II*, which visited Argentina in 1950, undoubtedly on a spy mission. (Ray Wagner)

The Boeing WB-29A registration 44-62090 (serial number 11567) of the USAF 53 Weather Reconnaissance Squadron, photographed over Burtonwood, England, in September 1954. Note the "Bug Catcher" on the rear of its fuselage and the dome of its weather radar in the belly. Due to its registration, it could have been the specimen that was photographed in Argentina in 1950. (R.A. Schoolfield)

or mission' and went up to 25 years in prison 'if the agent acted at the service or benefit of a foreign power'.

From the legislative debate on the bill proposed by Perón, it is clear that one of the objectives of national interest that was sought to be protected was the Bariloche Atomic Energy Pilot Plant. Furthermore, Perón sent his initiative for a law to repress espionage to the National Congress a few days after the Swiss-Italian professor Giovanni Pinardi, in charge of the Juan Perón Altitude Station (from which cosmic rays were studied in the Andes de Mendoza), was exonerated from his position and subjected to proceedings 'for having committed infidelity, before authorities of a foreign country, that compromise the secrecy of work carried out in ours.' Pinardi, who knew about the development of the Huemul Project, had travelled to the United States in 1950, for which reason, upon his return, he was accused of having passed secret information to the US government. Although he was fired from the National University of Cuyo, he could not be charged or punished for espionage because there was no typical figure in the Penal Code that was applicable to him, which is why Perón sent the National Congress the proposal for what became being Law 13,985. With this background, it is not surprising that Perón was unspeakably suspicious of US espionage and that he was uncomfortable with the presence of USAF planes in his country, which explains his decision to put an end to the US Air Mission in Argentina.[48, 49, 50]

The last indication that substantiates the suspicions of espionage by the Argentine government is that the decision to put an end to the US Air Mission was adopted by President Juan Domingo Perón before and not after the coup attempt on 28 September 1951. In other words, the decision was not adopted as retaliation for an internal political event in which the collaboration or assistance of a foreign power was suspected, but for an equally serious cause, but of an earlier date, taking into account that the decision had already It had been communicated by the Argentine Embassy in Washington to the US Department of State by note dated 2 March 1951.

In other words, both the attempt to overthrow President Perón and his suppression and the consequent purge in the three armed forces could have contributed to ratifying the decision to put an end to the US Air Mission, but under no circumstances were they the cause. The decision had already been made beforehand and was harshly implemented by both the new Minister of Aeronautics (Brigadier Juan Ignacio San Martín) and the new Commander-in-Chief of the Argentine Air Force (Brigadier Pedro Castex Lainfor). In the following years, and until the overthrow of President Perón by the coup d'état of September 1955, no US military aircraft returned to operate in Argentina, with the exception of the Douglas C-47 assigned to the US Embassy in Buenos Aires, which was flown with an officer of the Argentine Air Force always in the co-pilot position.

Whatever the motivation that led to the end of the US Air Mission in Argentina, what is certain is that the RB-29 and WB-29 radioactive reconnaissance and sampling planes that flew over Huemul Island did not find the slightest trace of gases resulting from a nuclear fission or fusion process, as well as no trace of a nuclear reactor that could produce atomic energy or atomic fuel on an industrial scale. That is because the entire secret project directed by Ronald Richter in Bariloche had been a farce. Oddly enough, Richter had deceived Perón by exaggerating the experimental results he had arrived at in his laboratory and playing with the president's political aspirations, given that obtaining nuclear energy in Bariloche (and especially by fusion of atoms) would place Argentina in the select club of the world's atomic powers.

The order to suspend all work on the alleged "reactor" on Huemul Island was given on 24 October 1952 after an inspection of the facilities between 5 and 8 September of that year by a scientific commission made up of Otto Gamba, Manuel Beninson, Mario Báncora, Juan Bussolini and José Antonio Balseiro. The scandal was huge and the government tried to keep it in the most absolute secrecy, not only because of the international embarrassment that that farce meant, but because the only political person responsible was Perón, who had blindly trusted Richter, on whose chest he had pinned the Peronist Loyalty Medal. As if the above were not enough, fortunes had been spent on the construction of the Bariloche Atomic Energy Pilot Plant without any practical benefit for the country having been achieved.[51]

USAF Boeing WB-29 parked in front of the Morón Airport terminal, Buenos Aires. The weather radar radome is partially visible on its belly and the upper machine gun turret has been removed, denoting its version. The size of the letters corresponds to the scheme used by the USAF during the Korean War (1950-1953), so the photo was taken in that period, which coincided with the development of the Huemul Project. (AGN)

But the scandal could not be covered up for long. On 5 December 1952, the New York Times newspaper published a two-column, front-page note by journalist Edward A. Morrow entitled 'Perón's atomic dream vanishes', in which he stated that 'the atomic energy project of the Argentina exploded with the force of a bursting soap bubble. According to engineers who participated in the top-secret project, all 300 workers at Argentina's pilot atomic power plant on Huemul Island, in San Carlos de Bariloche, have been laid off'.[52]

The veil of Bariloche's atomic secret had been completely lifted. Despite the fact that the scandal had not been caused at all by the US planes, the suspicion that the USAF flights suspected of spying had generated remained in the Argentine government, for which reason the US Air Mission in Argentina was not re-established despite the unquestionable fact that the alleged espionage activities

could not really have discovered anything since everything that happened on Huemul Island had been a great farce. However, Perón was somewhat right, since Unit 108 of AFOAT-1, set up in Puerto Montt to spy on Huemul's atomic secrets, was only deactivated by the USAF on 7 April 1955.

A gigantic mushroom cloud rises over Enewetak Atoll on 1 November 1952 following the Ivy Mike explosion, the first full-scale test for a thermonuclear bomb, which created a blast of 10.4 megatons, 700 times more powerful than Hiroshima. The United States had attained the technology to mass-produce truly doomsday weapons. (USAEC)

General Hoyt Sanford Vandenberg (24 January 1899 – 2 April 1954) was director of the CIA (1946-1947) and commander-in-chief of the USAF (1948-1953). In this capacity he visited Buenos Aires in 1950, but his presence was not enough to prevent the Perón government from putting an end to the Air Mission in Argentina, suspected of espionage. During World War II, Vandenberg had led the IX Air Force, one of whose units he was in charge of secret operations to capture radioactive particles to learn about the German potential to create nuclear weapons. (USAF)

Edward Teller (15 January 1908 – 9 September 2003) was the father of the hydrogen bomb and one of the greatest promoters of the Cold War arms race. In 1956 he received a job offer from Ronald Richter, which drew the following comment: 'reading one line, one has to think he's a genius. Reading the next, one realizes he's crazy'. (USAEC)

4

THUNDERBIRDS OVER EZEIZA (1953-1954)

For both the United States and the Soviet Union, 1953 was a pivotal year, since during its 12 months there were important changes in the political structure of both nations and, at the same time, a very marked increase in tensions in the Cold War. To begin with, on 20 January, retired General Dwight D. Eisenhower was sworn in as the 34th US president after having won the 1952 election by a wide margin. His victory in the election reflected the prevailing climate, since the average US citizen daily felt the danger of a third world war and the fear of a Soviet surprise attack, which was estimated to be nuclear. Eisenhower had served as Supreme Allied Commander during the Second World War and then as Supreme Allied Commander Europe between April 1951 and May 1952 (providing an important warning to the Soviet Union). His vice president, Richard Nixon, was a staunch anti-communist, which he considered antagonistic to the way of life of the Americans and a complete threat to the security of the country.

A little over a month after the formation of the new administration, and when executive positions were still being assigned in its extensive state organisation chart, unexpected news shook the country and the world. On 5 March 1953, after several days in a coma, the Chairman of the Council of Ministers of the Soviet Union, Josef Stalin, died in Moscow. He had been the builder of Soviet geopolitical power and one of the architects of victory in the Second World War. Already in the post-war period, he had not ceased efforts to expand the areas of influence of the Soviet Union, had increased the extent of the territory under its control and had endowed his country with fearsome nuclear weapons that equalled the United States in power. After the state funeral held in his honour, Stalin was succeeded by Nikita Khrushchev, First Secretary of the Communist Party, a very tough man who had taken part in the bloody defence of the city of Stalingrad during the war. Like Stalin, Khrushchev was suspicious of the Americans, from whom he expected an attack as surprising as it was imminent, since he assumed that the communist and capitalist political systems were antagonistic and that they would seek to cancel each other out, since they represented two completely different worldviews of the individual, of the state, of the community and of politics and the economy.

General Dwight D. Eisenhower, president of the United States from 1953 to 1961, prioritised the mass construction of cheap nuclear weapons for nuclear deterrence, while reducing funding for conventional military forces. His foreign policy was marked by a position of restraint and firmness before the Soviet Union, in the context of rivalry and tension typical of the Cold War. (Bachrac)

Khrushchev was right, since the American plans to attack the Soviet Union dated from the very end of the Second World War. Indeed, shortly after the dropping of the two nuclear bombs on Hiroshima and Nagasaki, US strategists began to analyse how many bombs of the same type would be necessary to, for example, prevail in a hemispheric conflict against the Soviets. Every armed force in the world is built on one or more conflict hypotheses, but the US hypothesis was not a mere game of soldiers, but the continuation of the war that was ending, which can give an idea of the growing suspicion of relation to Soviet expansionism. Joint Staff planners went so far as to consult with Major General Leslie R. Groves, director of the Manhattan Project, about the potential of new weapons being developed at the time, particularly nuclear weapons and long-range missiles. Groves explained that missiles were not technologically feasible in 1945, but that the bombs could be dropped relatively easily by a fleet of strategic bombers faster than the B-29s. However, he warned that the destruction of the Soviet Union's industrial capacity would not affect the outcome of a war, as the Allied strategic bombing of Germany had amply demonstrated.[1]

Far from being intimidated, the strategists adjusted their pencils and statistics. In 1946 a new conflict plan was presented with the Soviet Union in Europe (code name PLINCHER), in 1947 another more extended to Asia (code name BROILER), in 1948 one fully expanded to deep Soviet territory (code name HALFMOON). and in 1949 a definitive one that contemplated a total war on the continents and the oceans (code name OFFTACKLE). These plans were accompanied by corresponding budget adjustments, base

reinforcements, and training exercises. All contemplated the use of nuclear weapons, but the latter became more precise, since it was considered that the only way to defeat the Soviet Union was to pulverise all its cities with massive atomic bombings. In 1950, General Lauris Norstad, Commander-in-Chief of the US Air Force deployed in Europe, calculated that only 60 megatons of nuclear weapons, evenly distributed, were needed to wipe out all Soviet strategic targets with a sudden surprise air attack. between the cities chosen as targets.

Julius Robert Oppenheimer, the father of the atomic bomb, was much more pessimistic and viewed all these plans with concern, he considered them an unnecessary provocation towards the Soviet Union and, furthermore, a direct passport to an unbridled arms race. Far from making plans to build more nuclear bombs, Oppenheimer considered that the defence of the United States should be guaranteed with fewer bombs, since the destructive power of these weapons was so devastating that their mere existence was a deterrent for any adversary. Oppenheimer also warned that the military did not consider at all the main collateral effect of nuclear explosions, which was radioactive fallout or fallout, that is, the precipitation of radioactive waste resulting from the detonation.[2]

Since he was one of the few Americans informed of General Norstad's estimates, Oppenheimer believed that blasts with a yield of "just" 60 megatons at the start of a third world war would not only devastate the chosen targets, but would massive casualties from blast, fore and radioactive fallout. The radioactive fallout could be blown by the wind even towards allied countries or their own positions, where they would probably cause as many casualties as in the cities where the bombs had been dropped.[3]

Oppenheimer's opinion was based on the results of the GABRIEL project, a study begun in 1949 by Nicholas N. Smith Jr of the Oak Ridge Laboratory of the Atomic Energy Commission, with the aim of understanding the qualitative and quantitative properties of radioactive fallout, while documenting the types of isotopes that could pose a threat to human health on a global scale. The study was not military, nor was it aimed at military estimates, but it did raise two essential questions given the context of possible nuclear war: how many bombs could go off in the Soviet Union before lethal or dangerous amounts of radioactivity appeared in the air over North America? And what products resulting from the explosions posed the greatest threat? [4]

The first question was answered by the original 60 megaton yield limit set for the GABRIEL project, which matched General Norstad's estimate, a number that must have puzzled USAF analysts because it was highly accurate and did not come from a military analysis. The second question pointed directly to strontium-90, a radioactive isotope resulting from nuclear detonations, very abundant, with a half-life of 26 years and a dangerous tendency to accumulate in the bone marrow of mammals. To a lesser extent, the iodine-131 isotope, which could affect the thyroid gland of humans, was also analysed. Children with their developing hormonal systems were especially sensitive to exposure to this radioactive element. This led Oppenheimer to strongly advocate for the suspension or delay in the development of the hydrogen bomb, which allowed the release of exponentially increased amounts of energy compared to its atomic predecessor. His attitude earned him the suspicion of the USAF (which was very interested in developing a force of strategic bombers capable of projecting nuclear bombs at long distances) and also the suspicion of Edward Teller, the father of the hydrogen bomb, who began to secretly conspire to get Oppenheimer out of the USAEC and the entire nuclear programme, claiming he was a communist.

More than 1,500 B-47 Stratojet bombers were produced by Boeing, Douglas, and Lockheed for the USAF Strategic Air Command's deterrent nuclear arsenal. As the Cold War escalated, entire squadrons remained in flight and on continual standby, to deal a crushing and decisive first blow to the Soviet Union. (USAF)

By 1953 the predictions of the GABRIEL project had been carried over into the SUNSHINE project, which collected samples of bone, urine, and organic tissues from around the world. All these samples were analysed for radioactive fallout, but they were presented as a study on the nutritional importance and on the naturally occurring radon gas in the environment. Strontium-90 was determined to be a kind of "bone digger" as it was deposited in bone tissue and marrow after ingestion. For certain radiation tests, inmates from Utah state prisons were used and the corpses of stillborn babies were collected to determine the level of radioactivity due to strontium-90 accumulated in their bones.[5, 6, 7]

Another unforeseen event, which also occurred in 1953, sealed the fate of Oppenheimer and, with him, that of all moderates or critics of the arms race. On 12 August 1953, the Soviet Union secretly detonated its first thermonuclear bomb, codenamed Joe-4, with a yield of 400 kilotons, that is, 10 times more powerful than any previous Soviet nuclear detonation. As expected, the test was detected by the Air Weather Service atmospheric sampling planes operating for AFOAT-1 and, as was also expected, the development triggered hysteria in all official offices in Washington, since less than a year after the Ivy Mike explosion on 1 November 1952, the Soviets had achieved equivalent military technology. The only question seemed to be how many bombs they could make and in how long, because it was already known that they would have to be dropped with a new generation of strategic bombers: the Tupolev Tu-95 (NATO code name Bear) and the Myasishchev M-4 (NATO code name Bison), which entered service in 1953 and 1954 respectively.[8, 9]

Overnight, it became a top priority for the US government to determine what was the industrial capacity of the Russians in nuclear technology and aeronautics. Or, put another way, how many atomic bombs could they make, where would they make them, where were the factories for their strategic bombers, and how many did they have in their inventory? But getting that much information with an acceptable degree of certainty seemed an impossible task considering the geographic size of the Soviet Union and the fact that

the most important of its factories and laboratories were located beyond the Ural Mountains, beyond the reach of any traditional spy network that could be set up.

The only way to get this information was through aerial photography, but the United States did not have such long-range reconnaissance aircraft. Furthermore, penetrating Soviet airspace with spy planes could be considered an act of aggression, even more so considering that the 1941 Nazi invasion had been preceded by numerous reconnaissance flights by the Luftwaffe. Precisely those aerial photos taken up to 1943, captured by the American occupation forces from the Germans, were the only images that the CIA and the USAF could count on to estimate the location of the most advanced or sensitive Soviet infrastructure, but 10 years later and only in the European sector of the Soviet Union, not in its vast Asian region, where the Russians were known to have dispersed production after Hitler's surprise attack.

USAF officials had been pursuing the idea of high-altitude reconnaissance since January 1953, when Bill Lamar and Major John Seaberg, both from the Wright Air Development Center (WADC) in Ohio, drafted a design request to develop a highly specialised aircraft to be produced in small quantities. Surprisingly, they recommended skipping such prominent aircraft manufacturers as Lockheed, Boeing, and Convair and focusing on Bell Aircraft Corporation and Fairchild Engine and Airplane Corporation because, as smaller companies with relatively low output, they could give the project a higher priority. To provide a short-term option, they also asked officials at the Glenn L. Martin Company to look into modifying the B-57 light bomber model, already in production, with longer wingspans and improved engines. Such was the urgency that the three companies were asked to present the results before the end of 1953. The study project, codenamed BALD EAGLE, called for a subsonic aircraft with an operating radius of 1,500 nautical miles that was capable of reaching an altitude of 70,000 feet and carry a single crew member and a payload of between 100 and 700 pounds, that is, the weight of one or more cameras and their rolls of film.

The aircraft was to be equipped with available production engines (modified, if necessary) and have as low a gross weight as possible.[10]

The three summoned companies presented their respective studies in January 1954. Martin's model was a B-57 with extended wings, housing for cameras and sensors, and improved engines. Fairchild introduced the single-engine powered M-195 and Bell offered its Model 67, a delicate-looking, light twin-engine aircraft. Construction of mock-ups and prototypes of the selected designs proceeded smoothly through 1954, but the story of the future reconnaissance aircraft was to take a dramatic turn due to two events taking place in Washington and California, far from the drawing boards of Bell, Fairchild and Martin. First, CIA officials had learned of the USAF's aspirations and argued that clandestine reconnaissance over denied territories should be the function of a civilian intelligence agency and not an armed force, since in case of problems, the military nature of the operation could be denied. Second, Lockheed Aircraft Corporation chief designer Clarence L. Kelly Johnson had also heard about the spy plane project and had decided to submit an unsolicited proposal of his own to the USAF.[11,12]

Indeed, shortly after Lamar and Seaberg drafted their application for the spy plane design, Johnson was leaked from the Pentagon about the USAF study and the exclusion of Lockheed as a participant. The engineer managed to obtain a copy of the programme requirements and quickly developed a concept for an aircraft capable of a maximum altitude of 73,000 feet with an operating radius of 1,400 miles. The gross take-off weight would be just 13,768 pounds, including the payload of a 600-pound camera. To reduce weight, the aircraft would have no landing gear, would take off from a ground car, and land on a skid attached to the lower fuselage. In December 1953, Johnson appointed engineers Phil Coleman and Gene Frost to develop procedures to lighten the airframe and increase the area of its wings to achieve maximum altitude capability. They were soon joined by Henry Combs, a talented structural engineer and accomplished glider pilot.

Johnson's new design was given the designation CL-282 and was based on the airframe of the XF-104 Starfighter interceptor, saving time and expense. All unnecessary requirements for the spy plane, such as the fighter's load factor, armament and landing gear, were removed, while the general configuration of the fuselage and tail was retained. Johnson completely redesigned the wings and shortened the fuselage but managed to reuse all the XF-104's basic components, most of its manufacturing tooling, and nearly all the blueprints.

The biggest challenge was reducing the overall structural weight to allow the aircraft to perform its intended mission while carrying the cameras. Structurally, the CL-282 airframe was identical to that of the XF-104, except for the removal of a 62 inch section of the fuselage behind the cockpit. Since the CL-282 was designed for a 2.5g manoeuvring load factor compared to the XF-104's 7.33g, airframe strength requirements were reduced, allowing ribs and skins to use thinner aluminium, which in turn resulted in a reduction in structural weight. By dispensing with weapons, weight was also reduced and the same thing happened when the fighter's landing gear was completely removed, since the spy plane would land like a glider, that is, by sliding on a reinforced skid located on its belly.

In the forward part of the fuselage the pilot's accommodation was radically revised. The XF-104's cockpit included a downward ejection seat which on the CL-282 was scrapped entirely. This meant that in an emergency, the spy plane pilot would have to eject the Plexiglas upwards and get out under their own power. From the compressed air generated by the engine, the cabin would be pressurised to provide an equivalent pressure altitude of 25,000 feet when the aircraft was operating above 70,000 feet. Given that at an altitude of 25,000 feet the atmospheric pressure is very low and the air practically lacks oxygen, the pilot would be required to wear a special pressurised and oxygenated suit with a duration of seven hours.

Johnson conducted a limited study of wing configurations in search of the optimum planform. By considering the general weight and balance characteristics of the aircraft, he sought to determine the minimum area and aspect ratio necessary to reach a maximum altitude of 75,000 feet. The result was a configuration of thin, straight, high-lift wings, with a total area of 500 square feet. Unlike most conventional designs, the wings were sparless and bolted to the fuselage ring frames. This considerably limited the manoeuvring load factor, but Johnson included an innovative load distribution control system that prevented structural collapse. When flying at high speeds or in turbulent conditions at altitudes up to 35,000 feet,

In response to the USAF's request for a reconnaissance aircraft nearly unreachable by Soviet anti-aircraft defences, the Glenn L. Martin Company produced the RB-57D, a spread-wing variant of the B-57A tactical bomber. In the photo, the registered specimen 53-3977 flies escorted by a serial specimen, which makes it possible to compare the increase in wingspan. Later variants of the RB-57 flew in Argentina. (USAF)

the wing control surfaces could be raised (4 degrees for flaps and 10 degrees for ailerons) to reduce bending moments and tail loads by moving the centre of wing pressure in.

Each wing was designed to resist the bending moment at each surface by means of spars originating from the main joints of the fuselage frame. A structural rib in the wing root distributed torque to the fuselage frames. The wings also contained nylon bladder fuel tanks with internal tethers to prevent deformation of the airfoil from changes produced by steam pressure. Small, replaceable wingtip skids provided protection for the wingtips and ailerons during landing. Three power plants were studied: General Electric J73-X-52, Rolls Royce Avon RA14 and Wright TJ3B1 turbines. Finally, the first was chosen for its low weight and adaptability to the fuselage.

Johnson presented his CL-282 design study to Colonel Bernard Schriever at the Pentagon in March 1954. Schriever expressed great interest and requested a more specific proposal, which was approached a month later. But in the meeting that followed, the USAF generals were not enthusiastic because the design seemed too flimsy and had only one engine. Therefore, in April 1954, Martin received approval to proceed with his aircraft, called the RB-57D, which only needed to extend the wings of the successful B-57 light bomber. In June 1954 Lockheed's proposal was officially rejected by the USAF.

However, all was not lost. USAF Under Secretary for Research and Development Trevor Gardner was greatly impressed by Johnson's presentation of the CL-282 and, in May 1954, informed CIA Senior Intelligence Analyst Philip Strong of the project. The topic fell at just the right time as, with Cold War tensions mounting, President Eisenhower had tasked the intelligence agency with a comprehensive study of the Soviet threat, particularly its ability to build nuclear bombs and the strategic bombers to transport them. The panel of intelligence experts went around the matter several times and was reticent about the development, since it seemed unthinkable that the CIA would finance and operate a spy plane when, to do so, the United States had the largest Air Force in the world. But Gardner was convinced that it was possible and even necessary, so in October 1954 he met with Allen Dulles, the director of the CIA, to convince him of the need to act and the opportunity that was presenting itself.[13]

Gardner argued that with its own spy plane, the agency would be better prepared to conduct covert reconnaissance missions, to the point that USAF authorisation or involvement would not be necessary. They had to move fast, for the chance of a safe overflight of the Soviet Union might last a few years, until the Russians developed radar, guided missile defences, or interceptor aircraft that could reach the 70,000-foot region. Gardner's strong stance, coupled with fears of a possible third world war, convinced Dulles, so the matter was brought to the attention of President Eisenhower, who, in November 1954, approved development of the Lockheed CL-282. In addition, Eisenhower arranged for the new aerial reconnaissance programme to be controlled by the CIA, not the USAF, although both should work closely together, without absurd rivalries and in the utmost secrecy. On 26 November 1954, Allen Dulles assigned his special assistant, Richard Bissell, to take charge of organising the personnel, infrastructure, and resources to enable development of the CL-282 to proceed. Kelly Johnson promised to deliver the first plane in less than eight months. The CIA code-named the project AQUATONE and the USAF designated the future spy plane the U-2.[14]

The development of a spy plane unattainable by the Soviets was not the only preparation adopted by the US government to confront militarily what it considered a growing threat from the Soviet Union.

Brothers Allen Welsh Dulles (left) and John Foster Dulles (right) photographed at LaGuardia Field Airport, New York City in 1948. Staunch anti-communists, both wielded enormous power during the early years of the Cold War, first as director of the CIA (1953-1961) and the second was Secretary of State for President Eisenhower (1953-1959). (Jacob Harris, Associated Press)

After the Joe-4 thermonuclear explosion in August 1953, it was clear to Pentagon analysts that the country had to be prepared to face a future war, which would take place on all continents and all seas. Under this premise, the hemispheric defence format implemented for the Americas in the 1947 Inter-American Treaty of Reciprocal Assistance gained particular importance. However, the mere signing of a treaty did not mean that the Latin American armed forces were in a position effectively to confront to an open conflict, since modern warfare required logistics, coordination, communications, common tactics and weapons of a homogeneous technological level.

For the American hemispheric defence to be effective, the countries that signed the treaty had to have officers trained under the same doctrines, strategies, and tactics, they had to act in a coordinated manner, and they had to have compatible teams. Given that the Second World War and the recently ended Korean War had shown that dominance of airspace was critical to the success of land and naval deployments, Defense Department analysts recommended equipping the Latin American air forces with new aircraft, especially jets, whose squadrons could be subordinated under a unified US command in the event of a conflict. Of course, Latin American countries would not be supplied with state-of-the-art aircraft, but rather those that could satisfy their defence needs and increase technological dependence on US suppliers, without thereby compromising technologically sensitive information. In this regard, it was enough to provide used or second-line aircraft that were modern enough to replace obsolete inventories, and old enough to maintain technological leadership in the USAF.

The Pentagon plan, which was shared and accepted by the State Department, was functional from both a military and a political point of view. By having US weapons, US tactics and procedures, the Latin American countries would be better prepared militarily in a context of continental defence or hemispheric war led by the United States. In parallel, the United States would increase its political influence in Central and South America, given that the senior officers of all its

Four Republic F-84G Thunderjets of the USAF 3600th Air Demonstration Team. Its arrival in Argentina occurred through the Andes Mountain range, flying over Mendoza, en route from Santiago de Chile to Buenos Aires, on 28 January 1954. (USAF)

countries would be trained in US military institutes and academies, in addition to assigning themselves military instructors and advisers for full mastery of strategies, tactics and equipment. The local tools for the implementation of this foreign policy would be the air missions that the USAF had active in all Latin American countries with the sole exception of Argentina.

In this context and with these objectives, in January 1954 the USAF began a promotional tour that had no precedent in its history and which it conveniently called Wings for the Americas. The tour was announced by the Secretary of the USAF, Harold E. Talbott, as a way of strengthening the ties of friendship and camaraderie with the rest of the Latin American air forces although, as its name indicated, the purpose of the move was to show the flight equipment that the United States government was willing to supply for sale to Latin American governments that wished to acquire it, specifically Lockheed F-80 Shooting Star and Republic F-84G Thunderjet fighter jets, Lockheed T-33 training jet aircraft and, to everyone's surprise, North American F-86F Saber jet fighters recently used in the Korean War.

To brighten the deployment and to guarantee the massive attendance of the public in each of the capitals chosen for the tour, the USAF decided to mobilise its aerobatic demonstration team abroad for the first time, the Thunderbirds, members of the 3600th Air Demonstration Team with base at Luke AFB, near Phoenix, Arizona. The unit had been in existence for just over six months, having been activated on 25 May 1953, while the aerobatic team itself had been formed a few days later, on 1 June 1953. The Thunderbirds had performed 26 aerial demonstrations. since August 1953 but it was the first time she had deployed outside the United States. Since their F-84G Thunderjet aircraft were single-seaters, a Lockheed T-33 two-seater was added to the display team to support in-flight narrations, VIP outings, and press demos.[15]

The fraternity tour of South America began on 16 January 1954 from Kelly AFB in San Antonio, Texas. Four different types of jet aircraft participated: North American F-86F Sabre, Lockheed F-80 Shooting Star, Lockheed T-33 and Republic F-84G Thunderjets from the Thunderbirds aerobatic squadron. The deployment included the support of several transport, search, assistance and rescue aircraft, including two Douglas C-124 Globemasters and a Grumman Albatross. The tour began in Mexico City and continued through Managua (Nicaragua), where Captain Dean L.P. Ray suffered a fatal accident in which his plane, an F-86F, was also lost. Despite this altercation, the "air embassy", as it was called, continued to fly to Howard AFB in the Panama Canal Zone, and from there it continued to Talara and Lima (Peru), Santiago (Chile) and Buenos Aires.[16]

Argentine Air Force officers and USAF mechanics in front of the Republic F-84G-26-RE Thunderjet registration 51-16721 of the Thunderbirds aerobatic squadron. Ezeiza, 29 January 1954. (Atilio Marino via Vladimiro Cettolo)

Douglas C-47, FY-serial number 47-6275. This aircraft was used extensively by the United States Air Force in Argentina (whose titles are displayed on the fuselage) throughout the vast Argentine territory. It was photographed in such unlikely places as Ushuaia, on Tierra del Fuego Island, which shows the freedom with which it operated in Argentine territory. It crashed on 19 August 1950, in Rosario de la Frontera, Salta (North) during an unknown mission. (Artwork by Luca Canossa)

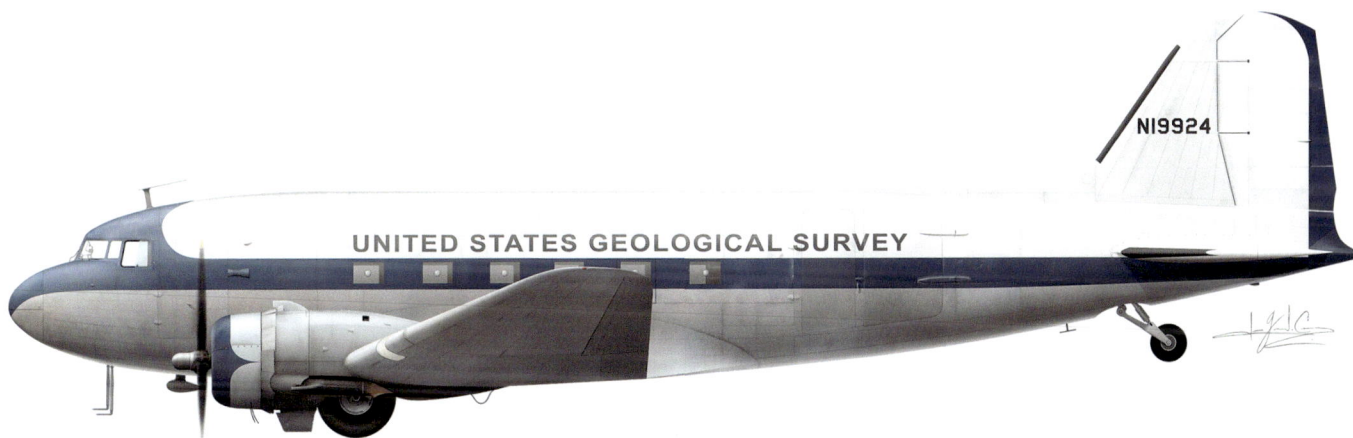

Douglas C-47A US Geological Survey, civilian registration N19924. This aircraft was among the first to incorporate airborne magnetometers to detect valuable subsurface resources in the areas it overflown, particularly uranium, by the US Geological Survey. USAAF aircraft were equipped with equivalent instruments to secretly detect strategic deposits in Latin American countries. (Artwork by Luca Canossa)

Douglas C-47D US Air Mission to the Republic of Argentina, FY-serial number 0-49533. This aircraft provided direct support to Lockheed WU-2A spy plane operations in Argentina, transporting crews and spare parts under the cover of its diplomatic status. After crashing on 22 May 1959, in Córdoba, it was sold to the Argentine Air Force for a nominal price and registered as TC-35. (Artwork by Luca Canossa)

De-militarised Boeing B-17G Flying Fortress, FY-serial number 44-85589, reconditioned for test purposes as QB-17G drone. With this unmanned aircraft, the USAEC obtained samples of radioactive particles directly from inside the mushroom cloud of the Zebra nuclear test, conducted on 14 May 1948, at Enewetak Atoll, as part of Operation Sandstone. The information obtained later allowed manned aircraft to approach the radioactive clouds. (Artwork by Luca Canossa)

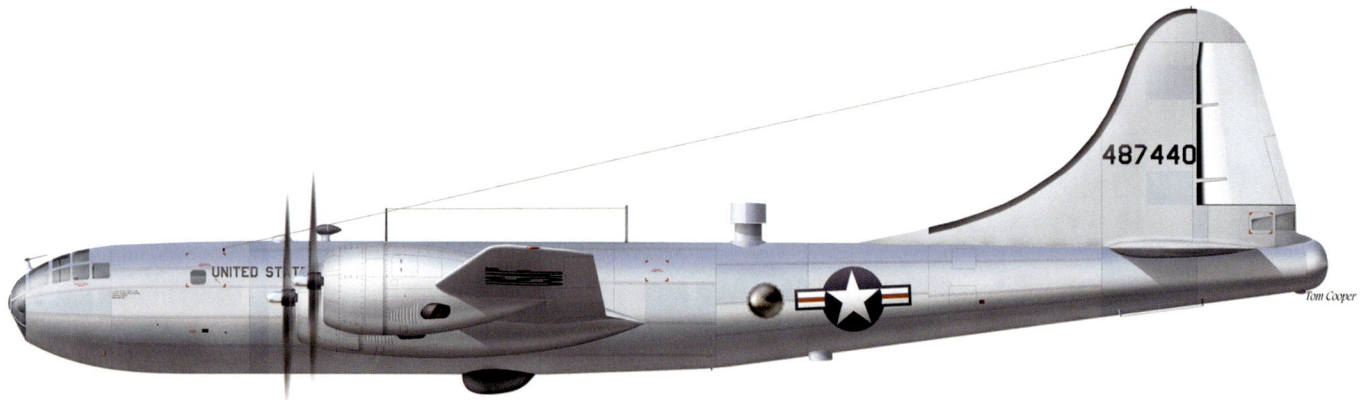

Boeing WB-29 Superfortress construction number 12543, FY-serial number 44-87440 (applied as '487440'). This aircraft was modified to collect radioactive particles and assigned to the 57th Strategic Reconnaissance Squadron, United States Air Force (USAF), based at Hickham AFB, Hawaii. It was used in 1951 to collect intelligence on the nuclear production capacities of the reactor built by the National Atomic Energy Commission (CNEA) on Huemul Island, Nahuel Huapi Lake, Bariloche. (Artwork by Tom Cooper)

Boeing KC-97G-105-BO Stratofreighter construction number 16583, FY-serial number 52-889 (applied as '2889'). This tanker aircraft was assigned to the 4060th Air Refuelling Wing of the United States Air Force (USAF), based at Dow AFB, Maine. The unit oversaw the first in-flight refuelling in Argentine airspace, during which this KC-97 transferred fuel to a Boeing B-57 Stratojet nuclear bomber. It is shown in the colours with which it was exhibited at the Ezeiza "Ministro Pistarini" International Airport on 15 November 1957. (Artwork by Tom Cooper)

Douglas C-54D-5-DC Skymaster construction number 10657, FY-serial number 42-72552 (applied as '272552'). This transport aircraft was assigned to the Caribbean Air Command of the United States Army Air Force (USAAF), based at Albrook Field, Panama Canal Zone. It was destroyed in an accident in the Mendoza mountain range on 12 November 1946, presumably during a geodetic or radiological espionage mission to the Soberanía uranium deposit. (Artwork by Luca Canossa)

Douglas C-54 FY-serial number applied as '49147'' on the fin. In 1945, the United States emerged from World War II as the sole nuclear superpower. In the immediate postwar period, the presence of its military aircraft became global, particularly in Latin American countries. This Air Transport Command aircraft was stationed at the U.S. Embassy in Argentina in 1947, operating from Palomar Air Base. (Artwork by Luca Canossa)

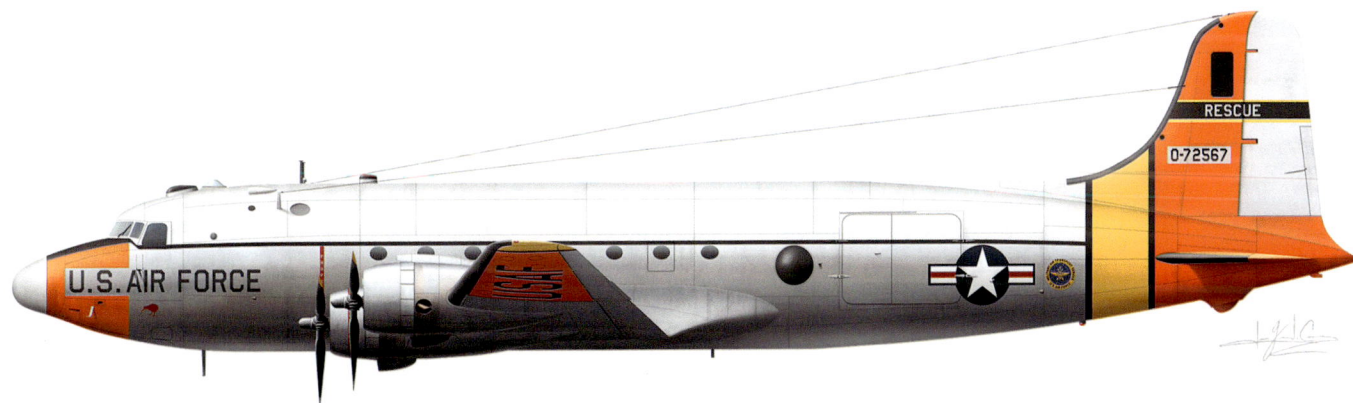

Douglas SC-54D-DC Rescuemaster, construction number 10667, FY-serial number 42-72567 (applied as 'O-72567'). This pararescue transport was reporting to the 2157th Air Rescue Squadron based at Ramey AFB, Puerto Rico. It was deployed to Argentina as search and rescue support for the Lockheed WU-2A. "Ministro Pistarini" International Airport, Ezeiza, 24 March 1959. (Artwork by Luca Canossa)

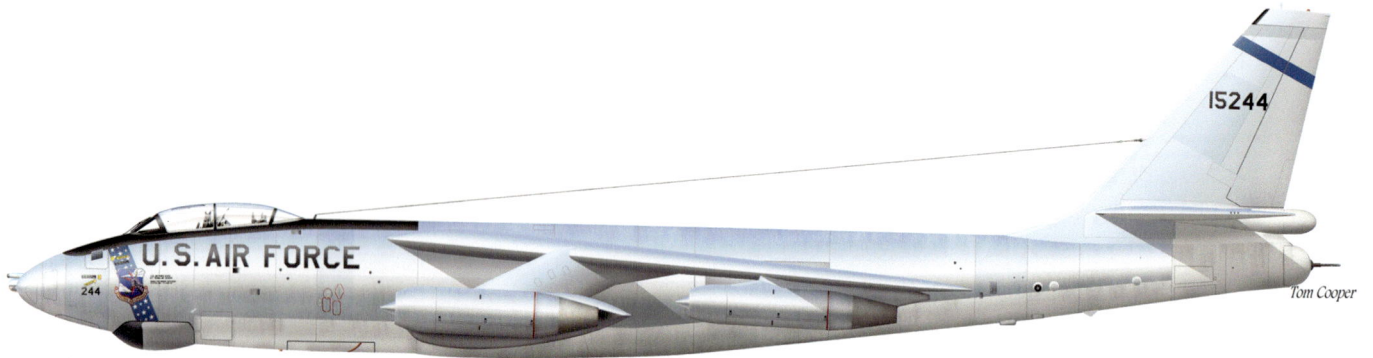

Boeing B-47E-65-BW Stratojet construction number 450529, FY-serial number 51-5244 (applied as '15244'). This strategic bomber was assigned to the 509th Bombardment Wing (Medium), of the Strategic Air Command, United States Air Force (USAF), based at Walker AFB, New Mexico. During its visit to Argentina within the framework of Operation LONG LEGS, it carried out demonstrations over Buenos Aires, Córdoba and Mendoza on 14 November 1957. (Artwork by Tom Cooper)

Lockheed WU-2A, construction number 383, registration 56-6716 (applied as '66715'). This intelligence-gathering aircraft was assigned to the 4028 Strategic Reconnaissance Squadron, United States Air Force (USAF) based at Laughlin AFB, Texas. It was operated in Argentina as a radioactive particle collection platform in the framework of Operation CROWFLIGHT. One of its pilots was Captain Gerald Eugene McIlmoyle, who on 25 October 1962 would be assigned to take aerial photographs of the island of Cuba during the Missile Crisis. International Airport "Ministro Pistarini", Ezeiza, 19 May 1960. (Artwork by Tom Cooper)

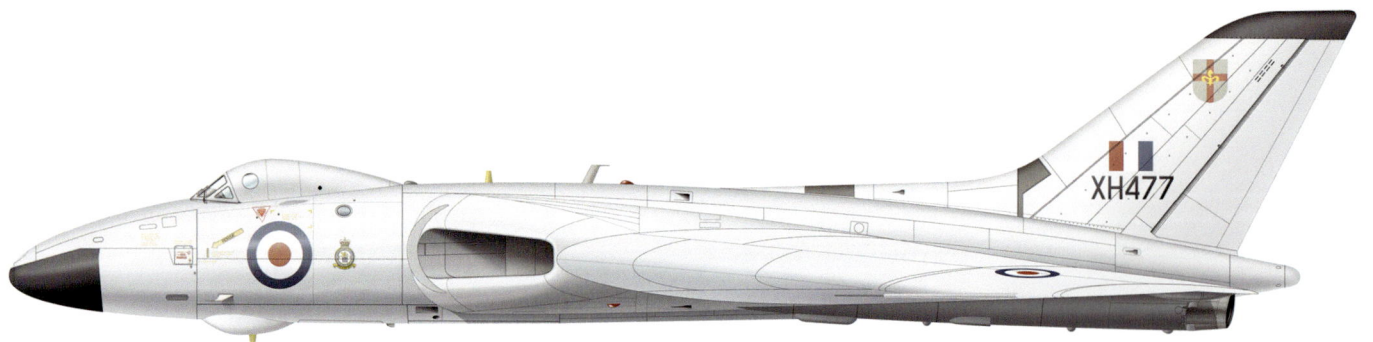

Avro Vulcan B. Mk 1 serial number XH477. During the Cold War, nuclear-capable powers conducted strategic exercises often disguised as goodwill visits. This AVRO Vulcan nuclear bomber from RAF 83 Squadron was sent to Buenos Aires, Argentina, in May 1958 under the pretext of celebrating the inauguration of President Arturo Frondizi. Argentine skies would see Vulcans again in 1982, during the Falklands War. (Artwork by Jean-Marie Guillou)

Two officers of the Argentine Air Force in front of the Lockheed P-80C-LO Shooting Star registration number 49-539 exhibited in Ezeiza on 29 January 1954. By then it was an obsolete model, removed from the USAF front line and reserved to the role of advanced trainer. For this reason, it was offered for sale to Latin American governments at bargain prices. (Atilio Marino via Vladimiro Cettolo)

One of the Lockheed T-33A-1-LO jet trainers deployed by the USAF to Argentina, registered 51-6737 (code TR-737), is preparing to carry out a public relations flight, with a special guest. At the controls is Major Charles Chuck Yeager, the legendary USAF test pilot. (Atilio Marino via Vladimiro Cettolo)

Captain William Lilley's F-86F Saber, registration number 52-4733 (painted 24733) after landing on 29 January 1954 on the "old runway" of the Punta Indio Naval Air Base. The Douglas C-54 Skymaster license plate 4-T-1 of the Naval Aviation Command can be seen in the image. (BAPI File via Fernando Jara)

45

The US planes landed at the Ezeiza International Airport on 28 January 1954. The first to do so, at 1:30 p.m., was a T-33 under the command of General Reuben Columbus Hood, Caribbean Air Commander since June 1953. and head of the Wings for the Americas mission. It was not the first time he had visited Argentina, as he had been to the country on two earlier occasions, the last in 1948, a detail that was expected to facilitate his approach to the Argentine government given the promotional nature of the tour in progress. The rest of the US delegation landed behind his T-33, up to a total of 20 planes, a not inconsiderable number that was unprecedented if compared with previous goodwill visits by US military aviation.

As expected, the USAF assigned its best pilots the responsibility of representing the institution abroad. The Thunderbirds were commanded by 32-year-old Major Richard C. Catledge, a Second World War veteran of Africa and Europe. On his twenty-third mission he had been shot down and captured in Naples, but he had managed to escape and return to his own lines. After the USAF was formed, he had become a Flight Instructor with units based in Alaska and Arizona. In the aerobatic team he led 29-year-old twins, Captains Cuthbert Augustus "Bill" Pattillo and Charles Curtis "Buck" Pattillo, also veterans of the war in Europe, who after the conflict had graduated in Aeronautical Engineering, later returning to the active service. The fourth Thunderbird was Captain Robert McCormick, 25, with over a hundred missions accumulated in the recent Korean War. The officers in charge of the other jet formations were no less experienced. Ernest Burnet, in charge of the Lockheed F-80s, was also a Korean veteran, while Charles Yeager, in charge of the Lockheed T-33s, was a living American aviation legend, having been the first man to cross the sound barrier, on 14 October 1947, flying the famous Bell X-1. As soon as their planes had stopped their engines on the commercial apron of the Ezeiza Airport, the programme of events prepared by the Argentine Air Force began, which began with a fellowship lunch at the headquarters of the Círculo de Aeronáutica, in Vicente López.[17]

The Argentine chapter of the Wings for the Americas exhibition took place on 29 January at the Ezeiza Airport, where an estimated 50,000 members of the public gathered. After having met General Reuben Hood early in the morning at Government House, General Juan Domingo Perón arrived at the airport at 11:00 am dressed in military uniform, a protocol formality that he reserved for court events of the State. In Ezeiza he was received by the Ministers of National Defence, Army, Navy, Aeronautics, Public Works and Foreign Relations, which can give an idea of the official significance that had been given to the USAF demonstration tour.

The official box was set up at the airport's international jetty, where President Perón was received by the United States Ambassador to Argentina, Albert F. Nufer, the Embassy's Air Attaché, Colonel Charles Roadmand, and the commander of the aircraft carrier USS *Franklin. D. Roosevelt*, which was sailing without planes from Norfolk, Virginia to the Puget Sound Naval Shipyard in Bremerton, Washington to undergo a conversion, and who had conveniently been diverted to Argentina to further emphasise the importance of the US military presence.[18, 19]

Now, while the Thunderbirds dazzled the public gathered at the Ezeiza airport, the rest of the Wings for the Americas mission component fulfilled its true promotional purpose. Thus, on 29 January 1954, a Lockheed T-33 was transferred to the Morón Military Air Base so that it could be tested in flight by several Argentine military pilots with experience in Gloster Meteor jets. The Chief of the VII Air Brigade, Brigadier Juan Carlos Ríos, and the Chief of the Naval Aviation Command of the Argentine Navy, Captain Gregorio Lloret, also flew in T-33s. Furthermore, one of the F-86F Sabers deployed to Ezeiza, the one commanded by Captain William Lilley, ended up landing at the Punta Indio Naval Air Base due to bad weather, which also served as a promotional action for the material against Naval Aviation. Once the objective was accomplished, all the USAF squadrons left Ezeiza at 9:30 in the morning of the following day, 30 January 1954, bound for Montevideo, where they exactly repeated

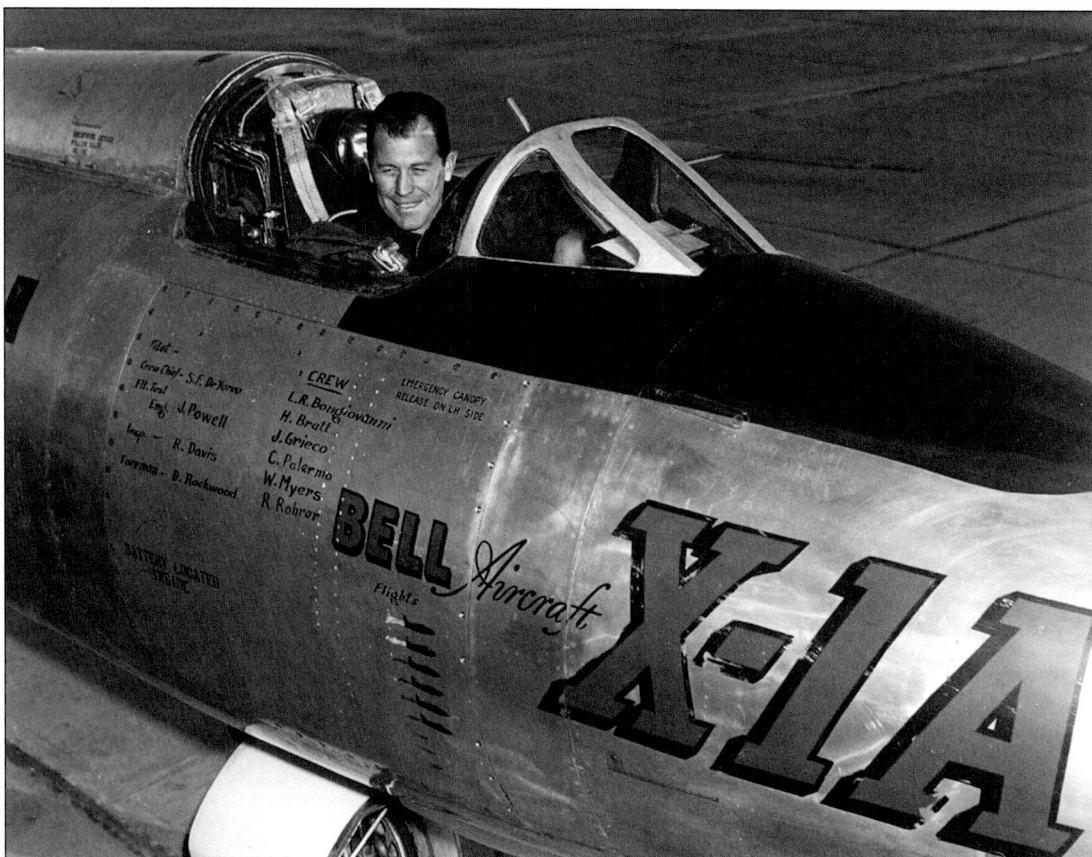

The USAF took care of every last detail to impress during the Wings for the Americas tour. One of the pilots called up was Major Charles E. Yeager, the first pilot to cross the sound barrier, on 14 October 1947, in a Bell X-1. On 12 December 1953, a few weeks before his deployment to Argentina, he had reached Mach 2.435 in the new Bell X-1A serial 48-1384, seen in the photograph. (USAF)

The aircraft carrier USS *Franklin D. Roosevelt* (CV-42) was sent to Argentina so that its visit coincided with the arrival of the Alas para las Américas squadron. It was a 65,000-ton displacement ship with the capacity to operate jet aircraft. (US Navy)

the exhibition held in Buenos Aires, with the only difference being that the pilot Maurice Nordlund crossed the sound barrier in a dive in an F-86, which could not be done the day before in Argentina due to bad weather. From Uruguay, the formations continued to Brazil.[20]

Within the framework of the Wings for the Americas exhibition, or as a result of it, the government of Washington offered the government of Buenos Aires 100 North American F-86F Saber fighters destined for the Argentine Air Force, plus a significant number of Lockheed T- 33 for the Military Aviation School and the Naval Aviation School. The proposal was extraordinary due to the number of aircraft committed and for what they represented from a technological point of view. However, by 1954 the Argentine coffers were exhausted and there was no longer liquid money to purchase expensive aeronautical material. The boom times of the immediate post-war period, when gold reserves and credit seemed inexhaustible, had passed, and now the country faced not only the retraction of its economy but also the beginning of a process of monetary inflation that had no precedent.

Thus, despite the demonstrations of friendship in favour of the USAF and the US government, and despite the relative low sale price of the material offered, Perón did not agree to buy any of the promoted jets. What's more, the president maintained his firm position of not allowing a USAF Air Mission to be formed again in Argentina. The Argentine refusal to buy the Sabers was not

The international terminal of the Ezeiza International Airport, in front of which the Wings for the Americas exhibition took place, on 29 January 1954. All the infrastructure was new and did not clash with the latest generation technology deployed by the USAF. (Pablo Luciano Potenze)

considered a slight. For the government in Washington, the mere presence of the Argentine president in Ezeiza had been a sufficient sign of commitment to US interests, even more so considering that just six months earlier, in July 1953, Perón had expressed to the presidential assistant Milton Eisenhower, brother of the president of the United States, that Argentina would be on the western side in the event of a world conflagration against the Soviet Union. Moreover,

The largest aircraft deployed by the USAF on the Wings for the Americas tour was a Douglas C-124A-DL Globemaster II troop transport. In the image it is seen parked on 29 January 1954 in front of the international jetty of the Ezeiza airport. In its enormous warehouse, the technical personnel and the necessary spare parts were transported to support the entire operation. (Atilio Marino via Vladimiro Cettolo)

Grumman HU-16B Albatross serial 51-7195, photographed in Ezeiza on 28 January 1954. Its primary function during the tour was to provide assistance and rescue to the aircraft involved in the Alas para las Américas tour. (Atilio Marino via Vladimiro Cettolo)

the alignment of Argentina with the United States for the defence of the Western Hemisphere in the event of a global conflict had already been analysed by the USAF since 1949.[21, 22]

In accordance with the climate of the time, a military collision with the Soviet Union seemed inevitable, to such an extent that references to a third world war with the use of nuclear weapons were omnipresent in the Western press, in the stories of politicians, and even in newspapers. In this context, on 1 March 1954, barely two months after the USAF visit to Argentina, the United States carried out the second test of a thermonuclear bomb, the one with the highest performance to date. It was called CASTLE BRAVO and it achieved a blast equivalent to 15 megatons, two and a half times more than calculated and anticipated by its designers and a devastating blast which was a thousand times more powerful than the atomic bomb dropped on Hiroshima.

The thermonuclear bomb from the CASTLE BRAVO test not only pulverised the coral atoll in the Marshall Islands on which it was detonated but also sent nuclear fallout falling over more than 18,000 square kilometres. Debris from the explosion precipitated in the form of white powder, remains of the atomised coral, saturated by unsuspected levels of radiation. The phenomenon prompted the emergency evacuation of hundreds of inhabitants of the nearby Rongelap and Utirik atolls, as well as USAF weather observation personnel, fearing that they would die from exposure to excessive and unprecedented radioactive doses.[23]

The extent of the fallout was kept top secret until a Japanese fishing vessel, the *Daigo Fukuryū Maru*, returned to port with its entire crew sick from fallout exposure. On 1 March 1954, at 6:45 in the morning, the sailors had seen, surprised, that the Sun was rising in the west. It was not the Sun, but the burst from the CASTLE BRAVO test, which matched it in size and brilliance. Hours later, the deck of the ship was covered in a thin film of wind-borne dust that burned skin on contact, irritated eyes and seeped into the respiratory tract and into the lungs. From that moment on, the unforeseen consequences of the thermonuclear explosion could no longer be hidden. To evade responsibility, the US government officially stated that the growth in the force of the atomic bombs was not accompanied by an equivalent growth in the radioactivity released, for which reason it denied that

the crew of the fishing boat had been affected by the radioactive fallout.[24]

Then it turned out that the wife of another of the sailors gave birth to a dead and deformed son, which showed that the matter was something very serious. In Japan, these episodes revived memories of the 1945 nuclear bombings and their immediate consequences for the civilian population. Amid the controversy, Polish nuclear physicist Joseph Rotblat, who had worked on the Manhattan Project and was then a researcher at St Bartholomew's Hospital in London, showed that the contamination caused by the CASTLE BRAVO explosion had been much greater than that officially declared. Rotblat deduced that the thermonuclear bomb tested had three stages and showed that the fission phase at the end of the explosion had increased the amount of radioactivity released a thousand times.

An immense fireball 7.2 kilometres in diameter rises over Bikini Atoll on 1 March 1954. The CASTLE BRAVO test was the most powerful ever detonated by the United States and its first lithium deuterium-powered thermonuclear weapon. The yield was 15 megatons, more than two and a half times the predicted 6 megatons, due to additional reactions. The leaders of the Soviet Union shuddered at this doomsday weapon and accelerated the strengthening of their own nuclear arsenal. (USAEC)

His investigative article escalated to the press and, when he arrived in Japan, there was talk of a second Hiroshima. The government in Tokyo made a formal protest to the government in Washington and, in the end, the Americans had to compensate the surviving victims of the *Daigo Fukuryū Maru*.[25]

This was what Julius Robert Oppenheimer had been warning about since 1949 after becoming aware of the results of the GABRIEL Project undertaken by the Atomic Energy Commission, according to which the accumulated radioactive depositions produced by the systematic explosion of nuclear weapons in a warlike context would affect the populations of the victim state, but also of the aggressor state, since the contamination of the environment would be global. These warnings by Oppenheimer about the potential threat posed to human health and the global ecosystem by the massive use of high-yield nuclear weapons were silenced in April 1954, when the scientist was separated from the atomic agency and from any project that involved the civil or military use of nuclear energy, due to his past affinity with students and scientists affiliated with the Communist Party.[26]

The USAF generals were relieved that Oppenheimer was ousted, and not because he was a communist. For an air force whose strategic purpose was to drop nuclear bombs (and whose main budget came from it), it was not pleasant to share space with a scientist of unquestionable prestige who advocated for the limitation of arsenals and moderation in the development of more powerful weapons. However, the results of the GABRIEL project were so evident that Oppenheimer's eloquence was not needed to understand that he was right with his warnings. Therefore, both the USAF and the Atomic Energy Commission decided to check the atmospheric dispersion mechanism of radioactive waste that could be released in a total nuclear war.[27]

For this it was not necessary to start a Third World War, but to obtain precise information from the nuclear test explosions that were subsequently carried out around the world. By detecting

To maximise their destructive power, nuclear bombs never touched the ground, but were detonated at a height. The image illustrates the explosion of the Grable test, with a yield of 15 kilotons, carried out on 25 May 1953 as part of Operation UPSHOT-KNOTHOLE. Points under the fireball are tanks, trucks and half-tracks set up in the desert to assess the effects a tactical atomic weapon would have on a battlefield. (USAEC)

certain radioactive isotopes, not only could the nuclear technological development of the Soviet Union be known by reverse engineering, but data could be loaded into a mechanical calculator that, at the end of its process, would provide information related to global radioactive fallout. This would allow the power of nuclear attacks to be "tuned" so that they only kill the population of the cities that were their target and not the populations of other cities (especially their own) due to the subsequent radioactive fallout. The desire was to avoid what was called overkill, or excessive death, which was considered morally unacceptable because the excess deaths would be from friendly or neutral countries. In the following years, a good part of the aerial data collection operations for the secret overkill calculations would be carried out from Argentina.[28]

5

AMBASSADORS IN BLUE

By January 1955, the United States already had its first spy plane. The U-2 prototype designed by Kelly Johnson, manufactured in secret by Lockheed, was an example of simplicity and innovation. The structure was built primarily from aluminium alloys machined to the thinnest gauges allowed within the structural strength requirements and, furthermore, with the fewest possible number of ribs, stringers and double plates. All metal cladding panels were flush riveted to prevent drag from even slight rivet protrusions. The aerodynamically balanced control surfaces had almost no gaps at any of the hinge points to ensure uninterrupted airflow across the wing assembly. To avoid the weight of hydraulic or mechanical systems, all controls were actuated by cables and pulleys, as would have happened in a racing glider. In this way, the hydraulic circuit was limited to the opening of the landing gear and the deployment of the airbrakes.[1]

Johnson spent two days designing a lightweight landing gear consisting of a bicycle-like configuration, with two tandem wheels, the rear one smaller, both mounted along the centreline of the plane.

To maintain lateral balance during take-off, the wingtips were fitted with span stabilisers, or pogos, small rubber wheels at the ends of two curved steel legs that released as soon as the plane left the ground. Like any glider, upon landing the U-2 would roll until it lost speed and fall sideways on either of its wingtips, which had therefore been fitted with a metal plate that acted as a skid, so that the wing that touched the ground would slide without affecting the structure.

The plane's only engine, a Pratt & Whitney J57 jet, received air through a split intake system. Since it was located on the centre chord of the wing to maintain balance for the entire aircraft, the main gear case had to be positioned between the air intake ducts, which was further forward than desirable. This meant that, at cruising altitude, the engine needed almost perfect ram air distribution to function, otherwise it would choke and generate what came to be called flameout.[2]

To expedite the commissioning schedule, the first flights of the U-2 prototype were made with a 10,500-pound-thrust J57-P-37 engine designed for the B-52 bomber. However, the production aircraft was

The first prototype of the Lockheed U-2 is unloaded from the hold of a Douglas C-124 Globemaster II on the dry lakebed adjacent to the US Atomic Energy Commission-administered test area north of Las Vegas, Nevada, on 25 July 1955. (USAF-CIA)

to have a more powerful version, the 11,500-pound thrust J57-P-31, the three-year development of which was compressed to enter service in less than one. The new engine had been designed to operate up to almost 74,600 feet before experiencing flameout. The turbine had a 16 stage compressor and was always running at full power during the flight to ensure it did not suffocate. Fuel consumption was 9,000 pounds per hour at sea level and a mere 700 pounds per hour at cruising altitude of 70,000 feet. In the event of a flameout, the engine could be restarted in high-altitude flight, descending to lower levels where there was greater atmospheric density, but without entering Soviet missile range areas, where the aircraft could be vulnerable. The missile issue was not taken lightly because a direct hit was not needed to bring down a U-2, given its relative structural fragility. It was enough for the explosive head of a missile or the casing of an anti-aircraft artillery shell to detonate nearby for the shock wave to disable the plane in mid-flight.[3]

The U-2's fuselage was like a very simple cylinder with a carefully organised interior. A pressurised compartment just forward of the main landing gear wheel, known as the Q-bay, contained the reconnaissance equipment. It was conceived as a modular bay, so that it could house the various types of cameras and instruments that had to be assembled and disassembled as required by each mission. Whatever the intelligence or espionage module, its lower part was flush with the belly of the plane, so as not to generate additional air resistance. Maintenance and removal of the equipment housed in the Q-bay was always done from above, through an upper hatch. Since the Q-bay consisted largely of empty space, only the centre spar of the fuselage supported the cockpit and nose section of the aircraft. That was another world in terms of design. The cockpit had been taken from the F-104 supersonic fighter and was therefore very cramped, but it did not have the controls of a fighter plane but rather the typical ones of a bomber or transport plane. The U-2 was to be flown with the smoothness of a glider, not the aggression inherent in a fighter plane. Given that it would be a spy plane and that its cameras would always be pointed downwards, a periscope viewfinder was placed in the centre of the control panel, which allowed the pilot to see the terrain over which he was flying. It was not necessary to incorporate convex-angle rearview mirrors to increase visibility to the rear, since at the altitude at which the U-2 would fly, it was estimated that it would never be pursued by any other aircraft.[4]

If the comparison is possible, the U-2 was like a racing car refined in all its aspects to achieve maximum performance, which was always to stay at an altitude unattainable by other aircraft. For the U-2, the refinement not only reached the design, weight or the

engines, but also the type of fuel that it used, which was specially formulated for use at high altitudes. The standard jet fuel, JP-4, had such a low vapour pressure that it evaporated at high altitudes. To prevent this, the Shell Oil Company developed a new kerosene-based fuel with low volatility and low vapour pressure for the U-2. The result was LF-1A or JP-TS, a broad mixture of aliphatic and aromatic hydrocarbon compounds with an initial boiling point of 315 degrees Fahrenheit (157 Celsius) at sea level and a freezing point of -164°F (-73°C). The production of LF-1A had an unexpected consequence for the insecticide market in the spring and summer of 1955, as its formulation required the use of additives and petroleum derivatives that Shell used to make Flit aerosol insect repellent. Consequently, there was a worldwide shortage of this insecticide at the same time that the tanks of the bases from which the new secret plane was to operate were being filled with fuel.[5]

The tendency of liquids to boil at high altitude had a significant effect on the design of the U-2's life support systems. Human body fluids vapourise at altitudes above 63,000 feet or 19,202 metres above sea level, unless the body is kept under the artificial pressure generated by a pressurised suit. Without adequate life support, the pilot could experience the collapse of his cardiovascular system (from lack of pressure) or respiratory system (from lack of oxygen). For this reason, it was contemplated that during the cruise the cabin of the U-2 would be pressurised to the equivalent of 28,000 feet or 8,534 metres above sea level and that the pilot would use a pressurised suit and a continuous supply of oxygen to the helmet at all times.

Assembly of the U-2 fuselage was complete by the third week of May 1955, but the wings were significantly behind schedule, so the Lockheed team implemented rotating shifts to work on the project twenty-four hours a day. In this way, the static tests were finished in June and by July the prototype of the plane was ready, which the USAF and the CIA called Article 341 so that there was not the slightest trace of its existence in the communications related to its construction.

Immediately thereafter, Lockheed technicians disassembled the U-2 and packed its various components onto a Douglas C-124 freighter, which transported it from the Lockheed plant in Burbank, California, to a dry lake adjacent to the Atomic Energy Commission test range, north of Las Vegas, Nevada. The site was ideal for test flights of the U-2 project given its remote location, excellent year-round climate, and the fact that it was already under the administration of the highly secretive US nuclear agency. The existing infrastructure was spartan as it had been built quickly and in secret. It consisted of a 1,500-metre long asphalt runway, a control tower, three hangars, an aircraft parking platform, various support facilities, and rudimentary amenities for personnel. The set became known as the Watertown Airstrip, although it would use other names in the future to mislead Soviet intelligence services.[6, 7]

The development and initial operation of the U-2 was a joint effort between the USAF, the CIA, and Lockheed as manufacturer. The CIA had overall control of the programme, as well as responsibility for developing security protocols and paying for all inputs. The USAF was in charge of logistics, the supply of engines, ground support equipment, maintenance and training personnel, air traffic controllers, operator transport, and fuel supply. To confuse, the secret project had different names, AQUATONE for the CIA and OILSTONE for the USAF, although new names would be used hereafter to ensure cover-up.

As Kelly Johnson had promised, the disassembled components of the first U-2 arrived in Nevada on 25 July 1955, less than eight

The first prototype of the U-2, with USAF markings and a "001" painted on the tail, was identified by the CIA as "Item 341." The photo was taken on 1 August 1955 before his first test shoot on the Nevada dry lake. The place was known as Groom Lake, but due to its secret nature, other names such as Dreamland, Paradise Ranch, Home Base, Watertown Strip, Homey Airport and Area 51 were used to mislead. (USAF-CIA)

months after Lockheed received contract approval. After reassembly the aircraft underwent ground vibration tests to re-measure its structural strength and frequencies for three different fuel load configurations. For these tests, the Article 341 was mounted on a ground transportation dolly and shaken at various frequencies, some as low as half a cycle per second. The results were satisfactory. The technicians then prepared the prototype for its first test run of the engine, which was also successful.

On 1 August, the first U-2 was towed to the dry lakebed for a first test run under test pilot Tony LeVier. In the second run, the plane took flight on its own, not initiated by the pilot, which may give an idea of the aerodynamic refinement achieved by the Lockheed team. The unplanned flight hinted at the airworthiness of the new aircraft, foreshadowing its tendency to stay airborne through ground effect at low speeds, while gliding long distances above the runway.

The true initial flight of the U-2, the one that was carried out at the will of the pilot and not of the aircraft itself, took place on 8 August 1955 under the gaze of representatives of the CIA, the USAF and Lockheed. The take-off was perfect and soon the plane surpassed in altitude the Lockheed T-33 that was following it for photographic record. Over the next few weeks, an additional 16 flights were completed during which Tony LeVier explored stall characteristics and pushed the U-2 to its maximum stress limits (+2.5g and -1.5g)

and maximum speed of Mach 0.85 (487 knots or 902 kilometres per hour). On 16 August, the U-2 reached an altitude of 15,850 metres, much higher than that of any aircraft built to date.

While in the Nevada desert the CIA and the USAF were successfully testing their first plane specifically designed to spy on the Soviet Union, in Argentina the political situation was rapidly deteriorating. The ruling Peronist government was unable to contain the inflation that it itself had generated by issuing unbacked paper money and that had been generating social discontent adding to the discomfort caused by the progressive encroachment on the individual liberties of citizens, especially if they were opponents. State intervention in practically all sectors of the economy, added to the drastic reduction of the enormous gold reserves accumulated during the Second World War, had placed the country in a very fragile situation. Peronism had set in motion forces that in a short time transformed Argentine society, but at the same time it had neglected macroeconomics and, in the process, had shaken traditional structures that saw their political influence and real power diminish. The opposition sectors took advantage of these structural weaknesses to oust the prevailing political model, which, on the other hand, had become unbearable due to the excesses and abuse of power by many of its officials.

By September 1955, the CIA had at least 10 U-2s in various stages of assembly at Lake Groom. Some of these planes began to bear USAF markings, such as this example identified as "36", photographed after its test flight in the dry lake. (CIA-USAF)

On the economic level, everything can be summed up in that the money that was left over in 1945 had begun to run out. Peronism, which from 1946 had used up the reserves accumulated during the Second World War, could not now maintain the level of investment and public spending that it had had in its first five years of government. Perón had produced large acquisitions for the state and had also nationalised companies. The oversizing of the public sector was not free, nor were the labour rights that its protectionist legislation had generated. When the public accounts did not balance, because the income from tax collection was lower than the expenditure from public spending, Perón resorted to the advice of his main economic adviser, Manuel Miranda, who had been president of the Central Bank of the Argentine Republic and the who he considered "the czar of finances". Miranda, at the head of the National Economic Council since 1947, suggested printing currency. In this way, the public accounts were balanced, but since the issue had no backing, an economic phenomenon hitherto unknown in the country was generated: inflation.

Inflation not only diluted the purchasing power of the middle class and the working class, for which Peronism had done so much, but also generated a state of social bad humour that the anti-Peronist sectors, which were varied and motivated by sectional interests, knew how to capitalise very well. The arc of disagreement went from the most rancid oligarchy to liberal intellectuals, passing through a business community increasingly hit by the abuses and outrages of bullies and social resentful people who thrived on the perks of the state. The entire anti-Peronist plexus was clear that it would not be possible to beat Peronism at the polls, because it was a mass movement with deep social roots, which is why conspiracies began to be hatched to depose Perón by force, in the same way that the constitutional presidents Hipólito Yrigoyen and Ramón Castillo had been deposed in 1930 and 1943.

The first hard blow against Perón came on 16 June 1955, when a combination of troops from the marines and the army tried to take the Government House, while naval aircraft, American Texan attack fighters, Beechcraft Kansan bombers and Consolidated Catalina seaplanes, bombarded the government headquarters and the Plaza de Mayo. Several squadrons of Argentine Air Force Gloster Meteor fighter jets took off to suppress the rebels, resulting in the downing of a Texan over the Río de la Plata (registration 0342/3-A-29) and the destruction of a Kansan bomber (registration 0273/3-B-11), which was concentrated at the Ezeiza Airport along with other rebel aircraft. In a dramatic turn of events, the Morón Air Base, from which the jets loyal to the Perón government had departed, passed

under rebel control for a few hours, enough time for several Meteors to be put into flight, now as rebels, they went to attack the loyal troops of the army that were advancing towards Ezeiza to quell the uprising of the naval aviation.

Three rebellious Meteors attacked the Government House and the police headquarters with cannon fire, after which they headed towards Uruguayan territory. The registration I-064 suffered an emergency due to lack of fuel and splashed down a few metres from the coast in the town of Carmelo. After the failure of the revolt, at least four other Meteors took refuge in Uruguay: I-058 landed at the Aero Club de Colonia, I-029 made an emergency landing with the gear retracted near the Ángel Adami aerodrome in Melilla, while that those registered I-094 and I-031 landed at the Carrasco Air Base (the latter without fuel).

After the bombing of the Plaza de Mayo and the Government House, all the pilots that rebelled against the constitutional government of President Juan Domingo Perón sought refuge in Uruguay. In the photo, taken at the Carrasco aerodrome, the Gloster Meteor fighter registration I-094 of the Argentine Air Force can be seen in the foreground and, behind, the Douglas C-54 Skymaster registration 4-T-2 of the Argentine Naval Aviation. (Life)

The uprising against Perón did not have any military success and ended up being a slaughter of innocent civilians, leaving 308 dead and more than 800 wounded. But it had an enormous political effect, since it clearly showed that Perón was not untouchable, that anti-Peronism was determined to overthrow him and that, to achieve this, all that was needed was greater cohesion among the rebel officers of the three armed forces. From then on, the conspiracy to forcefully remove Perón, which months before would have been unthinkable, began to take shape in the feverish minds of countless officers who never realised the tremendous historical mistake they were about to commit. Not least because presidential elections were scheduled for the 1958 elections and a military overthrow would

View of the Paseo Colón road and Hipólito Irigoyen corner, in front of the Government House with private and public transport vehicles destroyed. The fratricidal attack on 16 June 1955 left more than 300 dead and some 800 injured. (Argentine Federal Police)

only achieve what it ultimately did: turn into a victim, a political martyr, a constitutional president who, by 1955, was already very weakened in the face of Argentine public opinion.

The definitive uprising against Perón took place on 16 September 1955, exactly three months after the metropolitan bombardment and, like that attempt, it had the hardest anti-Peronist nucleus in the navy, concentrated under the iron command of Rear Admiral Isaac Rojas. Unlike what happened in June, this time the navy did not act alone, since in the three months that elapsed until September, many army and air force officers and non-commissioned officers had decided to join the conspiracy. As a result, the coup movement was triggered almost simultaneously in different military units located in various parts of the country.

By 20 September, the fate of the Revolución Libertadora[8] had not been decided. Although it is true that by then Perón already enjoyed political asylum (first in the Paraguayan Embassy in Buenos Aires, then in the Paraguayan gunboat *Paraguay* and finally in a Catalina seaplane from the same country that took him to the city of Asunción), it was no less true that the news caused a resurgence in the Peronist resistance, which reacted violently to the fate of its leader. It was not until 6 pm on 20 September that the heads of the Revolutionary Command and the (loyal) Military Junta began their eight-hour long meeting on the cruiser ARA *17 de Octubre* to decide the terms of a ceasefire. Hostilities across the country ended on the morning of 21 September. On 22 September, revolutionary control was secured throughout the country, on 23 September General Eduardo Lonardi assumed the position of Provisional President of the Nation and, the following day, Rear Admiral Isaac Rojas did the same as Provisional Vice President. On 4 January 1956, Commodore Julio César Krause was appointed as the new Minister Secretary of State for the Department of Aeronautics, replacing Brigadier Ramón Amado Abrahín, a "soft line" anti-Peronist.[9]

Vice Admiral Isaac Rojas, head of the insurgent Navy during the Revolución Libertadora, salutes from the deck of the cruiser ARA *17 de Octubre* in Puerto Belgrano on 23 September 1955. After the triumph of the coup that overthrew Perón the ship was renamed ARA *General Belgrano*. (General Archive of the Nation)

Krause, who would serve in the position until 2 April 1957, had been the retired officer of the Argentine Air Force responsible for having revolted the Córdoba Air Garrison against the constitutional government on 16 September 1955, that is, who lit the rebel spark that generated the bonfire of the Revolución Libertadora throughout the country. Krause was not only a staunch anti-Peronist, but an ultra-conservative Catholic who, by definition, was also an anti-communist. From his perspective, Argentina should align itself as

soon as possible with the interests of the United States, not only to ensure the individual liberties achieved by the revolutionary movement, but also to close ranks in the global opposition to the Soviet Union. His profile was closely taken into account by the Air Attaché to the US Embassy in Buenos Aires, Colonel Phineas K. Morrill, as well as by his Assistant Attaché, Lieutenant Colonel Lowell Earl May, who immediately transmitted this information to Washington. The head of the US State Department, John Foster Dulles, passed the information on to his brother Allen, CIA director. Both saw in Krause an excellent opportunity to extend the geopolitical influence of the United States in Argentina through the close rapprochement between their Air Forces.[10, 11]

General Eduardo Lonardi descends from a Douglas C-47 Skytrain of the Argentine Air Force at the Aeroparque in the City of Buenos Aires, on September 23, 1955, to assume as "provisional president" of the country, a position that does not exist in the Constitution. Behind him, Commodore Julio César Krause descends. (General Archive of the Nation)

In this context, on 3 October 1956, the Government of the United States, represented by its Ambassador in Buenos Aires, Willard Leon Beaulac, and the Government of the Argentine Republic, represented by its Minister of Relations and Worship, Dr. Luis A. Podestá Costa, and the Minister of Aeronautics, Commodore Julio César Krause, signed an agreement in Buenos Aires for the reestablishment of the permanent USAF Air Mission in Argentina.[12, 13, 14, 15, 16]

As soon as the diplomatic agreement for the re-establishment of the United States Air Mission in Argentina was sealed, the USAF took the first steps towards an organic landing in the country. To this end, on 18 October 1956, the commander of the USAF in the Caribbean, Brigadier General Truman H. Landon, was present in Buenos Aires, accompanied by Colonel Paul A. Zartman and Lieutenant Colonel Samuel H. Runyan. As soon as they touched Ezeiza they were led to the Ministry of Aeronautics by the Air Attaché of the US Embassy, Lieutenant Colonel Lowell E. May. The four members of the USAF were received in full by the Minister of Aeronautics (Commodore Julio César Krause), by the Commander in Chief of the Argentine Air Force (Brigadier General Heriberto Ahrens), by the Under secretary of Aeronautics (Brigadier Major Federico Fernando Antonio Ruiz), by the Chief of the Aeronautical Master General Headquarters (Brigadier Juan C. Pereira), by the Chief of the General Staff of the Argentine Air Force (Brigadier Alfredo Juan Vedoya), by the Director General of the Ministry of Aeronautics (Vice Commodore Eduardo Francisco McLoughlin) and by the assistant to Brigadier General Landon, Commodore Ernesto Tristán Hirthe. The conversation revolved around a single topic, specifically the implementation of the US

The first Globemaster II that arrived in Argentina with health care to combat the polio epidemic was in the 61st Carrier Group of the USAF, based at Donaldson AFB, South Carolina. The collaboration during the polio epidemic paved the way for the USAF to come closer to the government of the Revolución Libertadora. (Juan Carlos Cicalesi)

Air Mission and the "meteorological research" activities that were expected to be carried out in Argentina through it. Although they could not inform their Argentine hosts, the US officials already knew what would be the covert operations to be carried out in the country: survey of radioactive particles for the long-distance nuclear detection system administered by the AFOAT-1 agency and studies on radioactive fallout.[17, 18, 19, 20]

The agreement for the reestablishment of the US Air Mission in Argentina was negotiated and signed almost at the same time that the USAF carried out the last stage of the test programme for the U-2 spy plane and put the first examples into service. The existence of the plane was announced on 7 May 1956 by Dr. Hugh Dryden, director of the National Advisory Committee for Aeronautics (NACA), as a way to whitewash the high-altitude flights that would begin immediately in both the United States and Europe. Dryden informed the US public

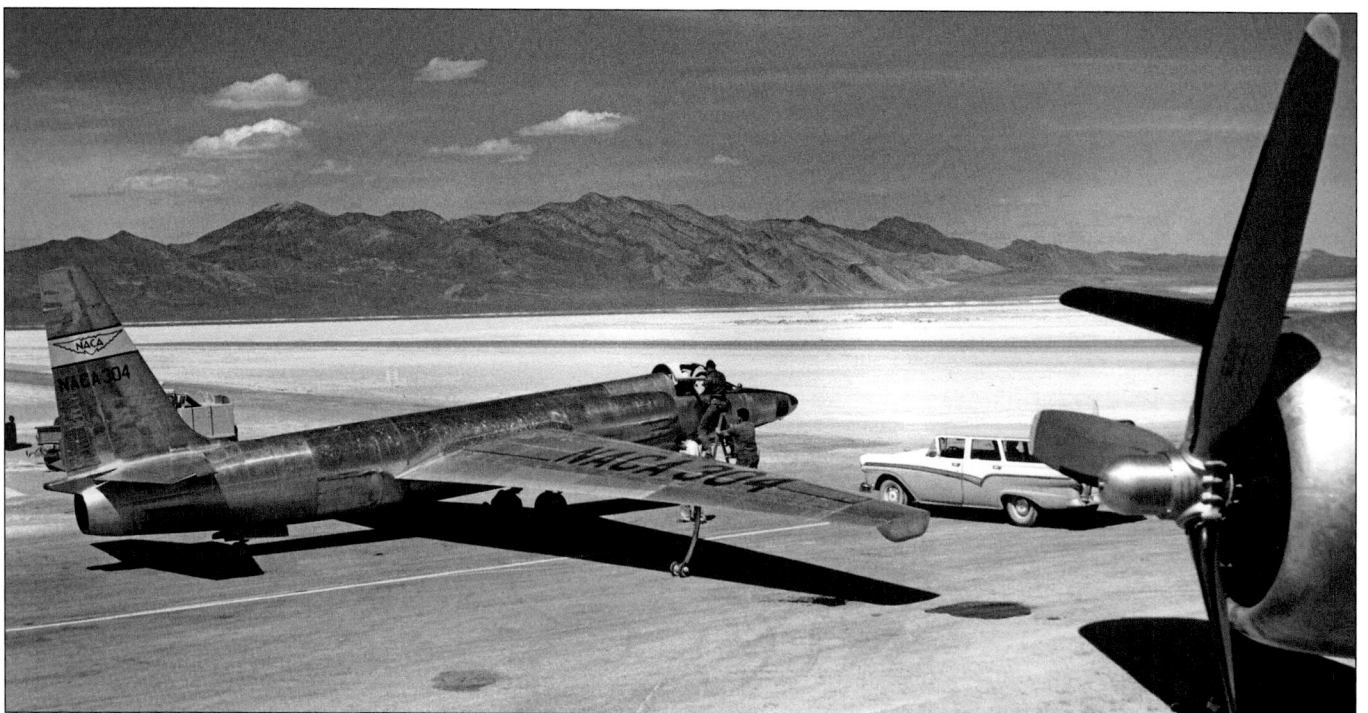

To conceal the true espionage purpose of the U-2s, the CIA painted several examples with National Advisory Committee for Aeronautics (NACA) lettering, logos, and numbers. This example, registered as NACA304, is preparing to carry out a test flight in Groom Lake, Nevada. (CIA)

that the U-2 would be used as a meteorological research platform for the study of the jet stream, the structure of the winds, temperature variations at high altitudes and the impact of lightning above 16,500 metres, although he was careful to make it known that by then the U-2 was already operating at 22,700 metres, about 74,500 feet.[21]

Dryden explained that the U-2 atmospheric reconnaissance flights would take place from Watertown Airstrip, Nevada, but in order to explain the presence of these aircraft in other parts of the world he added that 'USAF facilities abroad will be used as the programme gets underway, to enable the collection of research information necessary to accurately reflect conditions along tomorrow's high-altitude air routes around the world.' This declaration was timed to coincide with the deployment of the first U-2s to Europe. The civil nature of the U-2, its operation by civilian pilots and its exclusive use in meteorological studies related to the development of commercial aviation were emphasised.

Technicians from the USAF Special Weapons Center use an ion counter to check the radioactivity readings from a particle collector adapted to the wingtip of a Lockheed T-33 Shooting Star. The technology tested in proximity to nuclear explosions by tactical aircraft. Atmospheric sampling was later adapted to long-distance reconnaissance aircraft. Indian Springs AFB, Nevada, 20 April 1955. (USAEC via Robert Sullivan)

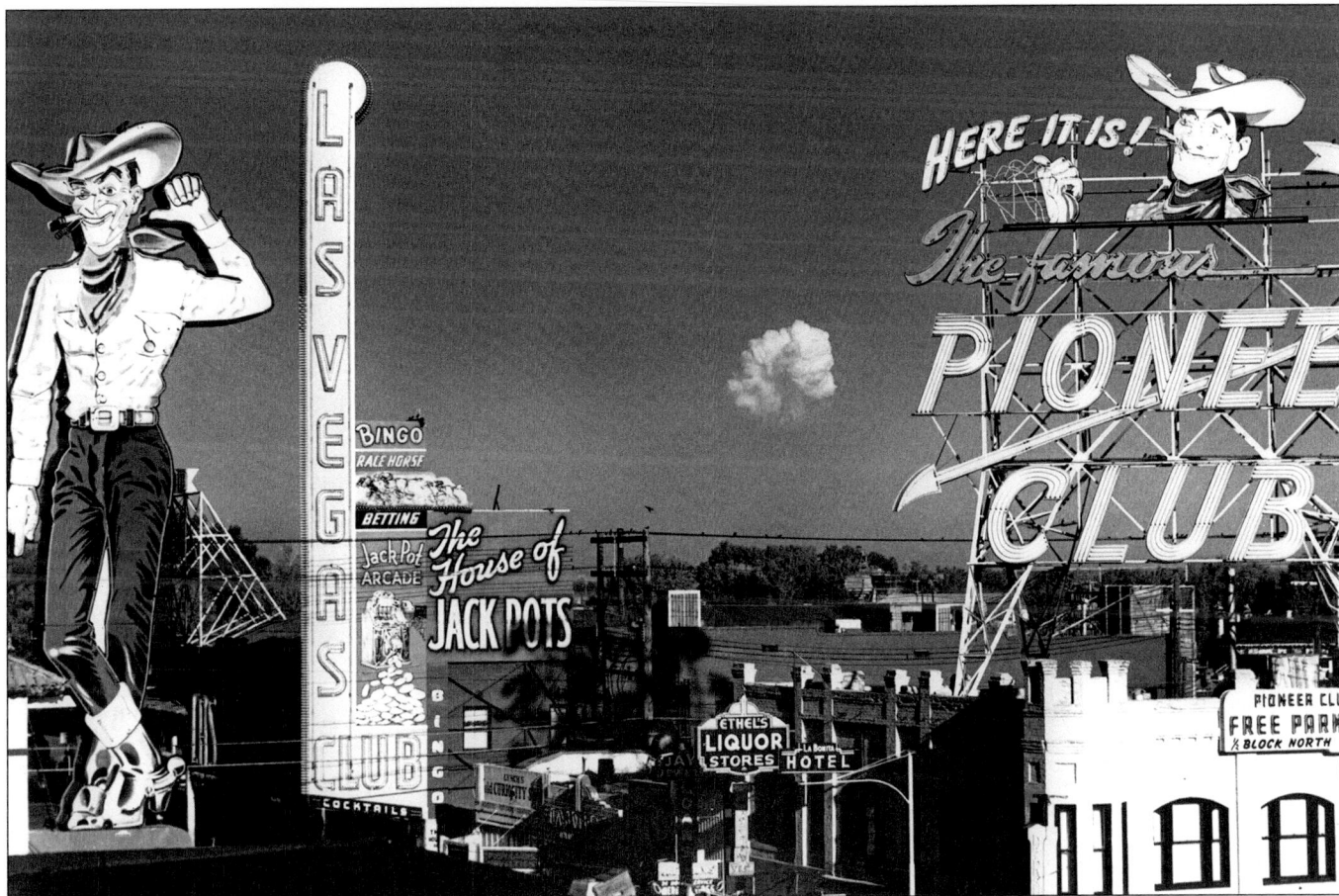

While the political situation in Argentina was rapidly deteriorating, the United States continued to test nuclear weapons in preparation for a potential global conflict. On 15 May 1955, the Zucchini test was detonated at the Nevada Test Site, with a yield of 28 kilotons. Its mushroom cloud is visible from Freemont Street in the city of Las Vegas, 105 kilometres away. (Smithsonian Magazine)

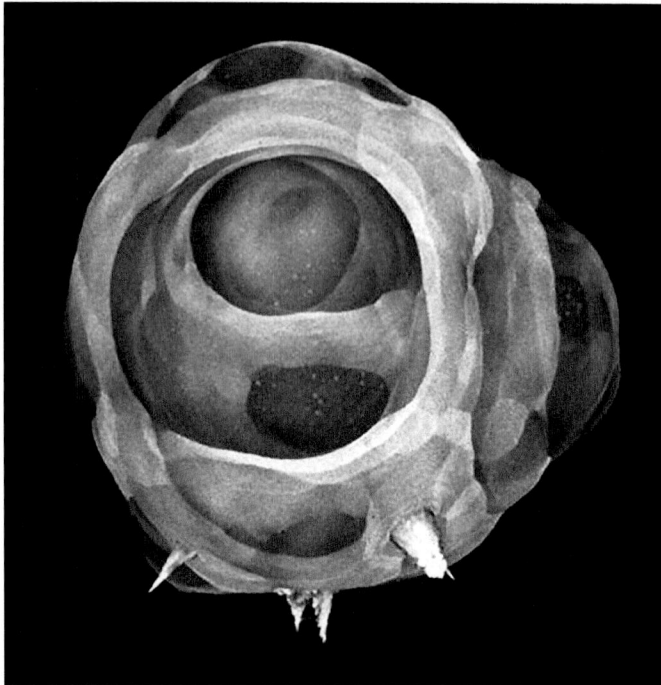

The fireball from the Turk nuclear test, with a yield of 44 kilotons, is captured by a high-speed camera milliseconds after the detonation, which occurred at the Nevada Test Site on 7 March 1955 as part of Operation TEAPOT. The device was detonated 150 metres above the desert and its effects were devastating. (USAEC)

Using this masquerade, the CIA managed to hide the spy flights that the brand new fleet of U-2 planes would begin to carry out frequently, first near the borders of the Soviet Union and then directly inside its territory. The planes flew at such an altitude that they were invisible from the ground to the human eye and also to radar. It did not take long for the first clandestine mission, which took place over Poland and East Germany on 20 June 1956. On 2 July, two more missions were executed into the heart of Czechoslovakia, Hungary, Bulgaria, Romania, and back to the heart of Poland and East Germany. The first overflight of the territory of the Soviet Union occurred on 4 July 1956, in the course of the fourth mission, after having confirmed that the U-2 had not been detected in any of the previous penetrations.[23, 24]

Boeing RB-52B-10-BO Stratofortress registration 52-013, christened *Barbara Grace*, assigned to the 4925th Test Group (Atomic), Air Force Special Weapons Center, Kirtland AFB, New Mexico. The photo shows him taking off from the runway at Eniwetok Atoll, Marshall Islands, on 20 May 1956 to drop the REDWING Cherokee test thermonuclear bomb on Namu Island. (USAF)

In June 1956 the initial U-2 task force, disguised as Weather Reconnaissance Squadron Provisional One (WRSP-1), deployed to Lakenheath in the United Kingdom, where its stated purpose was met with scepticism. Two sarcastic editorials in British Flight magazine belittled the excuse of weather research and questioned the excessive security surrounding the operation of the new planes. A NACA spokesperson announced, a month later, that preliminary weather data collection flights had been carried out from Lakenheath and that this had demonstrated the aircraft's value as a high-altitude research tool. The most significant fact of these coverage actions was that the U-2s carried the meteorological instruments that they had used during their test and training flights, thus allowing the public to be shown that data was actually being collected at altitudes hitherto unattainable for conventional aircraft. The transfer of this data to the scientific community reinforced the cover-up and in the process provided a veritable treasure trove of weather information applicable to the future of civil air transport.[22]

As CIA U-2s began flying over Soviet territory to determine the extent of its nuclear arsenal, the United States continued to hone its own through a new series of tests in the Pacific Ocean. Between May and July 1956, within the framework of Operation REDWING, 17 nuclear explosions were carried out on the Bikini and Enewetak atolls with the purpose of testing a new generation of thermonuclear devices. During the REDWING Cherokee test for the first time the actual ability of a B-52 bomber to drop a hydrogen bomb was demonstrated. Although the bomb ended up falling 6.4 kilometres away from its target, the effect was so devastating that its parameters could be perfectly measured as if it had hit the target. In practical terms, this

Namu Island, in the Marshall Islands, with the circle that marked the target for the REDWING Cherokee test. The crew of the B-52 in charge of the nuclear bombardment missed the target, but the test demonstrated the ability of a strategic bomber to hit the centre of a Soviet city with a thermonuclear weapon. (USAEC)

meant that, to vapourise an entire city, the USAF had only to place its atomic bombs anywhere in its urban radius and not necessarily in the centre, since the effect would be practically the same.[25]

The nuclear explosions of Operation REDWING were remotely monitored by the AFOAT-1 detection network, either to calibrate their detection equipment or to confirm the amount of radioactive isotopes released into the atmosphere, its permanence in the air, its precipitation rate and its planetary distribution in accordance with the mechanics of wind circulation. For this purpose, modified Boeing WB-29 bombers of the Air Weather Service were used, but also stratospheric balloons that could reach altitudes of 50,000 to 100,000 feet equipped with sensitive instruments. Hundreds of polyethylene balloons were launched as part of the ASHCAN Project (led by Dr. Lester Machta) and SUNSHINE (led by Dr. Willard Libby), both funded by the Atomic Energy Commission, the first to detect radioactive isotopes from Soviet nuclear tests and the second to study the effects of radioactive fallout.[26, 27]

In the southern hemisphere, these balloons were launched from different AFOAT-1 detachments located in Brazil, specifically in Porto Alegre (Unit 107), Recife (Unit 109), Sâo Paulo (Unit 158) and Rio de Janeiro (Unit 161). The results of these launches were not conclusive, largely because the balloons were at the mercy of the winds, they rose to different altitudes, they were displaced to different longitudes and they were very difficult to recover. In the planning tables of the Atomic Energy Commission, the idea of using the new U-2 spy planes as stable platforms to detect radioactive particles at defined geographical positions and altitudes around the planet gradually took shape. Coverage could be carried out perfectly in the northern hemisphere and, thanks to the reestablishment of the USAF Air Mission in Argentina, also in the southern hemisphere. In both cases, the flights in search of krypton-85 would be carried out in secret, under the cover of exclusively meteorological atmospheric soundings.[28, 29]

REDWING Dakota test explosion, 25 June 1956, at Bikini Atoll, Pacific Ocean. The test yielded a blast of 1.1 megatons. (USAEC)

To collect information on the precipitation of nuclear explosion debris and thus assess the consequences of acid rain worldwide, the USAEC funded Project SUNSHINE, consisting of the release of polyethylene stratospheric balloons. The southernmost launches were made from Brazil with balloons similar to the one seen in the image, captured at Holloman AFB, New Mexico, in 1955. Starting in 1956, the USAF began to consider Argentina as a prime location for launching these balloons. (Joseph T.Page II)

With the purpose of detecting the radioactive particles resulting from its own and the Soviet Union's nuclear explosions, the US Atomic Energy Commission financed the ASHCAN Project, which used balloons equipped with sensitive instruments built by Chicago Midway Laboratories. It soon became clear that the records were imprecise and random, so the possibility of conducting height surveys with the new U-2 aircraft began to be evaluated. (CML)

6

WARNINGS FROM BUENOS AIRES (1957)

In January 1957, the CIA decided to admit to the existence of the Lockheed U-2 spy plane. Since they could not declare the real nature of the aircraft's activities, they decided to describe it as a functional platform for exclusively meteorological air operations. It was not possible to have such a strange aircraft deployed in Europe without a plausible explanation being given, as the complete absence of information would arouse even more suspicion in the Soviet intelligence complex.

Bringing the U-2 to light meant not only publishing photos and data on its performance, but also generating a story, false of course, regarding the research and scientific tasks for which the plane was allegedly designed. After much discussion about it with CIA authorities, the director of the National Advisory Committee for Aeronautics (NACA), Hugh Dryden, arranged for the publication of the first official image of the plane, which came to light in early February 1957. The chosen specimen bore prominent NACA, not USAF, markings and codes, which was considered a good first step given the civilian nature of the stated activities and NACA's well-earned prestige as a scientific research agency.

A month later, in March 1957, researchers Thomas L. Coleman and Jack Funk published NACA Research Memorandum No. L57A11, titled Preliminary High-Altitude Atmospheric Turbulence Measurements as Determined from Aircraft Acceleration Measurements. Months later, Coleman wrote a second report with Emilie C. Coe, this time comparing turbulence data taken in the United States with that collected in England and western Europe. The information was true since it came from the U-2 flight recorders, but it had no relation to the actual espionage activities for which the plane had been designed.[1]

The coverage story that the U-2s were only good for weather research was furthered by the NACA. The agency issued an official statement announcing the publication of the first paper and stated that the high-altitude research programme was focused on statistical studies of turbulence. The main purpose of the new aircraft, the public was told, was to collect data on convective clouds,

temperature variations at different altitudes, wind shear, turbulence associated with the jet stream and other meteorological phenomena. According to what was falsely reported to the press, the NACA programme was developed in conjunction with the Air Weather Service, which provided state-of-the-art weather instruments, while the Geophysical Research Directorate used the collected data to develop methods to forecast major weather phenomena. for high altitude flights. According to what was said, the recipient of all that effort was the civil air transport of the future, since the information would be used to design faster, safer and more comfortable stratospheric range planes.[2]

In July 1957, the bogus cover story was amended. Dryden and his public information officer, Walter T. Bonney, met with CIA officials to jointly design a new facade that would explain the operation of the planes abroad, where they should fly with USAF markings and not NACA markings. The reason was very simple: a U-2 with civil licence plates and nationality marks was subject to the aeronautical control regime of any country in which it flew (for example, Argentina, where the operation was already being contemplated), while a military plane was not subject to such intrusions, even less in a country where a USAF Air Mission was based (as was the case in Argentina, which was precisely for this reason being considered an excellent foreign base for U-2 operations).

Lookout Mountain Centre specialists photograph the dirigible balloon that was to participate as a scientific sampling aircraft in the series of nuclear explosions of Operation PLUMBOBB, carried out at the Nevada Test Site in 1957. The tests mobilized a veritable army of technicians from different government agencies. (USAEC)

The airship arranged as a scientific instrument platform for the Priscilla test was anchored to the ground 8 kilometres from the epicentre to record the force of the explosion. The thermal wave instantly set it on fire and the pressure wave brought it down a few seconds later. The power of the nuclear weapon was immeasurable. (USAEC)

Test John, carried out on 19 July 1957 as part of Operation PLUMBBOB, consisted of the detonation of a nuclear-headed AIR-2 Genie air-to-air missile, the first designed to devastate entire formations of Russian bombers. The missile was launched by a Northrop F-89J Scorpion aircraft identical to the one seen in this photo, taken at Indian Springs AFB, 30 miles from the blast site. The light seen above the horizon is not the sun, but the explosion of the missile itself. (USAF)

The Boeing B-47E-20-LM Stratojet serial 52-0233 of the 306 Bombardment Group of the USAF parked in front of the passenger terminal of the Ezeiza International Airport on 10 November 1957. Its large size and its aerodynamic lines caused a sensation among the public present. (Martinito)

According to the new cover plan hatched between the NACA and the CIA, the U-2s would be used in the High Altitude Sampling Program (HASP) executed by the USAF Strategic Air Command and funded by the Air Force Special Weapons Project (AFSWP). The masquerade had a real core: the project involved the collection of atmospheric particle samples of radioactive fallout resulting from nuclear weapons tests, both in the United States and in other countries, to study their consequences on human health and wildlife, but the real purpose would be the collection of the strategic radioactive isotope krypton-85. The Air Weather Service would remain the executive agent and the pilots of the U-2 planes would remain civilians under NACA contract, an excellent cover for hiding the CIA pilots, all of whom were "civilian" with no connection to the CIA or the USAF. The false story was very solid because it made it possible to associate the high-altitude flights with the detection of fallout, a worrying effect of nuclear detonations, and it even made it possible to explain abroad what was the instrumentation that the planes would carry, but in no way revealed the true purpose of the operations, which was the detection of krypton-85.[3]

Events precipitated at the same speed that new examples of the U-2 were entering service. On 11 June 1957 the USAF 4028th Strategic Reconnaissance (Meteorological) Squadron received its first six U-2As for operational use. Three months later, in September 1957, the 4080 Strategic Reconnaissance Wing took delivery of five more aircraft modified to the WU-2A version for the declared collection of radioactive particles for the HASP programme and for the undeclared collection of the radioactive isotope krypton-85 for the top secret office AFOAT-1.

Project HASP flights began almost immediately, in October 1957, with aircraft deployed at Ramey AFB (Puerto Rico) and Plattsburgh AFB (New York). In parallel, and to support the exclusively meteorological use of the U-2, a few aircraft were used in real meteorological operations, which allowed for regular feedback on the stories that formed the cover-up. Thus, for example, on 14 November 1957, a CIA pilot assigned to Detachment C of the 3rd Weather Reconnaissance Squadron (Provisional), flew over the eye of Hurricane Kitt in the western Pacific Ocean, north of the Philippine island of Luzon. Using a Perkin-Elmer Model 501 tracking camera, he was able to photograph the storm from vertically above, thereby obtaining the first ever photo taken in the eye of a tropical cyclone. Several months later, Lieutenant Colonel Robert C. Bundgaard of the Air Weather Service published the results of that flight in a scientific paper that validated the aircraft's meteorological use.[4, 5]

Three USAF Douglas C-124 Globemaster IIs pass in formation over Aeroparque on 10 November 1960, at the start of the display inherent to Operation LONG LEGS. All of Buenos Aires witnessed the power of the USAF, whose planes could be seen from terraces and balconies. (Guido Ghiretti)

A Boeing KC-97 Stratofreighter tanker parades over Buenos Aires with a Boeing B-47 Stratojet bomber attached to its in-flight refuelling lance. The process had been repeated several times during the flight of the B-47s to Argentina, which was carried out non-stop over a journey of almost 7,000 kilometres. The last charge to the bombers took place over the Amazon. (Guido Ghiretti)

The Boeing B-47E-55-BW Stratojet serial 51-5244 of the Strategic Air Command, parked at the Buenos Aires City Aeroparque, within reach of the large public that took place there on 10 November 1957 on the opening day of the XII Aeronautical Week. (Martinito)

While the U-2s multiplied their photographic and nuclear espionage missions over Europe, Asia and the Pacific, secret tests of new atomic weapons, particularly warheads for the first generation of ballistic missiles, also multiplied on the continental United States. Medium-range and intercontinental-range missiles were expected to replace conventional bomber aircraft. That was precisely the purpose of most of the explosions tested at the Nevada Test Site between 28 May and 7 October 1957, within the framework of Operation PLUMBBOB. Twenty-nine explosions of variable power were carried out and were monitored by 21 laboratories and government agencies.[6]

The PLUMBBOB test series included 43 effects tests on civil and military structures, biomedical radiation studies, and aircraft structural tests. Almost 1,200 pigs were subjected to various biomedical experiments of variable cruelty, because they all basically consisted of burning them alive at different distances from the epicentre of the explosions. In the Priscilla explosion alone, which was a blast equivalent to 37 kilotons, more than 700 of these animals were used for various irradiation experiments on the Frenchman Flat plain. Some pigs were placed in raised cages and fitted with suits made of different materials, to test which provided the best protection against thermal radiation. The pigs survived, but with third-degree burns on 80 percent of their bodies. Less lucky were the animals placed in pens behind large sheets of glass, which died pierced by splinters generated by the pressure wave caused by nuclear explosions. In both cases, the aim was to verify with animals what would be the effects that a nuclear explosion could cause in human beings.[7]

General Curtis LeMay's Boeing KC-135 rolls over the Ezeiza platform on 12 November 1957, after setting an official non-stop or refuelling flight record of 10,175.64 kilometres from Westover AFB to Buenos Aires. Total flight time was 13 hours, 2 minutes, and 51 seconds. During the journey, and 3,500 kilometres from the starting point, a direct link was established with Thule Island, north of Greenland, and with the Little America US scientific base in Antarctica. (Joe Bruch)

The Fairchild (Kaiser-Frazer) C-119J Flying Boxcar registration 51-8137 (painted 18137), construction number 140, the second aircraft of its type deployed by the USAF to Argentina, displayed on the Ezeiza apron on 14 November 1957. (Fernando Benedetto)

Boeing B-47E-55-BW Stratojet serial 51-5244. Behind, a second bomber of the same type. Both are arranged on the Ezeiza platform on 14 November 1957. By far, they were the planes that most captured the attention of those present due to their size, beauty, speed and manoeuvrability. (Guido Ghiretti)

One of the most interesting tests in the PLUMBOBB series was the John shot, carried out on 19 July 1957, to test the capability of the Douglas AIR-2 Genie air-to-air missile. This was a nuclear warhead projectile specifically designed to destroy large formations of Soviet bombers in the air. It was fired from a Northrop F-89J Scorpion fighter over Yucca Flats and was spectacular not only because of the explosion itself, but also because the USAF used the test to show that nuclear bombs were harmless if detonated at high altitude. To this

end, five officers and a cameraman were positioned at ground zero, below the hypocentre, and remained there during the airdrop, flash, and explosion. They survived, but no one bothered to explain to the press that the Genie missile's nuclear warhead had exploded 5,639 metres above the surface and had a tactical yield of just two kilotons. If a thermonuclear bomb had been detonated at the same height, the six volunteers would have been vapourised on the spot.[8, 9]

The Boeing KC-97G-105-BO Stratofreighter registration 52-889, one of the four deployed in the framework of Operation LONG LEGS to provide in-flight refuelling to the B-47 and B-52 bombers sent to Argentina. The image was taken on the Ezeiza platform on 14 November 1957. Behind it appears the Douglas C-124A-DL Globemaster II registration number 50-099. (Atilio Marino via Vladimiro Cettolo)

The in-flight refuelling mechanism caught the attention of the press, as can be seen in this featured image of the KC-97G extendable lance serial 52-889, published by the Revista Nacional de Aeronáutica. (Martinito)

Left: Three Douglas C-124, a Boeing B-47 and a Fairchild C-119 on the wide platform of Ezeiza, on 15 November 1957. The public swarms around them in what was an unforgettable show. (Juan Carlos Cicalesi via Vladimiro Cettolo)

Below: A B-47 Stratojet escorted by four F-100 Super Sabers from the Thunderbirds squadron flies over the international breakwater of Ezeiza Airport at the closing of the air show on 15 November 1957. (RNA)

The tests of the PLUMBOBB series foreshadowed what would be the scenario of the nuclear war of the future, with nuclear warheads arranged at the end of large rockets and projected at a distance no longer by airplanes, but by ballistic missiles whose launch was impossible to detect and against which there was no possible defence. The USAF's first medium-range ballistic missile, the Douglas PGM-17 Thor, made its maiden test flight on 25 January 1957. Four months later, on 31 May, the more powerful Chrysler PGM-19 Jupiter was tested. Both had been developed in parallel to reach targets up to 2,400 kilometres away with individual 1.45-megaton thermonuclear warheads. To project nuclear destruction to targets between 2,500 and 14,500 kilometres, the USAF awarded Convair the design-build contract for the SM-65A Atlas, its first ICBM, which conducted its first flight test on 11 June 1957.[10, 11, 12]

Now, with all the potential represented by ballistic missiles under development and their new warheads being tested in Nevada, the truth is that, by 1957, the United States was a long way from being able to rest its national defence on the new technology, which had not even reached the state of maturity necessary to serve as an effective strategic deterrent against the Soviet Union. The infrastructure for the new missiles was still under construction and no model had yet reached operational level. Therefore, the USAF had to face the challenges of a potential global conflict with medium-range (Boeing B-47) and long-range (Boeing B-52) nuclear bombers, whose optimum performance required continuous training by their crews,

alert services, maintenance steps and tanker aircraft for in-flight refuelling.

Precisely to align all this complex machinery and send an unequivocal deterrent message to the Soviet Union, the USAF decided to carry out two very long-range operations in 1957, both with nuclear-capable strategic bombers. The first, called Operation POWER FLITE, took place between 16 and January 1957, and involved three Boeing B-52Bs that flew non-stop around the world replenished regularly by Boeing KC-97 tankers, allowing them to travel 39,165 kilometres in 45 hours and 19 minutes at an average speed of 864.25 kilometres per hour. The second operation, much more ambitious in scope than the previous one, was called LONG LEGS and was destined for Argentina. The choice was not accidental, since the distance between the main B-52 base at Loring AFB (Maine) and Moscow was equivalent to that between Washington and Buenos Aires. For this new operation, the B-52s would not only be refuelled in flight by the old KC-97s, but by the new Boeing KC-135 Stratotanker jets.

Unsurprisingly, the talks with the Argentine government began in secret and were conducted at the highest level through the USAF Air Mission in Buenos Aires. It was necessary to find an excuse for a whole formation of US strategic bombers to reach the Argentine capital and that excuse was found in the Argentine regulations themselves. Decree 288/45 of 4 January 1945, by which the Argentine Air Force had been created as an independent armed force, had granted the nascent

Together with the F-100s of the Thunderbids squadron, the USAF deployed a two-seater Super Saber to Argentina, the North American TF-100C-NA serial number 56-3765, which was repeatedly used to perform supersonic baptism flights with different personalities, such as the Minister of Aeronautics (Commodore Jorge Horacio Landaburu), the United States Ambassador to Argentina (Willard Beaulac), the British Ambassador to Argentina (Sir John Guthrie Ward) and some officers of the Argentine Air Force. The pilot of this plane was Captain William Scott. (Fernando Giró via Atilio Marino and Vladimiro Cettolo)

The Lockheed Hercules participating in Operation LONG LEGS was registered 55-0033 and corresponded to the C-130A-LM version, the first in series. It lacked auxiliary fuel tanks and was equipped with Allison T56-A-1A turboprop engines driving three-bladed propellers. In the distance, behind the plane, you can see the mobile radar station deployed by the USAF for the guidance of its aircraft. (Fernando Giró via Atilio Marino and Vladimiro Cettolo)

institution both the promotion of aviation and the creation of an aeronautical awareness in the community. Among other actions aimed at this end, the air force instituted the Aeronautical Week on 14 August 1945, which, since then, began to be held in the second half of September and during which all kinds of static and aerial demonstrations, exhibitions, conferences, promotion in schools and related cultural activities. Thus, the framework of the Aeronautical Week of 1957 was chosen to square the development of Operation LONG LEGS, which would be shown as a generous adhesion of the USAF to the programme of activities organised by the Argentine Air Force.

The traditional date of the Aeronautical Week changed according to the logistical needs of the USAF. On 27 September, the de facto president Pedro Eugenio Aramburu signed Decree-Law 11,849 / 1957 by which he created the Organizing Commission for the Aeronautical Week. On 16 October, Resolution 1,264/57 of the Ministry of Aeronautics set November 10 as the start date of the event. Never before had an Aeronautical Week deserved a presidential decree, nor did it deserve it in the following years, which allows us to infer the intense organisational effort that, behind the scenes, the USAF Air Mission was making.[13]

The curtain was lifted on 2 November 1957 when the Buenos Aires newspapers announced that, on the occasion of Aeronautical Week, on 16 November, six Boeing B-52 Stratofortress strategic bombers were going to arrive in Argentina on a direct flight from their base at Loring AFB (Maine). Without landing in Buenos Aires, these planes would return to their starting point to cover a journey of more than 22,000 kilometres in almost 23 hours, for which they would be refuelled in flight by tanker planes, demonstrating their ability to fly around the world. Operation LONG LEGS was already underway and, as was immediately known, it would not only include the B-52s, but an entire "extraordinary embassy" that would commit almost 400 men, 10 Douglas C-124 Globemaster II transport planes, five North American F-100 Super Saber supersonic fighter jets from the Thunderbirds aerobatic squadron, two Fairchild C-119 Packet freighters, one Lockheed C-130 Hercules transport plane, five Boeing KC-97 Stratofreighter tankers, one Boeing KC-135 Stratotanker, two Grumman SA-16 and SA-54 Albatross amphibious aircraft for search and rescue, four Boeing B-47 Stratojet bombers and a supersonic TF-100 Super Saber two-seater. The USAF released to the Argentine press a large number of photos alluding to all these models that were distributed by the United States Information Service (USIS), the foreign news agency of the United States.[14, 15]

Operation LONG LEGS began on 8 November 1957, when a formation of 35 aircraft arrived at Ezeiza responding to what was described as "an invitation made by the Argentine aviation authorities." The USAF not only deployed the planes, but everything

General Pedro Eugenio Aramburu, with the presidential band, sings the Argentine National Anthem in the Government House together with Rear Admiral Isaac Rojas. He took office as "provisional president" of the Nation on 13 November 1955 after a palace coup against General Eduardo Lonardi, whom he considered too soft on overthrown Peronism. Aramburu had served in 1952 as a military attaché to the Argentine Embassy in the United States. (General Archive of the Nation)

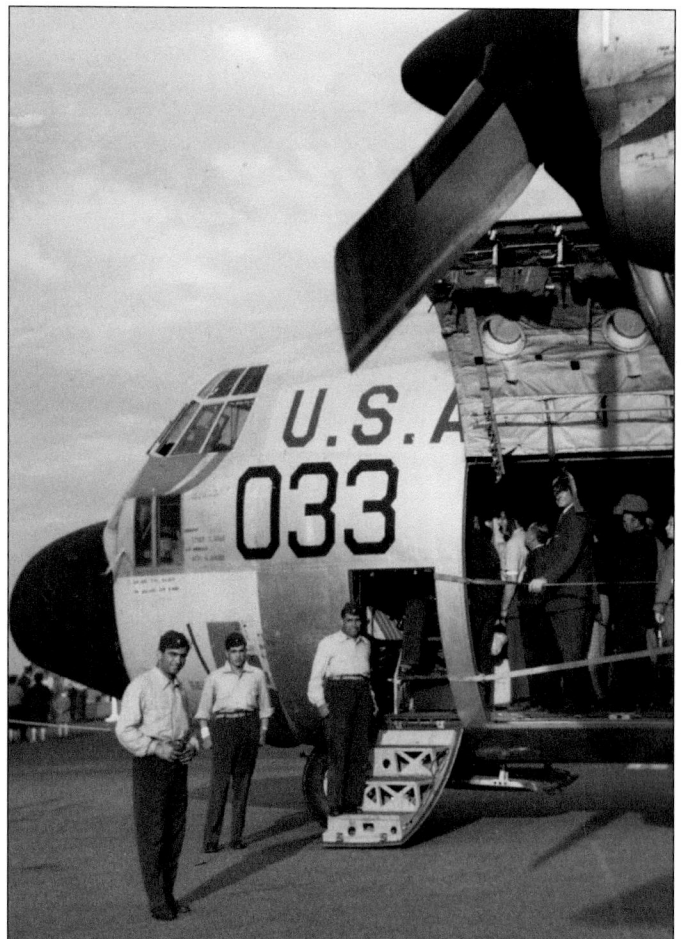

The public crowds inside the cargo hold of the C-130 to visit the very large cockpit of the plane, while conscript soldiers from the Argentine Air Force ensure security that, in reality, it was not necessary to protect due to order and self-control that prevailed throughout the XII Aeronautical Week. (Martinito Collection)

The TF-100 Super Saber registration number 56-3765 was the first plane to cross the sound barrier in Argentine airspace. It did so on 10 November 1957 over the Buenos Aires City Airport, at the controls of Captain R. McIntosh, who was accompanied in the back seat by Captain Febo Ippolito, of the Argentine Air Force. (Fernando Giró via Atilio Marino and Vladimiro Cettolo)

necessary for their self-sufficient operation, including maintenance, repair, communications, air traffic control, and administrative support. The officers of the Argentine Air Force were struck by the fact that their US counterparts brought even pencils and office supplies. At the head of the mission was General Paul Stanely Emrick, commander of the VI Air Division based at Mc Dill AFB (Tampa, Florida), who arrived aboard a KC-97, after 8,600 kilometres of flight with stops in Ramey AFB (Puerto Rico), Georgetown (British Guiana), Fortaleza and Rio de Janeiro (Brazil).

Emrick, a mechanical aeronautical engineer who graduated in 1938 from Purdue University, knew full well what Operation LONG LEGS meant. During the Second World War he had served as deputy chief of planning on the General Staff of General Curtis LeMay (whose B-29 bombers dropped the nuclear bombs on Hiroshima and Nagasaki) and between 1950 and 1953 he had dealt with the air defence of the countries NATO Europeans. As of 1956, he was in command of the 6 Air Division of the USAF, which administered four Bombardment Wings formed, at the same time, by several squadrons of B-47 and B-52, all of which had the sole purpose of carrying nuclear devastation to the Soviet Union.[16, 17, 18]

The XII Aeronautics Week began on 10 November 1957. The symbolic cutting of the inaugural ribbon took place at the Aeroparque of the City of Buenos Aires and was overseen by the vice president of the provisional government, Rear Admiral Isaac F. Rojas, who was accompanied by the Minister of Aeronautics and other high authorities. In his presentation speech, General Paul Stanely Emrick did not shy away from showing the extraordinary power of the Strategic Air Command and assured that "the USAF can bomb any part of the world with the help of radar, whatever the weather conditions". The media that would be shown to the public from that day on would make it possible to confirm it. The static display at the Aeroparque included a Douglas C-124 Globemaster II and a USAF Grumman SA-16 Albatross amphibian, which attracted the public due to their large size. Less attention was given to two missiles on display by the USAF, a Boeing IM-99 Bomarc for air defence and a Lockheed X-17 for high-atmosphere scientific applications.

The air show over the Aeroparque began with the passage of two squadrons with 24 Gloster Meteor planes from the Argentine Air Force, followed by four F4U Corsairs from Naval Aviation and three civilian Aerocommander 500s. The signal to start the show was given by a roaring bomb that, when it exploded overhead,

released a parachute with the Argentine flag. At 11:31 a.m., the USAF delegation made its thunderous presentation with the first supersonic speed flight in Argentina, led by Captain William Scott in a silver two-seater TF-100 Super Saber.

The demonstrations carried out at Aeroparque on 10 November 1957 were of such magnitude that the public turned en masse to the

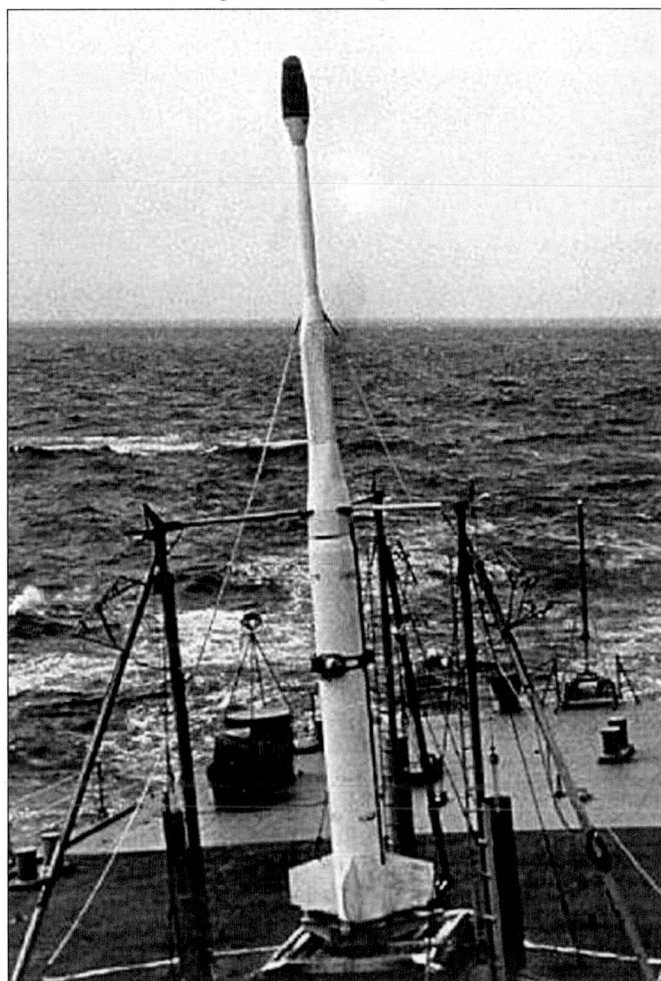

One of the X-17A missiles from Operation ARGUS ready to be launched from the deck of the USS Norton Sound. The first launch took place on 27 August 1958 and its 1.7 kiloton warhead exploded 170 kilometres above sea level. The launch was tracked by COZI radar and radiometers from the support ship USS Albemarle; and by the USAF-installed MSQ-1A Missile Tracking Equipment aboard the USS *Tarawa*. (US Navy)

The two Fairchild C-119 Flying Boxcar deployed to Ezeiza are visible in this image, the first wearing the colours of the Thunderbirds squadron. They were superb and ubiquitous aircraft for all kinds of tactical and logistical tasks, largely thanks to their rear cargo gate. (Juan Carlos Cicalesi via Vladimiro Cettolo)

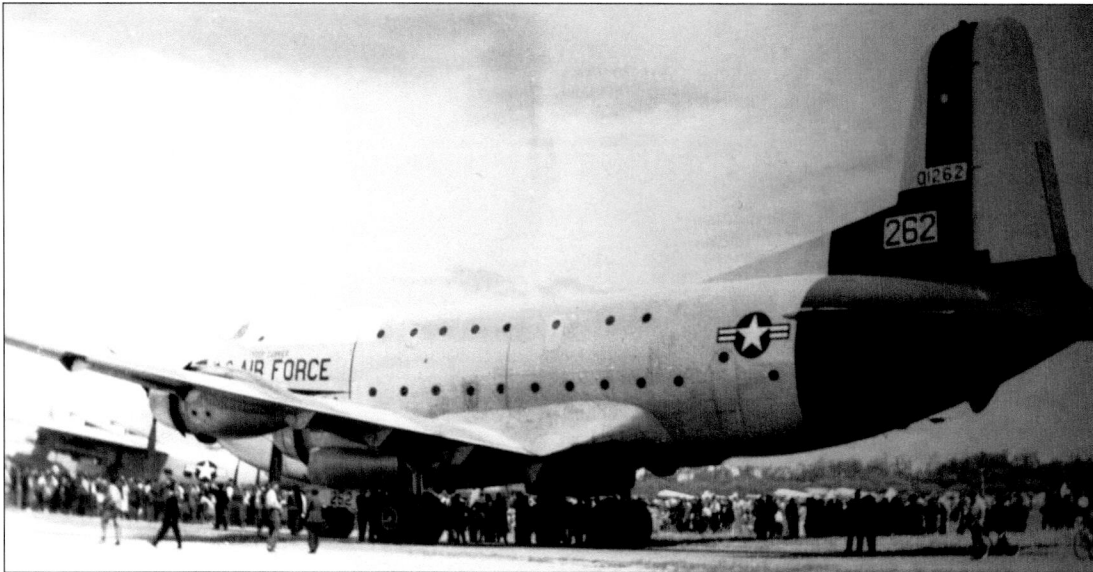

The formidable size of the Douglas C-124 Globemaster II becomes apparent when compared to the crowd around it. The aircraft had two decks and could accommodate 200 soldiers or 123 stretcher patients. The photographed example is C-124A-DL registration number 50-1262. (Martinito Collection)

Ezeiza Airport the following day. There the USAF carried out several supersonic flights in the TF-100 two-seater manned by Captain William Scott Jr., which took several officers of the Argentine Air Force beyond the sound barrier. The first Argentine to join the Mach Buster's Club was the Minister of Aeronautics, Commodore Jorge Horacio Landaburu.[19]

On 12 November, early in the morning, the Boeing KC-135 commanded by General Curtis E. LeMay, deputy chief of the USAF General Staff and architect of the Strategic Air Command, which he had headed since its creation, arrived in Ezeiza. He was accompanied by Major General Arno Luehman, Director of Information for the USAF. The plane flew over Ezeiza at 7:45 and landed at 7:51. It completed an exceptional time of 13 hours, 3 minutes and 30 seconds over a distance of 10,140 kilometres, without stops or refuelling from its starting point at Westover AFB, Massachusetts. Thus, two world records were established to be recorded in the respective categories of the Federation Aeronáutique Internationale (FAI): distance record for a flight without stages or refuelling and distance in a straight line with time calculation between the ends of the route. The flight took place at a maximum speed of 888 kilometres per hour and at an altitude of between 9,500 and 12,000 metres.[20]

It was not the first time that LeMay was in Buenos Aires, since in 1948 he had integrated the mission carried out by the 2nd Heavy Bombardment Group with the Boeing B-17 Flying Fortress that attended the inauguration of President Roberto Marcelino Ortiz. General LeMay was received by authorities from the Argentine Air Force and the Argentine Army, the United States Ambassador

(William Beaulac), the head of the USAF mission in Argentina (Colonel Richard Welztin) and by his friend the head of the USAF delegation to the Aeronautical Week (General Paul Stanley Emrick). LeMay left for the United States at 6:27 a.m. the following day, 13 November, and covered the 8,350 kilometres that separate Ezeiza from Washington in just 11 hours and 7 minutes, at an average speed of 751.2 kilometres per hour. In this way, the first non-stop flight between the capitals of Argentina and the United States was completed with a new world speed record.[21]

The day of exhibitions and supersonic flights was repeated in Ezeiza the following day. Minutes after the landing of the TF-100 that had led new personalities to fly beyond the speed of sound, four KC-97 tankers they took off from Ezeiza to meet the B-52 bombers that were flying in from Homestead AFB (Florida). An hour later they met them and refuelled them on the source of the Río de la Plata, near the Uruguayan city of Carmelo. It was the second time that the bombers received fuel in flight, since they had been resupplied over the Caribbean by six Boeing KC-135 Stratotankers taken off from Castle AFB (California), far enough away to show that they could go to any geographical point in that might be required, a clear message to Soviet strategic analysts.[22, 23]

The bomber formation was commanded by General W.K. Martin, head of the 45th Air Division of the USAF, who greeted the operators of the USAF radar which, installed in Ezeiza, monitored the entire operation by radio. With good horizontal visibility (10 kilometres in Ezeiza) the B-52s completed their in-flight refuelling and returned to their combat position, consisting of two groups of three aircraft

The C-124A-DL registration number 51-5192, another of the Douglas Globemaster II deployed to Argentina, on the Ezeiza platform. No public flights were made on these planes, but the USAF allowed access to their huge cargo holds. (Juan Carlos Cicalesi via Vladimiro Cettolo)

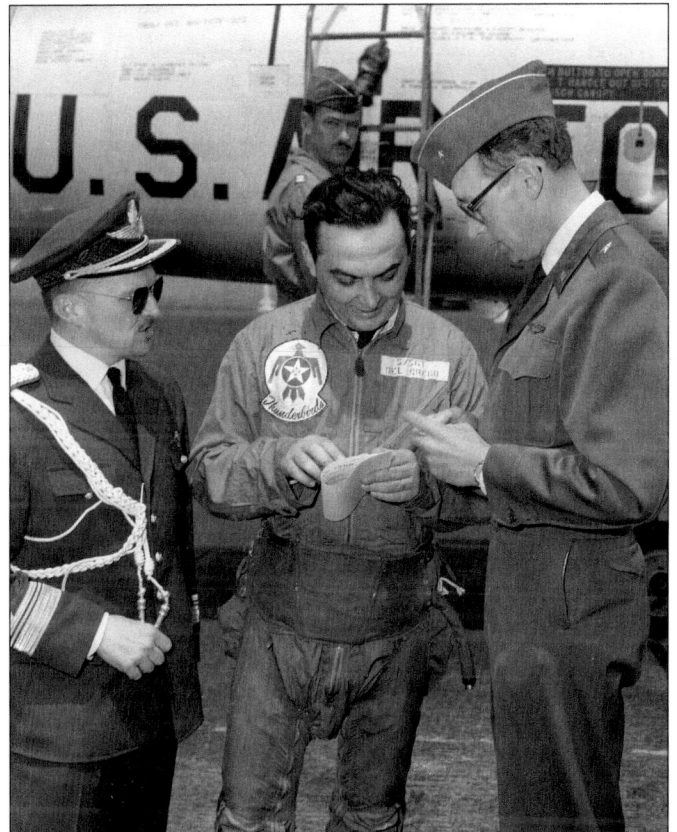

Above: Captain William Scott Jr., using Commander Ernesto Axel Niethardt as a translator, instructs President Pedro Eugenio Aramburu on the correct way to adjust the anti-G suit belt that was supplied to him by the USAF, prior to the supersonic flight of the president, on 15 November 1957. The Minister of Aeronautics, Brigadier Jorge Horacio Landaburu, attends the preparation. (Fernando Benedetto)

Right: Brigadier Jorge Horacio Landaburu, Minister of Aeronautics, receives a briefing from General Paul Stanley Emrick prior to his supersonic flight in the USAF TF-100. Landaburu was the first officer of the Argentine Air Force to cross the sound barrier. In the background, Captain William Scott, narrator for the Thunderbirds and pilot of the TF-100. Landaburu wears Sergeant Del Grego's flight jacket. (Fernando Benedetto)

Part of the freighter fleet deployed to Argentina is visible in this image, with four C-124 and one C-119 spread out on the Ezeiza platform, in front of the international jetty. (Fernando Giró via Atilio Marino and Vladimiro Cettolo)

each. This is how they approached the city of Buenos Aires, in a straight line coming from the Uruguayan city of Colonia.[24, 25, 26]

Six orange dots then appeared on the green screen of the radar, revealing the location of the two B-52s, so that both their height and the distance in a straight line to the checkpoint located in Ezeiza could be determined. From 6,000 metres the formation began its gradual descent, thus successively flying over the towns of Escobar, Vicente Casares and Ensenada. From there, and changing their formation to that of single file, they passed at 300 metres and at very high speed over the Aeroparque de la Ciudad de Buenos Aires. Then followed a wide turn at the same level, thereby facilitating the observation of the large audience that in the metropolis looked up to follow his step. The presentation ended when the six large bombers stormed the Ezeiza airport. After two passages they quickly regained height, heading back to their base at Loring AFB (Maine), almost on the border between the United States and Canada. The landing occurred at Plattsburg AFB (New York), after a new in-flight refuelling over the Caribbean and after having completed 16,897 kilometres of crossing in 21 hours with 40 minutes of continuous flight.[27, 28]

Operation LONG LEGS more than fulfilled the objective of its planners, not only because it showed the capacity for autonomous deployment of the USAF's most dangerous aircraft thousands of kilometres from their bases, but also because it confirmed in fact that the B-52 bombers of the Strategic Air Command could easily reach Moscow (and any other city located within its radius of action) thanks to the in-flight refuelling provided by the new generation of tanker aircraft, the KC-135. It may not be surprising that, during their approach to Buenos Aires, the B-52s placed the city in the centre of their bomb sights and that they carried out all the nuclear attack procedures on the Argentine capital. It was never disclosed whether the planes had transported thermonuclear bombs in their bomb bays, but training with armed B-52 bombers was commonplace throughout the Cold War, since not only was the operation of the machines or the navigation capacity of the crews evaluated, but rather the logistics of transporting the bombs, their safe handling and their assembly.[29]

The political objective of Operation LONG LEGS was also fully achieved, both for the government in Washington and for the

The six B-52s deployed to Argentina within the framework of Operation LONG LEGS received in-flight refuelling over the Caribbean by the new USAF tankers, the Boeing KC-135 Stratotanker, far superior to the slow KC-97 Stratofreighter. In the image, the B-52D-70-BO registration 56-0582 is refuelled by the KC-135A-BN registration 55-3127. (USAF)

The Air Attaché to the Embassy of the United States in Argentina, Colonel Albert Frances Fahy Jr., photographed in Ezeiza at sunset on 15 November 1957 together with the Assistant Air Attaché Lieutenant Colonel Vergil Nick Nestor and members of the Air Mission of the USAF in Argentina, the "Ambassadors of Blue". They are Colonel Richard F. Weltzin, Lieutenant Colonels Lawrence R. Poundstone, Kenneth A. Omsted, and John D. Mattie; Majors Raymond J. Herdzina, Joseph E. Cosgrove, Jack Terzian, and Jack D Shattuck; Captains E.O. Andrews and Raphael Bentachner; and Petty Officers William O. Todd, Charles E. McGinty, and Michael R. Schuster. (Fernando Benedetto)

government in Buenos Aires. President Eisenhower confirmed that Argentina was a trustworthy country for US geostrategic purposes in the context of the Cold War, while President Aramburu perceived complete and total support for his domestic and foreign policies, both markedly anti-Peronist. It is not surprising, therefore, that at 7:40 p.m. on 15 November 1957, hours after having crossed the sound barrier in the USAF TF-100, President Aramburu addressed the country by national radio broadcasting channel to announce the end of the political cycle of the Revolución Libertadora based on a democratic opening that would take place through general elections called for 23 February 1958. The elections would be held throughout the country with Peronism outlawed, that is, without the participation of candidates or political parties that represented or alluded to the regime deposed in 1955. The handover to the new civil government was set for 1 May 1958.

Operation LONG LEGS, which was a resounding success in all its stated purposes, was also a success in its veiled objective, that is, the one that was not made known to the Argentine authorities. So it was that, at the end of the XII Aeronautical Week, when embarking all the equipment and supplies in the holds of the C-119, C-124 and C-130, the technicians of the VI Air Division omitted to load the tower mobile control unit, portable radar, and approach guidance control (GCA) that they had brought from the United States. These pieces of equipment were not forgotten, much less donated to the Argentine Air Force, but placed in the care of the USAF Air Mission in Buenos Aires. It was not by chance because, by then, the ultra-secret AFOAT-1 agency was already planning to extend the krypton-85 tracking flights to Argentina. Operations with U-2 spy planes had to start, precisely from Ezeiza, no later than the second half of 1958.

Three Boeing B-52 Stratofortress bombers on the apron at March AFB, California. The examples deployed to Argentina in the framework of Operation LONG LEGS belonged to the 52nd Bombardment Group (Heavy) based at Loring AFB, Maine, much further north. Their licence plates were never disclosed, but the communication codes with which they presented themselves before the USAF control arranged in Ezeiza were: L-58, R-23, R-28, R-30, R-47 and R-79. (USAF)

Three B-52 Stratofortress paraded in formation over Ezeiza after having flown low over the City of Buenos Aires a few minutes earlier. It is estimated that the six bombers deployed to Argentina in the framework of Operation LONG LEGS had nuclear weapons in their holds, because that was the standard deterrence procedure of the Strategic Air Command throughout the Cold War. (Guido Ghiretti)

7

SILVER CROWS IN THE SOUTHERN SKY (1958-1959)

By the end of 1957, the ultra-secret krypton-85 radioactive isotope detection programme with U-2 aircraft was extremely advanced, to such an extent that the AFOAT-1 office demanded that it be extended to the southern hemisphere in order to achieve global tracking of radioactive waste. In parallel, the Atomic Energy Commission was very interested in also extending its studies on the precipitation of radioactive fallout and its potentially dangerous effects on human life, to estimate what should be the limit of use of nuclear weapons in the event of a global nuclear conflict. The Weather Bureau, for its part, expressed interest in knowing and specifying the general circulation mechanisms of the atmosphere in the southern hemisphere, in order to generate increasingly accurate forecasts from numerical models fed with data collected on a global scale.

All these initiatives and demands converged in December 1957 on the Air Force Special Weapons Project (AFSWP), the US government agency in charge of planning and developing the most advanced military projects, which was already financing the High Altitude Sampling Program (HASP), the weather screen concocted with the CIA and the NACA to cover up the krypton-85 detection missions over Europe and Asia. After a brief evaluation, the AFSWP analysts concluded that the most convenient way to achieve all the intended objectives simultaneously was to extend HASP operations to the south by redefining the phases and expanding the declared objectives, which from that moment would become:

1. The determination of the amounts of strontium-90 and other dangerous radioisotopes in the stratospheric reservoir, and its global precipitation as a function of latitude, altitude, and time.
2. The determination of the residence times of these radionuclides in the stratospheric deposit at a global level.
3. Estimation of the mechanism and rates of mixing and transfer of radioactive waste within the stratosphere and into and through the troposphere.

In addition to the pursuit of these objectives, the HASP programme included investigations of other aspects of radioactive fallout, such as the physical nature of stratospheric radioactive particles, evaluation of studies of concentrations in rainwater and soil, the amount of strontium-90 already precipitated stratospheric and the potential danger for the human population of this isotope and other radioactive nuclides present in radioactive fallout worldwide.

Unsurprisingly, the AFSWP never stated or published the main objective of the HASP Project, which was to detect traces of krypton-85 in order to determine the nuclear capabilities of the Soviet Union. Consequently, the entire programme was a huge front to cover the real purpose of the studies, even considering the veracity of the stated objectives, which would also be pursued as a scientific cover.

The HASP Project was conceptually divided into five phases. The first, started in 1957, included the development of an atmospheric sampling mechanism, the planning of flight operations, the establishment of scientific facilities, and the contracting of the

During 1958 and 1959 the USAF tried to show that the U-2 was a scientific research plane designed to learn about high atmosphere meteorological phenomena. But the real goal was to detect particles of krypton-85 and other radioactive isotopes derived from nuclear explosions. The image shows a WU-2A, easily recognisable by the pressurised "bottle" attached to the front of its fuselage. (Guido Ghiretti)

laboratories and universities that were to participate. The second phase, also begun in 1957, included the establishment of a sampling network in the northern hemisphere, the analysis of flight profiles to measure the accuracy of the sampling, and the calibration of the stratospheric tracking balloons developed by the USAEC. Phase 4, developed from the requirements of AFOAT-1, consisted of extending the sampling network to the southern hemisphere and studying the rates of lateral mixing of debris resulting from the nuclear explosions developed in the Pacific Ocean during Operation HARDTACK in 1958. Phases 4 and 5, to be carried out in 1959 and 1960, consisted of the continuation of the sampling, detailed studies of the mixing processes and atmospheric transfer, particle captures at the North Pole, recalibration of equipment and random controls at the two hemispheres.

The HASP programme was designed to achieve the highest possible sampling density over a single cross section of the planet. It was based on the fact that the normal circulation of the atmosphere should transport an entire mass of air in a uniform way, so it was decided to systematically search for particles on a strip located on a single meridian, up to 70,000 feet.

The U-2's range made it impossible to sample the entire length of the southern corridor at any one time, and furthermore the aircraft could only fly safely through regions where navigation could be accomplished with the assistance of the U-2's magnetic compass. Therefore, the HASP project was designed to cover up to 71° North Latitude and 57° South Latitude. Approximately 90 percent of Earth's atmosphere was assumed to lie between the mentioned latitudes, so the scan was virtually global in scope. Extrapolation of the results to the upper stratosphere would be possible using data obtained by weather balloons from the ASHCAN Project, run by the Air Weather Service and the Atomic Energy Commission.

SAM Launch Complex Zones 1 & 2

Behind the cover of the meteorological research flights that were carried out within the framework of the HASP Project, the U-2 photographic espionage of the USAF and the CIA multiplied their secret operations over the Soviet Union. The image, taken in 1958, corresponds to the Kapustin Yar polygon, where nuclear-headed ballistic missiles were launched. (CIA)

The HASP Project involved a major scientific effort. The first steps for the formation of the team of brains were taken in 1956, for which purpose the resources and laboratories of the company Isotopes Incorporated (of Westwood, New Jersey), the Institute of Paper Chemistry (of Appleton, Wisconsin) and Stanford University were employed. The contract between DASA and Isotopes was signed in February 1957 and through it the company was entrusted with providing the scientific direction and the radiochemical analysis of the radioactive elements impacted in the IPC-1478 model paper filters developed by the Institute. The flights of the HASP programme were entrusted to the USAF Strategic Air Command, with logistical support provided by the Military Air Transport Service and the preservation of the samples by the Air Research and Development Command.

The main analytical programme was led by Dr. Johannes A. Van den Akker of the Institute of Paper Chemistry, in charge of developing and processing the paper used for in-flight sampling. Herbert W. Feely, Jerome Spar, Philip W. Krey, Alan Walton,

DASA 532B

HASP MASTER

Special Report on

High Altitude Sampling Program

Maj. Albert K. Stebbins, III Ed.

RADIATION DIVISION

1 JUNE 1960

Cover of the Special Report prepared in 1960 to detail the operations carried out by WU-2 aircraft in Argentina within the framework of the High Altitude Sampling Program (HASP). The report was published by the Defense Atomic Support Agency (DASA), a new name given in 1959 to the Air Force Special Weapon Project (AFSWP). DASA was a difficult organisation to categorise because it undoubtedly had a secret military function, although it sometimes published the results of its activities at the request of the United Nations, which was interested in monitoring the effects of nuclear radiation. (DASA)

James P. Friend, and J. Laurence Kulp of the Atomic Energy Commission and Isotopes Incorporated conducted the separation of the particles, their radiochemical analysis, and the determination of its stratospheric distribution. The Weather Bureau through Lester Machta, Robert J. List and Kosta Telegadas provided the weather models and weather analysis of the results. The work team for the analysis of radioactive fallout and global fallout of nuclear waste was made up of Joshua M. Holland and Harold A. Knapp (US Atomic Energy Commission), Edward A. Martell, Christian E. Junge, Marvin I. Kalkstein, and James E. Manson (Air Force Cambridge Research Laboratory) and Willard F. Libby (University of California). The recalibration of the U-2 pipelines was led by Hugh Dryden, Dr. Smith of France and George Holden of the National Aeronautics and Space Administration (NASA), Professor Elliott G. Reid of Stanford University and Captain Budd Knapp of the USAF Flight Test Center. DASA personnel who played key roles in the HASP programme included Colonel R. Maxwell, Lieutenant Colonel H. Rose, Major L.E. Trapp and Dr. F.H. Shelton.

Project HASP formally began when six Lockheed U-2s were assigned between August and September 1957 to the 4080th Strategic Reconnaissance Wing of the USAF Strategic Air Command, which code-named their operation CROWFLIGHT. The six U-2s were converted to the WU-2A weather research version by incorporating nose samplers and "bottles" with air intake hatches attached to the

sides of the fuselage. The U-2's nose air intake could carry four filters, while the hatch intake six. Hatch filters could only be exposed in sequence, but nose filters could be exposed out of sequence or twice during a single mission.

After an initial phase of training and testing between August and October 1957 at Laughlin AFB (Texas) the sampling aircraft were based at Plattsburg AFB (New York) and Ramey AFB (Puerto Rico). From these two bases, a North-South sampling corridor coincident with the meridian 70° West Longitude, from 66° North Latitude to 6° South Latitude, was systematically monitored from November 1957 to May 1958. During June and July 1958 sampling was carried out only in the vicinity of Puerto Rico, with the hope of extending operations much further south as soon as possible.

The USAF Air Mission in Buenos Aires had pursued this purpose since at least November 1957. Diplomatic relations with the Argentine government were solid and the reconstructed ties with the officers of the Argentine Air Force were also close enough for atmospheric tracking operations to start in December of that year. However, the ultra-secret nature of the radioactive particle tracking did not allow any loose ends to be left, so the CIA recommended that the deployment to Argentina be carried out only after the new constitutional government took office after the general elections called for the 23 February 1958 by Decree-Law No. 15,100/57 signed by the de facto president Pedro Eugenio Aramburu.

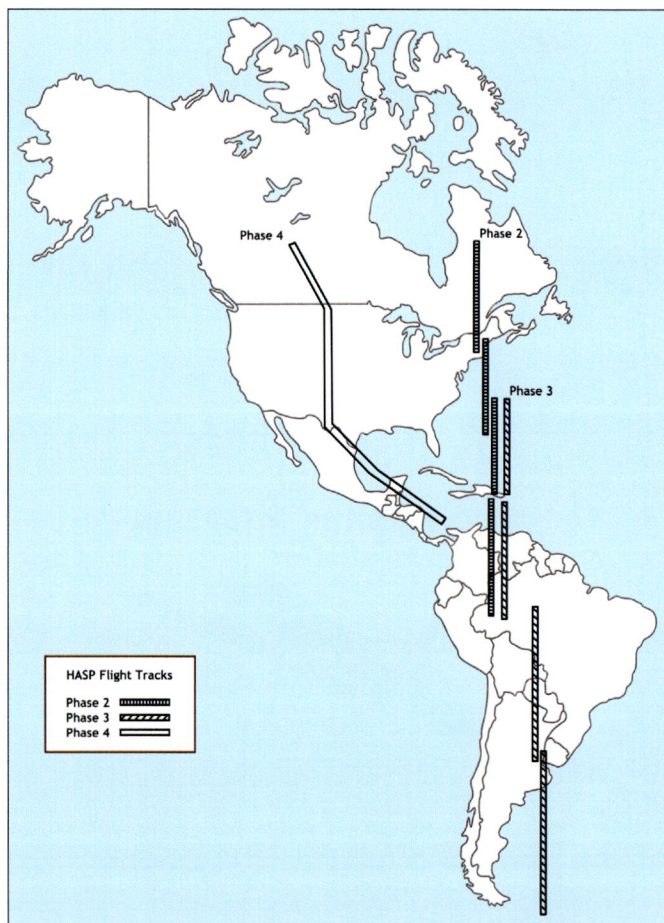

A map with the planned trace for the atmospheric sampling flights of the HASP project. As can be seen, the USAF WU-2As, involved in Operation CROWFLIGHT, always followed the same atmospheric survey pattern to intercept and capture radioactive particles in the Northern and Southern hemispheres. The graph was published in 1960 in the DASA 532B-1 report. (Map by b.b.h.illustrations, based on DASA)

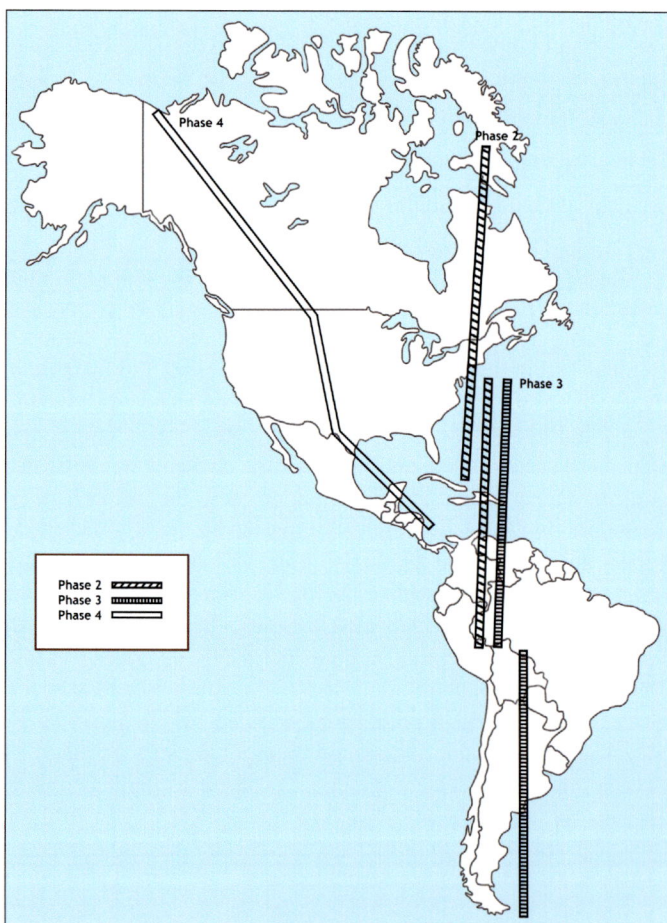

A map of the flights of the HASP Project in charge of the USAF. Phase I began in October 1957 at Plattsburg AFB (New York), followed by Phase II the same year at Ramey AFB (Puerto Rico) and Phase III at Ezeiza starting in September 1958. The operation lasted a total of seven years, it took 45,000 flight hours and carried out missions in a dozen locations around the world. The first foreign destination of the HASP Project was Argentina. The map was prepared by Isotopes Inc. and published in the DASA 1300.1 report. (Map by b.b.h.illustrations, based on DASA)

The provisional Argentine vice president, Rear Admiral Isaac Rojas, euphorically receives in Ezeiza the vice president of the United States, Richard Nixon, sent by President Dwight Eisenhower to attend the inauguration ceremony of Arturo Frondizi on 1 May 1958. The new government would be "guarded" by the anti-Peronist hawk who three years earlier had led the Revolución Libertadora. (Life)

The elections took place on the indicated date and were carried out throughout the country with complete normality, but with Peronism outlawed from the electoral process. The winning slate, with 44.79% of the votes, was made up of Dr. Arturo Frondizi as president and Alejandro Gómez as vice president, leaders of the Intransigent Radical Civic Union (UCRI). Despite winning the election, the new presidential team was not supported by the leaders of the armed forces. In spite this, his victory should have been recognised because the commitment of the provisional government of the Revolución Libertadora had been to democracy and the electoral victory had been achieved by a large majority. Frondizi apparently enjoyed an unshakable position, but it was only a legal fiction because, in reality, General Aramburu gave him only the formal insignia of command. The armed forces retained real power, assuming the role of zealous inspectors of the government, which under no circumstances would they allow to return to the "intoxication" of Peronism.

The inauguration ceremony of the new president took place on 1 May 1958 and took place in a context of real optimism, since Argentina seemed to return forever to the democratic world from which it should never have left. To give an idea of the geopolitical importance that the United States gave to the event, it is enough to indicate that President Eisenhower sent his Vice President, Richard Nixon, to Buenos Aires to participate in the act and offer his express support to Frondizi.

It remained to be seen whether the new Argentine president would be willing to collaborate with the US government regarding the permanent establishment of "atmospheric reconnaissance" planes in his country, but the CIA quickly found a weighty argument in favour of authorisation, thanks to the commitments assumed by the Argentine Republic for the execution of the International Geophysical Year 1957-1958. This was a scientific event held between July 1957 and December 1958, during which more than 30,000 university students and technicians from 66 countries had agreed to cooperate in a series of observations on Earth and outer space to investigate solar activity, cosmic rays, geomagnetism, northern lights and ionospheric physics.[1]

As soon as authorisation was obtained from the Argentine government to base "scientific" military aircraft on its territory, the CIA and the State Department gave the USAF the green light to arrange for the deployment of WU-2 spy planes to Argentina. Consequently, starting in May 1958, the USAF Air Mission in Buenos Aires began talks with the highest authorities of the Argentine Air Force to define the place of operation and the necessary security requirements. The US proposed the Ezeiza Airport from the outset, not only because its runways offered excellent operating conditions,

President Arturo Frondizi was a researcher who well understood the importance of maintaining strong relations with the United States, although he also consolidated ties with many other countries in the region. He had to lead the country at a time convulsed by anti-Peronist hatred, Peronist resistance, and the beginning of communist infiltration. (AGN)

On 1 May 1958, on the occasion of the inauguration of Dr. Arturo Frondizi, the Royal Air Force was present in Argentina with two AVRO Vulcan bombers from 83 Squadron RAF based at RAF Waddington. In addition to protocol, the deployment was the British counterpart to Operation LONG LEGS, executed six months earlier by the USAF, and conveyed the same message to the Soviet Union: that the Vulcans could hit any Soviet city with a thermonuclear bomb. (Guido Ghiretti)

but also because it was an entirely civilian location, which made it possible to show that the "scientific meteorological research flights" to be carried out from there were innocuous. However, no one could approach the area assigned to the USAF, only members of the CROWFLIGHT team with access credentials could circulate in it, and under no circumstances could the planes or their personnel be photographed. The same security measures should be adopted in the hangars of the state company Aerolíneas Argentinas where the USAF

technical personnel provided maintenance service to the planes in segregated and carefully delimited areas with paint lines on the floor that no one could cross without the corresponding accreditation.

The first US officers linked to Operation CROWFLIGHT arrived in Argentina on 16 June 1958. They were Colonel Jack Nole, commander of the 4028 Strategic Reconnaissance Squadron and his deputy, Major Rae A. Behrens. In less than a month, both received eight Douglas C-124 Globemaster II and two Douglas

The pressurised sample collection container attached to the fuselage of the U-2 (making it the WU-2A) was developed from aerodynamic studies conducted by Elliott G. Reid of Stanford University. Lockheed Aircraft Corporation then designed and built the device, which could sequentially expose six paper filters. These devices were installed on aircraft beginning in the summer of 1959. (USAF)

During most of CROWFLIGHT III, the WU-2As were only capable of collecting four paper samples per flight. Each plane had inflatable neoprene seals that secured the paper discs against the portafilters to prevent leakage around them. Beginning in 1959, collecting probes designed by the USAF Cambridge Research Center Geophysical Research Directorate were installed. The image shows a technician placing a filter in the nose port of the WU-2A registered 56-6718, one of the examples that flew in Argentina. (Guido Ghiretti)

Only six U-2s were converted to the WU-2A atmospheric sampling version, but it was enough to cause a real revolution. The planes not only served as a cover for the photographic missions of their twins operated by the USAF and the CIA, but also determined the Soviet nuclear production capacity in the midst of the Cold War and made it possible to determine the global mortality due to radioactive fallout in the event of a nuclear war. (USAF)

The mechanic of a WU-2A shows the locks removed from the small wheels called 'pogos', which prevented the plane's long wings from touching the ground during take-off roll. The pogos were ejected to avoid induced drag on the airfoil. When take-off occurred with low fuel, the wings remained straight and the pogos were practically in the air, not touching the ground. (USAF)(Guido Ghiretti)

C-54 transport planes full of cargo in Ezeiza and, with them, the staff of their unit: Majors Robert Hackman, Hamilton Blakahear, John P. Cordova, Russell J. Leibfarth and Harry Pedersen, Captains Robert B. Downs, Jack Griffin, Robert T. Holmes, Lloyd Thomas L. Smith and Warrant Officer Winton D. Lunceford. As officially reported by the Argentine Air Force, the purpose of the presence of the US contingent was to 'obtain precise information on clear air turbulence, cloud formations, wind systems, and the exhaust jet at an altitude of 55,000 feet, as well as information on cosmic rays and concentration of elements in the atmosphere, such as ozone and water vapour, wind friction, etc'.[2, 3]

The forecasts for the deployment of the WU-2 to Argentina not only reached the safety of the aircraft, but also the right to use an entire building at Ezeiza Airport, the rights to use Argentine airspace and that of all those countries that could be flown over for the planes to reach Ezeiza, specifically Mexico, Venezuela, Brazil, Bolivia and Paraguay. Accommodation was contracted in different hotels for all the personnel that would be deployed, about 150 people. The US placed a lot of emphasis on the legal status that corresponded to granting the pilots and mechanics, which were analogous to the diplomatic status of the members of the USAF Air Mission itself in Argentina, which made them practically untouchable. One of the most sensitive aspects was the transportation logistics and the collection of the necessary fuel for the WU-2, since the General Electric J-73 turbine did not work with commercial kerosene but with additive fuel specially refined by Shell.[4]

The first three WU-2s deployed to Argentina belonged to Detachment 4 of the 4028 Strategic Reconnaissance Squadron of the 4080th Strategic Reconnaissance Wing, based at Plattsburg AFB (New York) and were flown to our country by Majors Richard Dick

By 1959, the HASP Project had processed one billion standard cubic feet of air between 57° South Latitude and 71° North Latitude, up to 70,000 feet altitude. Information from the ASHCAN stratospheric balloon programme was used to extrapolate the results to higher levels of the atmosphere. All the information ended up being reprocessed at the Los Alamos Scientific Laboratory in New Mexico, the most important atomic complex in the United States. (LASL)

Atkins, Edwin Ed Emerling and Lloyd Leavitt. They first landed at Ezeiza on 12 September 1958, marking the start of Phase 3 of Operation CROWFLIGHT.[5,6]

For the USAF, Ezeiza was not an air base itself (AFB, Air Force Base) but an operation location (OL, Operating Location) where a detachment (Det, Detachment) was based and it appears as such in the few official sources available since the WU-2 operations carried out from Argentina were always considered top secret. Thus, Ezeiza was "Detachment 4" for the USAF, to which the Lockheed WU-2 based at Plattsburg AFB that should participate in the HASP project were deployed.[7]

Everything connected with Operation CROWFLIGHT was secret. Not even the personnel involved in the piloting and maintenance of the WU-2s were clear about the real purpose of the missions or what was the use of the radioactive samples they were collecting.[8]

Before the start of the "scientific" flights of Operation CROWFLIGHT and to explain the tasks that the support WU-2 and Douglas SC-54 Rescuemaster aircraft would have to carry out from Ezeiza, the USAF prepared a lengthy description of the profile of a typical flight, which was delivered in a dossier to the Ministry of Aeronautics and later published in the Special Report that was supplied, in English, to the Argentine government. Both documents stated the same thing:

As is customary in the USAF, the mission actually begins a few days before take-off. Extensive planning is necessary to ensure the success of the mission. As you must act as pilot, radio operator, navigator, flight engineer and survival expert, in addition to the scientific observer, each moment of the flight and each action that the pilot must perform is detailed in advance. Since celestial navigation is performed, the sextant angles are pre-calculated based on the time take-off, upper winds, forecast weather observation, and expected true airspeed. Position lines are then drawn on a strip map based on these pre-calculated angles. These lines of positions are also indicated if measurements are taken at a specific time period before or after. In addition, a composite record of navigation is prepared, co ammunition and aircraft together with the HASP flight data card. When air rescue support is to be used in the mission, extensive coordination of emergency services is required and communication procedures are carried out.

Several hours before the U-2 pilot is due to wake up for an early breakfast, the air rescue plane takes off and continues along the defined course. Since the U-2 flies almost twice as fast as the air rescue aircraft, this procedure allows for maximum coverage of the U-2's route.

On the day of the mission, the U-2 pilot must breathe oxygen for several hours before take-off. This procedure prevents decompression sickness if the U-2's cabin depressurizes during flight. Considerable precautions are taken to ensure that pilots' personal equipment and survival kits are in proper condition.

A partial pressure suit is worn in the event of cabin depressurization, as exposure to ambient pressure at 70,000 feet would be fatal within minutes. Since the pilot is subjected to considerable physical stress during prolonged high-altitude flight, a careful examination is performed by the flight surgeon before take-off and after landing. Meanwhile, the filter papers are inserted into their holders and installed in the charger. This mechanism is then given a last-minute operational check.

When the flight is ready to depart, the pilot is assisted on board. His personal equipment is checked again and the aircraft is inspected by another pilot. A portable oxygen cylinder is used when boarding the plane to enhance the effectiveness of pre-breathing.

At the appointed time, the pilot starts his engine and heads to the runway. After aligning the aircraft for take-off, a ground crew member removes the stabilizer gear safety pins that keep the wingtips off the ground. During take-off, the wings flex upward and the stabilizers droop. The pilot then climbs steeply to the sampling altitude.

While flying the sample route, the pilot maintains his logs and flight data card and periodically changes filter papers. He also sends position reports to ground stations and maintains radio contact with air rescue aircraft. This has a paramedical team to help the pilot in case he falls. In addition, this aircraft provides normal communications and navigation assistance, as well as emergency assistance.

At the end of the route, the U-2 pilot reverses course and changes altitude to take the return sample. The air rescue plane usually changes course at about the same time. At the end of the flight, the aircraft is stopped with the help of a drag chute and the stabilizers are reinstalled before leaving the runway. Wingtip skids protect the aircraft if the wings droop before coming to rest. A full debriefing of the pilot is performed and the exposed filter papers are removed and placed in mailing envelopes. The mission ends when the air rescue plane returns, usually a few hours after the U-2.[9]

From 12 September 1958 to November 1958, all sampling flights from Ramey AFB and from Ezeiza were scheduled for an altitude of 60,000 feet. In December 1958 the flight plans were changed to provide periodic sampling at altitudes ranging from 48,000 to 65,000 feet in the south polar stratosphere. The missions were always carried out along the same corridor, which followed the meridian 63° West Longitude, between 38° North Latitude and 57° South Latitude, at a rate of two missions per week, each of which had to collect 40 samples. Detected remnants of Soviet explosions in the northern hemisphere were minimal.

With speed brakes and flaps extended, and pogos removed, WU-2A serial 56-6705 of the 4080th Strategic Reconnaissance Wing lands at a US base after a flight of more than six hours in Phase I of Operation CROWFLIGHT. The Loco Crow logo is visible on the tail. (USAF)

WU-2A serial 56-6715 slows down its landing run by using parachutes at a US base. This aircraft operated in Argentina during Phase III of Operation CROWFLIGHT. According to DASA reports, this plane suffered an engine flame-out, over the Drake Passage, which gives an idea of the southern reach of the HASP Project. (USAF)

Since the U-2 missions were to be flown over subarctic, oceanic, and rainforest areas, without airfields or aids to navigation, each sortie was accompanied and assisted by a Douglas SC-54D Rescuemaster search and rescue aircraft of the 64 Air USAF Rescue Squadron with two paratrooper medics per plane belonging to the USAF 2157th Air Rescue Squadron.[10]

During the CROWFLIGHT flights made from Argentina in 1958, tritium was detected. Natural tritium in the atmosphere results from the spallation of atmospheric nuclides by energetic cosmic ray particles. Satellite measurements also indicated that tritium could also be a component of solar flares. The half-life of tritium is relatively short (approximately 12.4 years), therefore there could be a noticeable gradient of natural tritium in the stratosphere. However, it was discovered that tritium was also introduced into the stratosphere by the explosion of thermonuclear weapons, either because tritium was initially present in the weapon or because tritium was produced as a result of thermonuclear reactions.

During the development of the HASP project and the CROWFLIGHT missions, samples of precipitated water were taken at various locations around the world in an attempt to detect strontium isotopes. On 1 July 1959, between 20° and 90° South Latitude, strontium-90 particles were uniformly detected. These

latitudes comprised the entire territory of the Argentine Republic and almost all of its Antarctic sector, which confirmed the suspicions that were held regarding the devastating global effect that a global war fought with nuclear weapons could have, since the resulting contaminated rain would precipitate across the whole planet.

Carbon-14 samples taken by the Ezeiza-based WU-2s were compared with samples of the same radioisotope obtained by the ASHCAN Project's stratospheric sounding balloons from readings taken in Minneapolis (45° North Latitude), San Angelo (32° North Latitude), Panama Canal Zone (9° North Latitude) and Sao Paulo (23° South Latitude).

To provide information on stratospheric concentrations between the northern limits of the HASP sample and the North Pole, three sampling missions were conducted between 60° and 90° North Latitude, one in April 1959 with 14 samples, another in August 1959 with 15 samples and another in October 1959 with 15 samples. For that, a Boeing B-52 bomber equipped with hatch samplers was used.

The B-52 polar flights confirmed the validity of the assumption that there were no significant variations in the concentration of nuclear waste as a function of latitude at a given altitude. It was deduced that the same effect occurred in the southern polar

The CROWFLIGHT operations carried out from Ezeiza made it possible to collect radioactive remains from the atomic tests carried out by the Soviet Union on 1 November 1958 (code name Joe 73) and 3 November 1958 (code name Joe 74), both with R-5M Pobeda tactical missiles (NATO Code SS-3 Shyster) launched from the Kasputin Yar firing range, part of which can be seen in the image. (Roscosmos)

To publicise Operation CROWFLIGHT in Argentina, the USAF provided the Argentine Air Force with this photo, which was published in December 1958 in the Revista Nacional de Aeronáutica. The image corresponded to the example registration number 56-6696 (painted 66696), the first aircraft delivered to the 4080th Strategic Reconnaissance Wing on 11 June 1957, and was carefully selected not to show the air intake of radioactive particles. (USAF)

stratosphere, although the Ezeiza-based U-2s never flew over the Antarctic circle.

The U-2 missions were individual, that is, only one aircraft flew accompanied much lower altitude by the support and rescue Douglas SC-54D Rescuemaster. However, from Ezeiza two planes were used on several occasions flying in the same direction at different heights. Vertical soundings and spiral tracking orbits cantered on the airport were also carried out from Ezeiza. The flights south of Ezeiza were made through the polar stratosphere and were scheduled to be executed at 40,000, 48,000 and 55,000 feet.

For the construction of the cross sections of each of the flights projected from Ezeiza, a meteorological analysis was prepared based almost entirely on radiosonde observations (RAOBS) launched from 44 meteorological stations located in the vicinity of the sampling corridor. Each RAOB used in the analysis was plotted on a meteorological sounding diagram (tephigram), which showed temperature as a function of altitude and pressure changes. The radio soundings also provided data on the speed, intensity and direction of the high-altitude winds, shears and other phenomena detected by the rising weather balloons. The combined upper wind and radiosonde measurement system became known as the "rawisonde" and the wind observation was called the RAWIN report. In addition to the weather stations set up for radiosonde in the northern hemisphere, during Phases 3 and 5 of HASP the following stations were added in the southern hemisphere:

Station	Latitude	Longitude
Guayaquil, Ecuador	02° 09′ S	79° 53′ W
Lima, Perú	12° 01′ S	77° 06′ W
Antofagasta, Chile	23° 26′ S	70° 26′ W
Resistencia, Argentina	27° 27′ S	59° 03′ W
Córdoba, Argentina	31° 18′ S	64° 12′ W
Quintero, Chile	32° 47′ S	71° 31′ W
Ezeiza, Argentina	34° 50′ S	58° 32′ W
Neuquén, Argentina	38° 57′ S	68° 05′ W
Puerto Montt, Chile	41° 27′ S	72° 50′ W
Comodoro Rivadavia, Argentina	45° 47′ S	67° 30′ W
Port Stanley, Falklands Islands (Malvinas), UK	51° 41′ S	57° 51′ W
Argentine Island, Antártida	65° 15′ S	64° 16′ W

The CROWFLIGHT operations carried out in the northern and southern hemispheres during 1958 collected information from the atmospheric explosions registered that year by the United States and the Soviet Union. The HASP missions launched from Ezeiza also made it possible to collect atmospheric samples from the Grapple X thermonuclear explosion, carried out on 8 November 1957 on Kiritimati Island (Christmas Island). This was the first successful thermonuclear bomb detonated by Britain, with an explosive yield of 1.8 megatons. It was launched from about 7,380 feet (2,250 metres)

The Douglas SC-54D Rescuemaster registration number 42-72464, one of the aircraft assigned by the 64 Air Rescue Squadron of the USAF to support the HASP/CROWFLIGHT missions carried out from Argentina. (USAF)

USAF officers display the flight gear of the 2157th Air Rescue Squadron paramedics, analogous to those of WU-2A pilots. Paramedics were to launch from the search and rescue Douglas SC-54 Rescuemaster to assist the pilot of the U-2 that eventually crashed and provide first aid. Ezeiza, 18 March 1959. (RNA)

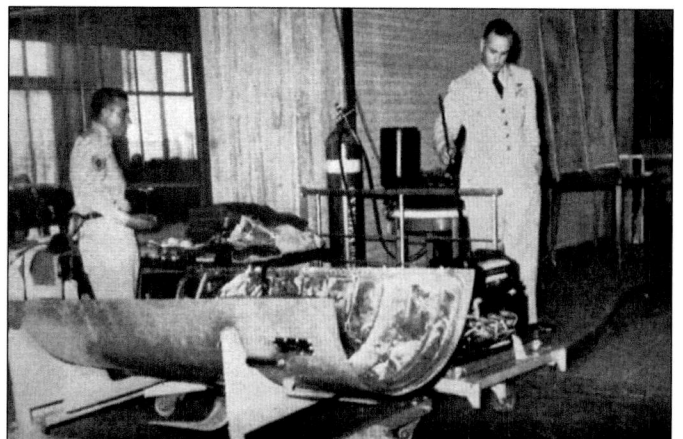

Major Atkins displays the complex suite of recording and scientific instruments mounted on the WU-2As of Operation CROWFLIGHT. It was the first time that the USAF presented to the press the capabilities of its most secret aircraft and, of course, limited the explanation to meteorological sampling. Nothing was said about the HASP Project, nor about the aircraft's photographic reconnaissance capabilities. (RNA)

The mushroom from the Grapple Z1 explosion rises above Kiritimati (Christmas Island), central Pacific Ocean, on 22 August 1958. The Pennant nuclear device, developed by Britain, achieved a yield of 24 kilotons. Traces of this explosion were detected by the WU-2As operating from Ezeiza, which made it possible to confirm the accuracy of the remote detection capabilities of the ultra-secret AFOAT-1 agency. (RAF)

The British Dickens thermonuclear bomb, detonated under the code name Grapple Y, achieved a yield of three megatons on 28 April 1958 on Christmas Island. The rising fireball injected large amounts of radioactive debris into the equatorial stratosphere, which was slowly transferred to the southern hemisphere. It was detected months later by the WU-2A based in Ezeiza, which made it possible to adjust the general circulation model of the atmosphere, showing air movements that were unknown up to now. (BBC)

by a Vickers Valiant bomber of 49 Squadron RAF, the registration XD824, flown by Squadron Leader Barney Millett.[11, 12]

During 1958, the WU-2 flights made from Ezeiza took samples of the dispersion in the southern hemisphere of radioactive residues from the Teak and Orange explosions, the atmospheric detonations of Operation HARDTACK I, which were carried out on Johnston Island, the main one of the homonymous atoll located in the northern Pacific Ocean, on 31 July and 11 August 1958.[13]

Both tests consisted of launching two Redstone ballistic missiles from Johnston Island itself. Their W-39 thermonuclear warheads exploded at their predicted height, both with an individual yield of 3.8 megatons. The missile launched for the Teak test exploded at an altitude of 81.3 kilometres over the island itself, while the one launched for the Orange test did so at an altitude of 45.5 kilometres and some 41 kilometres away. To give an idea of the energy released into the atmosphere, it is enough to indicate that the explosions could be seen from Hawaii, 1,297 kilometres away, in both they were visible for half an hour.[14]

After both explosions, high-frequency radio communications were disrupted throughout the Pacific and could only be resumed when the electromagnetic pulses dissipated. The Ezeiza-based WU-2s not only searched the air for traces of krypton-85 resulting from this explosion, but also for a radioactive tracer specifically injected into the stratosphere as part of the HARDTACK nuclear tests, specifically rhodium-102. These particular samples were analysed by the USAF Air Force Cambridge Research Center (AFCRC).[15, 16]

The CROWFLIGHT operations launched from Ezeiza in 1958 also allowed the WU-2 to collect radioactive remains from the atomic tests carried out by the Soviet Union on 1 November 1958 (code name Joe 73) and 3 November (code name Joe 74). In both cases, R-5M tactical ballistic missile launches were launched from the Kasputin Yar range, in both cases the explosions took place more than 12 kilometres above western Astrakhan and in both cases yields of 10 kilotons were recorded. These two shots occurred in top secrecy, shortly after 31 October 1958, the date on which the Soviet Union, the United Kingdom, and the United States agreed to a three-year temporary moratorium, during which they pledged not to test any more nuclear weapons.[17, 18]

The caesium-144 and strontium-90 samples from the Teak and Orange tests obtained in 1958 by the Ezeiza-based WU-2s were compared and compared with identical samples taken from the Soviet explosions, so that explosive yield, the type of bombs used, and the technological level reached by the Soviet Union.

One of the lesser-known aspects of Operation CROWFLIGHT consisted of the collection of tracer debris introduced into the nuclear warheads detonated over the South Atlantic in the framework of Operation ARGUS, carried out secretly by the US Navy between 27 August and 9 September 1958. The tests were aimed at studying the electromagnetic effect proposed by the Greek physicist Nicholas Constantine Christofilos at the Lawerence Livermore National Laboratory (LLNL), according to which high-altitude nuclear detonations would create a radiation belt in the extreme regions of the Earth's atmosphere, with an effect similar to the Van Allen radiation belts. For Christofilos it was possible to defend against Soviet nuclear missiles by exploding a small number of nuclear bombs high up in the south Pacific. This would create a disk of electrons over the United States that would fry the electronics of the Soviet warheads as they descended. It was also possible to use the effect to blind Soviet radars, which meant that Moscow would have no defence against a US counterattack. Operation ARGUS was carried out with nine ships and 4,500 crew members. The tests

One of the two RS-50 Redstone missiles used to execute the Teak (1 August 1958) and Orange (12 August) tests at Johnston Island, as part of Operation HARDTACK I. Each of these missiles carried a W-39 thermonuclear warhead with a yield of 3.8 megatons, which exploded at altitudes of 81.3 and 45.5 kilometres respectively. Debris from both explosions, including krypton-85 and the tracer isotope rhodium-102, were detected by Ezeiza-based WU-2As. Note in the photo the presence of a Martin RB-57D, one of the planes involved in taking "hot" samples of the radioactive clouds. (Art LeBrun)

showed that the expected effect did occur but also revealed that it dissipated too quickly to be militarily effective. The ARGUS tests came to light on 19 March in a story published in the New York Times by Hanson Baldwin and Walter Sullivan, who called them the 'greatest scientific experiment ever performed'.[19, 20, 21, 22]

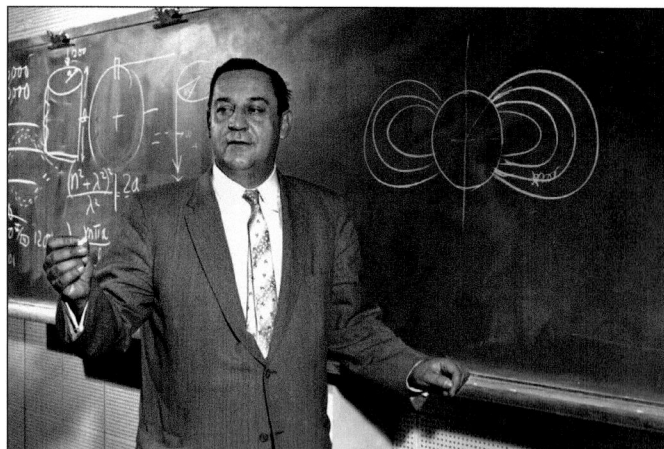

The Greek physicist Nicholas Christofilos shows the magnetic field that surrounds the earth, generated by its core of liquid iron, which, being a metal, generates positive and negative polarisation. When a nuclear bomb is detonated at height, some of the radiation is trapped and travels along magnetic lines of flux, to then spread across the Earth in a thin shell of electrons. According to Christofilos, thanks to this electromagnetic effect, the offensive capacity of Soviet missiles could be cancelled and their ground radars blinded. Washington, 30 March 1959. (Life)

Since the CROWFLIGHT missions were by definition secret, it has been very difficult to reconstruct the activity displayed by the Ezeiza detachment. However, the scientific reports of the results shed some light, albeit partially, on its scope. Indeed, all the samples obtained around the world were processed in two laboratories, that of the company Isotopes Inc (under AFSWP contract) and that of the USAF itself (Air Force Cambridge Research Laboratory, AFCRL). In the reports of finding barium-140, strontium-89, zirconium-95. caesium-144, strontium-90 and tungsten-185, the places, dates and altitudes where the samples were obtained are indicated.

U-2s registration 56-6705, 714 and 715 were based at Ramey AFB during Phases 2 and 3 of Operation CROWFLIGHT. The three with registrations ending in 716, 717 and 718 were based at Plattsburg AFB during Phase 2 and at Ezeiza during Phase 3. In mission reports, Ezeiza was identified with a letter "E" and the missions as "ES Flights" in reference to "Ezeiza Sampling Flight". To identify the transfer flights between bases, the letters of the departure and destination aerodromes were simply joined, for example "ER" if the route was made between Ezeiza and Ramey AFB, or "RE" if it was the other way around. The first recorded flight of the WU-2 in Argentina within the framework of Operation CROWFLIGHT took place on 12 September 1959 (Mission 1, USAF codes WP1055 and WP1046) and consisted of a transfer flight between Ramey and Ezeiza of the WU-2 with registrations ending in 718 and 716. The last flight of this stage took place on 8 August 1959 (Mission 84, USAF code WE1548, WE1552 and WE1580) and consisted of the return to Ramey of the WU-2 with registrations ending in 716, 717 and 718.

The Oak thermonuclear test, conducted on 28 June 1958 at Enewetak Atoll, as part of Operation HARDTACK I. The bomb achieved a yield of 8.9 megatons. The HASP Project sought to know with certainty the actual amount of radioactive waste injected into the stratosphere by this type of explosion, how long it lasted, and how far it precipitated as acid rain. The dangerous radioactive isotope strontium-90 resulting from this explosion was detected in the air, water and soil of Argentina under the HASP Project. (USAEC)

The air operations of the HASP project were given different code names depending on their purposes. Thus, for example, the operations Test Hop 717 (14 June 1958) and Mission of Opportunity (10 June 1959) were carried out to verify the operation of the equipment, while Special 1 (19 March 1958) and Special 2 (20 November 1958) were additional operations that obtained some atmospheric samples. Operations Minney 1 and 2 (6 March 1958) were flown from Minneapolis in conjunction with a stratospheric balloon for the purpose of intercalibrating the results of the samples obtained by the ASHCAN project balloons and the HASP project aircraft. The Sea Fish Special missions (14 April, 21 August, and 14 October 1959) were flown to the North Pole by Boeing B-52 aircraft to provide samples of the polar region far beyond the range allowed by the U-2s of Operation CROWFLIGHT. Samples were also collected in the Arctic Circle during Operation North Flight in U-2 aircraft that departed from Eielson AFB on 12 September and 2 October 1958, and 22 to 29 April 1959. The missions launched from Ezeiza do not appear to have received any special name, simply a mission identification number.[23]

During Phase 3 of Operation CROWFLIGHT, carried out from Ezeiza, 1,423 samples of radioactive debris were collected. Two groups of isotopes were measured: those potentially dangerous (such as strontium-90, caesium-137 and plutonium) and those that could provide information about the mixing and transfer processes of atmospheric air by showing the mobility of air between layers and between hemispheres. Caesium-137 was not only dangerous because of its radioactivity, but also because of its long half-life (29 years). Even more dangerous were plutonium-239 (a half-life of 24,300) and plutonium-240 (a half-life of 6,600), which could be original components of some weapons or could have been formed by neutron activation of uranium-238 in others. Some 300 samples obtained from the flights made from Ezeiza showed traces of caesium-137 and Plutonium, a fact that was taken into account by analysts when predicting the scope of radioactive fallout resulting from total nuclear war.[24]

The atmospheric flow information obtained from Ezeiza was obtained from the analysis of the calcium-145 and sodium-22 isotopes. The first, with a half-life of 160 days, was formed by the activation of neutrons from calcareous rocks, such as coral, during nuclear explosions in the ocean. The second, with a half-life of 2.6 years, was formed by the neutron activation of sea salt during the explosion of a nuclear weapon in contact with oceanic waters. Their traces were sufficient to generate a general model of atmospheric air circulation and to show that concentrations of radioactive waste were not uniform throughout the stratosphere as they changed over time as a result of re-injections and subsequent mixing. With the beginning of the moratorium on nuclear weapons testing, in November 1958, it also became clear that, even without further injections, changes in the stratospheric distribution of nuclides occurred as a result of seasonal weather factors.[25]

A Lockheed WU-2A receives maintenance in the Aerolíneas Argentinas hangar provided to Operation CROWFLIGHT. Note that the tail assembly has been removed to facilitate access to the turbine. (Oscar Luis Rodríguez via Pablo Potenze)

Above: The GCA/AN-CPN4 radar installed by the USAF at Ezeiza Airport for air control and instrument approach control of the Lockheed WU-2As involved in Operation CROWFLIGHT. (Guido Ghiretti)

Right: A Lockheed WU-2 takes off from Ezeiza to fulfil a CROWFLIGHT mission in April 1959. The image was published in Revista de Aviación number 2, May 1959. The angle of the photo, taken by the USAF, obscures the radioactive sample capture device. (Aviation Magazine)

Two Lockheed WU-2A of the HASP Project, one of them registration number 56-6716, photographed at the Tandil Military Aeronautical Detachment on 24 March 1959. (Atilio Marino via Vladimiro Cettolo)

The first WU-2s that operated in Ezeiza retained their photographic espionage capacity, since their cargo bay had not been modified and the "bottles" that allowed the collection of samples had not yet been incorporated. There is no evidence regarding the use of the U-2 in photographic missions over Argentina. But being by nature a spy plane, the most evolved in the world at its time, it is naive to imagine that it would not have been used to photograph at high altitude various locations of interest to US intelligence, not only military but also refineries, laboratories and factories. For the rest, the 4028th Strategic Reconnaissance Squadron, to which the U-2s operating in Argentina were attached, simultaneously executed sensitive reconnaissance missions and more public HASP flights, in parallel with the missions flown by the U-2s. It was common practice for atmospheric sampling and photographic surveillance to be incorporated into the same mission, just in case they found something interesting to capture on film.[26, 27, 28]

Although extremely discreet and far from public scrutiny, the activities of the CROWFLIGHT Detachment in Ezeiza did not escape the critical eye of some officers of the Argentine Air Force as soon as they began. It is not surprising, therefore, that, as early as February 1959, the nationalist weekly *Azul y Blanco* questioned the secrecy, the loss of sovereignty and the extraterritoriality involved in the operation of the USAF unit:

Our readers know that the characteristics of the occupation of the scientific-military establishment that the United States forces occupy in Ezeiza have been maliciously hidden from public opinion. They also know, through a recent confession by the Foreign Ministry, that there are some "reversal letters" of confidential content whose objective is to ensure the execution of the more or less revealed technical agreement in detail. Lastly, they know that the Americans, thanks to this set of secret forecasts, enjoy, in practice, an extraterritorial regime similar to that of diplomatic headquarters. And that is why your establishment has direct communication with the United States and its activities escape the comptroller of the jurisdiction of our country. Even the reversal letters authorize the occupants to guard the base with a double guard —internal and external—, uniformed and without weapons or without uniform and with weapons. We do not know if, in fact, the North American forces make regular and ostensible use of these privileges, which are certainly unusual. We know

that usually the external guard is also fulfilled by soldiers of our Aeronautics. We will add that these guests bring and carry very diverse documents and materials. They use for this and for troops, the transport of DC-4 (C-54) aircraft and sometimes Globemaster (C-124) with three floors and 115 tons. Between officers and troops, it is estimated that there are two hundred individuals at the base. They live in the Hotel de Ezeiza and most are subjected to a regime of military life. It should be added that his conduct is absolutely correct. We insist: is there or is there not in Ezeiza an American establishment that has been granted an extraterritorial regime? And we also once again invite our Armed Forces to go to the North American establishment to verify the truth of what we say.[29]

Azul y Blanco was a weekly publication directed by Marcelo Sánchez Sorondo, an opponent of the governments of General Pedro Eugenio Aramburu and Dr. Arturo Frondizi. Therefore, he was very critical of government decisions, particularly those that allowed the interference of foreign interests in Argentina or that entailed a loss of sovereignty. What followed was a true scandal, which required the parliamentary intervention of the Minister of Aeronautics in the National Congress.[30, 31]

The commotion caused by the *Azul y Blanco* magazine and the subsequent parliamentary questioning motivated the USAF to hold an open day in Ezeiza, to highlight the absolutely scientific nature of the flights that were being carried out from there. The decision was important because the U-2 had never been presented in public. It had made only one demonstration flight during an open day held in the spring of 1958 at Ramey AFB, Puerto Rico, which could be considered US territory, since, since 1952, it had been a commonwealth of the United States. With this background, on 18 March 1959, the first presentation of the U-2 was held in Ezeiza before the world press.[32, 33]

The host from the Argentine Air Force, Captain Alejandro Urbano Rojas, introduced USAF Major Richard Atkins, who repeated the official script on the upper atmosphere investigation. In his own words: 'operation Crow Flight is intended to achieve accurate data on cloud formations, turbulence, winds, jet streams and air gusts that can vary from day to day. It also seeks to collect data on the existence in the upper atmosphere of cosmic rays, ozone and humidity; it looks for the presence of radioactive elements and tries to follow the trajectory of the remnant or residual products of atomic explosions.

Another photo of the WU-2A pair stationed in Tandil on 24 March 1959, taken from the opposite angle. Note that the planes lack the sampling "bottle" located on the forward side of the fuselage. Partially visible behind is the Douglas SC-54D Rescuemaster for logistics support, search and rescue. (Atilio Marino via Vladimiro Cettolo)

The rapprochement between the Argentine and US governments after 1955 not only strengthened ties between the Argentine Air Force and the USAF, but also between the Argentine Navy and the US Navy. This photo taken at the end of 1958 shows a Grumman F9F-2B Panther fighter acquired by the Argentine Naval Aviation, still in the colours of the US Navy, during its assembly process in Hangar No. 6 of the Comandante Espora Naval Air Base. (Juan Carlos Cicalesi)

This information, it must be said, is sent immediately to the different US laboratories in charge of interpreting it'.

Then, the head of the USAF Air Mission in Argentina, Colonel Howard Shidal, reported that the flights planned within the framework of Operation CROWFLIGHT would last a total of 18 months. Two weekly missions would be carried out on Tuesdays and Fridays, with a total of 150 flight hours per month. At the time of the conference, there were 157 men and three U-2s in Argentina. No further details were provided about the personnel, but the normal U-2 crews were made up of four or five pilots and about 15 support men, who stayed at their destination for about 15 days, without family accompaniment. The management of the flight plans before the air traffic control and the meteorological information was in charge of an Argentine pilot hired for this purpose. Presentations by Atkins and Shidal were followed by a demonstration of the Lockheed U-2.[34, 35]

The U-2s involved in Operation CROWFLIGHT did not only operate in Ezeiza. According to oral tradition, they also did so in 1958 from the Mendoza Airport runway and, according to documentary sources, also from the Ushuaia aerodrome runway, to where an unarmed specimen was transferred in the hold of a Douglas C-124 Globemaster. On 24 March 1959, two U-2s (one of

them commanded by Major Richard Atkins) and his supporting Douglas SC-54 Rescuemaster landed at the Tandil Aeronautical Detachment, probably due to bad weather in Ezeiza. The USAF pilots and mechanics stayed for two days in the unit's officers' and NCOs' cabins, until weather conditions allowed them to travel to Ezeiza.[36]

The last flights of Phase 3 of Operation CROWFLIGHT were made from Ezeiza on 8 August 1958. A month earlier the Secretariat of Aeronautics awarded honoris causa decorations and titles of Military Aviator to all members of the Task Force that had participated in the "high atmosphere studies in Argentina, on the occasion of the International Geophysical Year 1958". After reading the decrees, the Secretary of Aeronautics, Brigadier Ramón A. Abrahín, presented the decorations of the Order of May to Aeronautical Merit, in the rank of commander, to Colonels Jack D. Nole and Howard G. Shidal and in officer rank to Major Richard A. Atkins.[37]

Decorations were also presented to Majors Robert E. Allen, Warren J. Boyd, Edward B. Dixon, Joe R. King, and Lloyd R. Leavitt; Captains Edwin B. Emerling, John T. McElveen, James D. Sala, Robert D. Downs, Phillip H. Voge, Daniel R. Durbin, Charles Jones, Joseph E. Ramage; First Lieutenants Anthony P. Bevacqua, Roger H. Herman, Robert D. Pine, Clinton A. Clark, James J. Dipalma, William P. Kerman, Richard E. Porter, Kenneth S. Smith, Archibald

S. Walker, and Gerald D. Young. The title of Military Pilot honoris causa was also awarded to technical sergeant Margarito Garza. In this way, completely unexpectedly, the identities of all the officers involved in one of the USAF's most secret missions came to light.[38, 39]

On 7 July 1959, shortly after the return to the United States of the CROWFLIGHT team stationed in Argentina, the ultra-secret AFOAT-1 agency was dissolved and reorganised as the Air Force Technical Applications Center (AFTAC), after which it began a new, much more ambitious stage of long-range detections. For its part, the Air Force Special Weapons Project (AFSWP) changed its name to the Defense Atomic Support Agency (DASA), with expanded functions and budget. The organisational restructuring, like everything related to the remote detection of Soviet technology, was kept in the strictest secrecy.[40, 41]

Next page:
Top: The registration 56-6718 is clearly visible in this photo of one of the two Lockheed WU-2As landed in Tandil on 24 March 1959. This particular aircraft was transferred to the CIA in August 1964. It was destroyed on 5 January 1969 in the Yellow Sea between mainland China and the Korean peninsula, killing its pilot, Hseih Billy Chang. (Fuerza Aérea Argentina)

Centre: In addition to a Douglas C-124 Globemaster used as logistical support for Operation CROWFLIGHT, the USAF Air Mission in Argentina was permanently assigned the Douglas C-47B-15-DK Skytrain serial O-49533, which it wore on its fuselage legends alluding to its affectation. The plane was assigned to the Caribbean Air Command (5700 Air Base Group) and had been assigned to Buenos Aires on 4 August 1957, shortly before the flights of the HASP Project began in Ezeiza. (Atilio Marino via Vladimiro Cettolo)

Bottom: On 22 May 1959, the C-47 O-49533 suffered an accident on the runway of the Military Aviation School of Córdoba, crewed by Lieutenant Colonel Raymond J. Hedzina and Major Robert E. Gardner, both members of the Mission Air of the USAF in Argentina. (Atilio Marino via Vladimiro Cettolo)

The Explorer 4 satellite is launched into space on 26 July 1958 from Cape Canaveral by a Juno I carrier rocket. The mission of the satellite was to study the Van Allen radiation belts, particularly during Operation ARGUS. (NASA)

One of the WU-2As of the HASP Project, which landed at the Tandil Aeronautical Detachment on 24 March 1959 for meteorological reasons, is prepared for take-off to Ezeiza, for which purpose the pogo sticks are already installed under the wings. (Fuerza Aérea Argentina)

ENDNOTES

Introduction

1   William Burr, *Documents on the U.S. Atomic Energy Detection System (AEDS): National Security Archive Electronic Briefing Book No. 7.* https://nsarchive2.gwu.edu/NSAEBB/NSAEBB7/nsaebb7.htm, accessed 11 January 2021.
2   Charles A. Ziegler and David Jacobson, *Spying Without Spies: Origin of America's Secret Nuclear Intelligence Surveillance System* (New York: Praeger, 1995).
3   Air Force Systems Command, *History of Air Force Atomic Cloud Sampling: AFSC Historical Publication Series 61-42-1* (Air Force Systems Command, 1963).

Chapter 1

1   R.G. Hewlett. and O.E. Anderson Jr., *A History of the US Atomic Energy Commission—Volume I, The new world, 1939/1946* (University Park: Pennsylvania State University Press, 1962).
2   US Atomic Energy Commission and US Geological Survey, *Prospecting for uranium* (Washington DC: US Government Printing Office, 1951).
3   T.J. McCormick, *America's half century—United States foreign policy in the cold war and after* (Baltimore: Johns Hopkins University Press, 1995).
4   W.D. Johnston Jr., *The United States Geological Survey in the other American Republics: The Record* (Washington DC: US Department of State Interdepartmental Committee on Scientific and Cultural Cooperation, 1947).
5   Mary C. Rabbitt and Clifford M. Nelson, *Minerals, Lands and Geology for the Common Defence and General Welfare, Volume 4, 1939 – 1961.* (Renton, Virginia: US Geological Survey, 2009). https://pubs.usgs.gov/book/2015/rabbitt-vol4/pdf/vol4_chapter5.pdf, accessed 18 July 2021.
6   J.E. Helmreich, *Gathering rare ores—The diplomacy of uranium acquisition, 1943–1954.* (Princeton: Princeton University Press, 1986).
7   Martin Carotti, *Las oportunidades perdidas de Mendoza.* San Rafael, Mendoza, Argentina, 20 de mayo de 2021. https://diadelsur.com/las-oportunidades-perdidas-de-mendoza/, accessed 18 July 2021.
8   'Mina Soberanía', *Fotos Antiguas de Mendoza, Argentina y el Mundo de cada década desde 1880,* https://mendozantigua.blogspot.com/2016/02/instalaciones-de-una-mina-de-uranio.html, accessed 18 July 2021.
9   *United States of America, Department of State, Executive Agreement Series (EAS) No. 175 – 54 Stat. 2320* (Washington DC: Government Printing Office, 1940).
10 *Military aviation instructors agreement, Department of State, Executive Agreement Series (EAS), Catalog of the Public Documents of the Seventy-sixth Congress and of all Departments of the Government of the United* States *for the period from 1 January 1939 to 31 December 1940* (Washington DC: Government Printing Office, 1945), p. 2267.
11 *Military Aviation Mission Argentina, Publications of the Department of State, 1 October 1929 to 1 January 1953. Department of State, Executive Agreement Series (EAS) 211, 55 Stat. 1284* (Washington DC: Government Printing Office, 1953).
12 *Military Aviation Mission Argentina, Publications of the Department of State,1 October 1929 to 1 January 1953, Department of State, Executive Agreement Series (EAS) 340, 57 Stat. (part 2) 1068* (Washington DC: Government Printing Office, 1953).
13 William Z, N. Slany, Stephen Kane, William F. Sanford, Jr. (eds), *Foreign Relations of the United States, 1952-1954. Volume IV. The American Republics, Department of State Publication 9354* (Washington DC: Office of the Historian, Bureau of Public Affairs, 1983).
14 Carlos Abella, 'Una baja de la USAF en Corrientes', *Roll Out,* https://aerospotter.blogspot.com/2018/12/una-baja-de-la-usaf-en-corrientes.html, accessed 2 October 2022.

15 Henry Bieniecki, 'Airplane Crash Paraguay', *Aerial Survey & Photomapping History,* http://www.1370th.org/7gcs/7gcs.html, accessed 2 October 2022.
16 Secretaría de Aeronáutica. Parte de prensa, Buenos Aires, Argentina, 8 December 1945, Dirección de Estudios Históricos de la Fuerza Aérea Argentina (DEH-FAA) (Buenos Aires, 2020).
17 Sidney DeBoer, 'C-47 Crash In Argentina, *Aerial Survey & Photomapping History,* http://www.1370th.org/7gcs/7gcs.html, accessed 2 October 2022.
18 Secretaría de Aeronáutica. Subsecretaría de Informaciones. Parte de prensa, Buenos Aires, Argentina, 7 December1945.
19 Secretaría de Aeronáutica. Subsecretaría de Informaciones. Parte de prensa, Buenos Aires, Argentina, 12 December 1945.
20 Embassy of the United States of America in Argentina, *Military Attache Buenos Aires. Special Order No. 16* (Buenos Aires, 1945).
21 Embassy of the United States of America in Argentina, *Office of the Military Attache. Report of activities in connection with search for United States Army Douglas aircraft C-47, No. 8603* (Buenos Aires, 19 December 1945).
22 U.S. Army Air Forces, *Military Intelligence Division. Report on Crash of C-47 No. 8602 in Province of Corrientes, Argentina, 3/Dec/45* (Military Attache, Montevideo, 28 December 1945).
23 Presidencia de la Nación. Parte de prensa, Buenos Aires, Argentina, 13 November 1946, Dirección de Estudios Historicos de la Fuerza Aérea Argentina (DEH-.FAA) (Buenos Aires, 2020).
24 'Crash of a Douglas C-54D-5-DC near Mendoza', *Bureau of Aircraft Accidents Archive,* https://www.baaa-acro.com/crash/crash-douglas-c-54d-5-dc-near-mendoza, accessed 24 July 2021.
25 'Un avión norteamericano cayó cerca de Casa de Piedra', *Diario La Libertad,* 14 November 1946 .
26 'Cayó y se incendió un avión norteamericano', *Diario Los Andes,* 14 November 1946.
27 'Nos confirma uno de los pilotos que la causa del accidente fue la falta inicial de altura', *Diario La Libertad,* 15 November 1946, p.3.
28 Atilio Baldini, 'La caída del espía radiactivo. Serie Grandes accidentes aéreos de Mendoza', *Diario UNO de Mendoza,* 21 May 2000, pp.4-5.
29 Howard W. Penney, 'A Brief History of the Defense Mapping Agency', *Photogrammatic Engineering & Remote Sensing,* 39:5 (1973), p469.
30 Bart Barnes, 'Frederick J. Doyle, photographic mapping specialist for NASA, dies at 93', *Washington Post,* 18 May 2013, https://www.washingtonpost.com/local/obituaries/frederick-j-doyle-photographic-mapping-specialist-for-nasa-dies-at-93/2013/05/18/6019566e-bdac-11e2-89c9-3be8095fe767_story.html, accessed 26 July 2021.
31 Brian Haren, 'Inter American Geodetic Survey', *Northing & Easting* https://oldtopographer.net/2011/01/23/inter-american-geodetic-survey/, accessed 26 July 2021.
32 Frank W. Stead, *Airborne radioactivity surveying: USA,* Paper presented to the Nuclear Engineering and Science Congress in Cleveland, Ohio, December 12-16, 1955.
33 James A. Pitkin, *Airborne measurements of terrestrial radioactivity as an aid to geologic mapping. Geological Survey Professional Paper 516-F. US Atomic Energy Commission.* (Washington DC: Government Printing Office, 1968).
34 J.R. Balsley Jr., *The airborne magnetometer. US Geological Survey Geophysical Investigations Preliminary Report* (Washingtoin DC: US Geological Survey, 1946).
35 J.R. Balsley Jr., D.L Rossman, C.L Rogers and E.M. Canfield, *Aeromagnetic map showing total intensity 1000 feet above the surface of part of the Oswegatchie quadrangle, St. Lawrence County, New York. U.S. Geological Survey Geophysical Investigations Preliminary Map 1, scale 1:31,680* (United States: US Geological Survey, 1946).
36 'Continúan en grave estado cuatro de los aviadores del Douglas', *Diario Los Andes,* 15 November 1946, p.3.
37 'Estados Unidos agradece el auxilio a los ocupantes del C-54', *Diario Los Andes,* 24 November 1946, p.3.

38 United States Air Force, *Lieutenant General Stanley J. Donovan* . https://www.af.mil/About-Us/Biographies/Display/Article/107224/lieutenant-general-stanley-j-donovan/, accessed 7 August 2021.

39 United States Air Force, *Brigadier General Charles Caldwell.* https://www.af.mil/About-Us/Biographies/Display/Article/107430/brigadier-general-charles-h-caldwell/, accessed 7 August 2021.

40 John Wiley, 'Doyle, Frederick Joseph, obituary', *The Photogrammetric Record*, 28:143 (2023), pp.326-330.

41 Luis Walter Alvarez, *Alvarez: Adventures of a Physicist* (New York: Basic Books, 1987).

42 Luis Walter Alvarez, Walter Álvarez, Frank Asaro and Helen Michel, 'Extraterrestrial cause for the Cretaceous-Tertiary Extintion; Experiment and Theory', *Science*, 208:4448 (1980), pp.1095-1108.

Chapter 2

1 Chauncey E. Sanders, *Redeployment and Demobilization, USAF Historical Study 77* (Maxwell Air Force Base: Air University, 1952).

2 Edwin L. Williams Jr., *Legislative History of the AAF and USAF, 1941-1951, USAF Historical Study 84* (Maxwell Air Force Base: Air University, 1955).

3 Herman S. Wolk, *The struggle for Air Force independence, 1943 – 1947* (Washington DC: Air Force History and Museums Program, 1997).

4 R. Earl McClendon, *Autonomy of the Air Arm* (Maxwell Air Force Base: Air University, 1954).

5 Bill Yenne, *The History of the US Air Force* (New York: Exeter Books, 1984).

6 David A, Anderton, *The History of the U.S. Air Force* (London: Aerospace Publishing Limited, 1981).

7 *British – U.S, Communication Intelligence Agreement, signed 5 March 1946. Approved for Release by National Security Agency on 8 November 2014. MDR, Case#78775.* https://www.nsa.gov/Portals/70/documents/news-features/declassified-documents/ukusa/agreement_outline_5mar46.pdf, accessed 31 July 2021.

8 Kai Bird and Martin J. Sherwin, *American Prometheus: The Triumph and Tragedy of J. Robert Oppenheimer* (New York: Alfred A. Knopf, 2005).

9 Michael R, Lehman, *Nuisance to Nemesis: Nuclear Fallout and Intelligence as Secrets, Problems and Limitations on the Arms Race, 1940-1964* (Urbana- Champing: University of Illinois Press, 2016).

10 United States Air Force, *Report of Operation FITZWILLIAM, Volume. I. Introduction. Copy No. 35. Design of Operation and Summary of Results. AFMW-1* (Washington DC: 1948).

11 L H. Berkhouse, S.E. Davis, F.R. Gladeck, J.H. Hallowell, C.R. Jones, E.J. Martin, F. W. McMullan, M.J. Osborn and W.E. Rogers, *Operation Sandstone: 1948* (Washington DC: Nuclear Nuclear Defense Agency, 2008).

12 It was precisely the accidental fall of one of these balloons on the outskirts of the town of Roswell, New Mexico, on 2 July 1947, which marked the beginning of the legend of the unidentified flying objects (UFO). The purpose of the MOGUL project was so secret that the USAF could not afford to make it known, but they were nothing more than formations of stratospheric balloons applied to intelligence tasks, shining at high altitudes.

13 Michael Young, 'The U.S. Air Force's Long Range Detection Program and Project MOGU', *Air Power History* 67:4 (2004).

Chapter 3

1 William Burr, *Documents on the U.S. Atomic Energy Detection System (AEDS): National Security Archive Electronic Briefing Book No. 7.* https://nsarchive2.gwu.edu/NSAEBB/NSAEBB7/nsaebb7.htm.

2 Michael S. Goodman, *Spying on the Nuclear Bear: Anglo-American Ingellience and the Soviet Bomb* (Palo Alto: Stanford University Press, 2007).

3 Martin B. Kalinovsky, Johan Feichter, Mika Nikkisen and Clemens Schlosser, 'Environmental Sample Analysis', in Rudolf Avenhaus, Nicholas Kyriakopoulos, Michel Richard and Gotthard Stein (eds), *Verifying Treaty Compliance: Limiting Weapons of Mass Destruction and Monitoring Kyoto Protocol Provisions* (Berlin: Springer, 2010).

4 'Memorandum by R. C. Maude and D.L. Northrup, AFOAT/1, for Mr. Robert LeBaron, Deputy to the Secretary of Defense for Atomic Energy, "Notes on Technical Cooperation with British and Canadians in the Field of Atomic Energy Intelligence", 21 March 1951', *The National Security Archive, George Washington University*, https://nsarchive2.gwu.edu/NSAEBB/NSAEBB7/nsaebb7.htm, accessed [date].

5 *Diario La Nación*, 29 March 1951.

6 *Diario La Nación*, 26 March 1951.

7 *Mundo Atómico*, March 1951 p.66.

8 'Perón pode, mas não quer ordenar a fabricação da bomba atômica', *Jornal Correio do Ceará*, number 12288, 26 March 1951, p.1.

9 Phillip Davenport, 'When the Argentines tamed fusion', *The New Scientist*, 97:1343 (1983), p. 322.

10 Tácito Thadeo Leite Rolim, *Brasil e Estados Unidos no contexto da "Guerra Fria" e seus subprodutos: EraAtômica e dos Mísseis, Corrida Armamentista e Espacial, 1945-1960. Aprovada em março de 2012*, Rio De Janeiro: Universidade Federal Fluminense, Instituto de Ciencias Humanas, 2012).

11 Robert Arnoux, 'Proyecto Huemul: the prank that started it all', *Iter*, https://www.iter.org/newsline/196/930, accessed 27 June 2021.

12 Hans Thirring, 'Is Perón's A-Bomb a Swindle?', *United Nations World*, May 1951.

13 Ronald Richter, 'Argentina does not have an atomic bomb', *United Nations World*, June-August 1951.

14 'Perón não tem a bomba atômica', *O Cruzeiro*, 22 September 1951, pp.3-18, 50, 48.

15 *Jornal Correio do Ceará*, number 12341, 1 June 1951, p.5.

16 Edward Teller and Stanislaw Ulam, *On Heterocatalytic Detonations I: Hidrodynamic Lenses and Radiation Mirrors* (Los Álamos Scientific Laboratory, University of California, 1951).

17 Defence Nuclear Agency, *Operation Greenhouse (DNA-6043F)*, (Department of Defense, 1951).

18 US Department of Energy, *United States Nuclear Tests: July 1945 through September 1992. DOE/NV-209 REV15*, (US Department of Energy, 2000).

19 William Mizelle, 'Peron's Atomic Plans', *New Republic*, [ ] (24 February 1947), pp.22-23.

20 William Mizelle, 'More about Peron's Atoms Plans, [ ] *New Republic*, (31 March 1947), p.20.

21 Regis Cabral, 'The Perón-Richter Fusion Program: 1948-1953', in Saldaña, Juan José (ed.), *Cross Cultural Diffusion of Science: Latin America* (Berkeley: Sociedad Latinoamericana de Historia de las Ciencias y la Tecnologia, 1987, pp.77–106).

22 Alwyn T Lloyd, *B-29 Superfortress in detail and scale. Part 1. Production versions* (Fallbrook: Aero Publishers Inc, 1983).

23 Michael R. Lehman, *Nuisance to Nemesis: Nuclear Fallout and Intelligence as Secrets, Problems and Limitations on the Arms Race, 1940-1964* (Urbana- Champing: University of Illinois Press, 2016).

24 Jeffrey T Richelson, *Spying on the Bomb: American Nuclear intelligence from Nazi Germany to Iran and North Korea* (New York: WW Norton, 2006), p.96.

25 Paul Ozorak, *Underground Structures of the Cold War: The World Below.* (Barnsley: Pen and Sword, 2012).

26 *Diario La Nación*, 22 September 1950.

27 *Aeronoticias*, 10:102/3 (1950), p.11.

28 J. Rickard, '7th Reconnaissance Group', *History of War*, http://www.historyofwar.org/air/units/USAAF/7th_Reconnaissance_Group.html, accessed 3 July 2021.

29 Andrade, John M., *US Military Aircraft Designations and Serials, 1909 to 1979* (Leicester: Midland Counties Publications, 1997).

30 Robert A. Mann, *The B-29 Superfortress: A Comprehensive Registry of the Planes and Their Missions* (Jefferson: McFarland and Company, 2004; pp.108-109.

31 Oscar Francisco González,, *Vigilancia y Control Aéreo en Argentina. Historia de la Especialidad VYCA en la Fuerza Aérea* (Buenos Aires: Ediciones Argentinidad, 2014), p.87.

32 Rita Markus, Nicholas Halbeisen and John F. Fuller. *Air Weather Service, our heritage, 1937-1987.* Military Airlift Command Historial Office Special Study. United States Air Force, Scott AFB, Illinois, United States of America, July, 1987.

33 Tom Robinson, 'The B-29 in Weather Reconnaissance', *B-29 Superfortress Then and Now*, http://www.awra.us/The%20B-29%20in%20Weather%20Reconnaissance%20by%20Tom%20Robison.htm, accessed 28 June 2021.

34 John F. Fuller, *Thor's Legions; Weather Support to the U.S. Air Force and Army, 1937-1987* (Chicago: University of Chicago Press, 1990).

35 United States of America, Department of State. Notes filed under references 735.58/3-251 and 735.58/3-1651, Washington DC, 1951.

36 United States of America, Department of State. Nota archivada bajo decimales 735.58/10-1151. Washington DC, United States of America, 1951.

37 United States of America, Department of State. Nota archivada bajo decimales 735-58/12-1251. Washington DC, United States of America, 1951.

38 Ralph R. Goodwin, N Stephen Kane and Harriet D. Schwar (eds), *Foreign Relations of the United States, 1951. Volume II. The United Nations; The Western Hemisphere* (Washington: Government Printing Office, 1979), p.1085.

39 In 1944 General Vandenberg served as commander of the IX US Army Air Force based in Europe. He was one of the few officers who knew the nature of the xenon-133 gas detection flights carried out by Douglas A-26 Invader aircraft over Germany, for the Foreign Intelligence Sector of the Manhattan Project.

40 *Aeronoticias*. 3:5 (1950), p.70.

41 *Diario La Nación*, 3 May 1950.

42 Diario *La Nación*, 5 May 1950.

43 Roberto García Baltar, *El abuelo aviador*. Asociación de Tripulantes de Transporte Aéreo, Buenos Aires, Argentina, 2020. http://asociacionatta.com.ar/pdf/El%20abuelo%20aviador.pdf. Retrieved 4 January 2021.

44 'Crash of a Douglas C-47B-50-DK Skytrain near La Poma: 8 killed', *Bureau of Aircraft Accidentes Archives*, https://www.baaa-acro.com/crash/crash-douglas-c-47b-50-dk-skytrain-near-la-poma-8-killed,accessed 13 October 2022.

45 Carlos Abella, 'Una baja de la USAF en Salta', Roll Out, https://aerospotter.blogspot.com/2019/02/una-baja-de-la-usaf-en-salta.html, accessed 13 October 2022.

46 Andrew Pentland, 'Civil Aircraft Register – United States', *Golden Years oif Aviation,* http://www.airhistory.org.uk/gy/reg_N3.html, accessed 13 October 2022.

47 Secretaría de Aeronáutica, SISA-Departamento III, *Comunicado de la Secretaría de Aeronáutica N° 132-E* (Buenos Aires: Secretaria de Aeronautica, 21 February 1949).

48 República Argentina, Congreso de la Nación, Honorable Cámara de Diputados. Dirección de Información Parlamentraria. Departamento de Coordinación de Estudios. Antecedentes de la ley 13.395 sobre represión del espionaje, sabotaje y traición. https://www4.hcdn.gob.ar/dependencias/dip/wdebates/Ley.13985.Debate.Represion.Actos.Espionaje.Sabotaje.y.Traicion.pdf, access 4 July 2021.

49 República Argentina, Congreso de la Nación. Ley N° 13.985. Boletín Oficial de la República Argentina, 16 de octubre de 1950.

50 Adrián C. Rovero, *Historia de la Astronomía de altas energías en Argentina. En Historia de la Astronomía Argentina, Asociación Argentina de Astronomía, Book Series. AABS, Volume 2* (La Plata: Asociación Argentina de Astronomía, 2009), p.365.

51 José Antonio Balseiro, *Informe referente a la inspección realizada en la isla Huemul en setiembre de 1952.* Buenos Aires, Comisión Nacional de Energía Atómica, 1988. (Informe CNEA, 493) Energía Nuclear; Historia; Argentina; 621.039(091)(82) Buenos Aires, Argentina. 1988.

52 Edward A. Morrow, 'Peron's Atom Dream Fades; Director reported arrested: Argentine dream on Atom Explodes', *New York Times*, 5 December 1952.

Chapter 4

1 Walton S. Moody, Jacob Neufeld and R. Cargill Hall, *The Emergence of the Strategic Air Command. A Winged Shield, Winged Sword: A History of the United States Air Force.* (Washington, DC: Air Force History and Museums Program, 1997).

2 J. Robert Oppenheimer, 'Atomic Weapons and American Policy', *Foreign Affairs*, 31: 4 (1953).

3 Kai Bird and Martin J. Sherwin, *American Prometheus: The Triumph and Tragedy of J. Robert Oppenheimer.* (New York: Knopf Publishing, 2005).

4 Richard G. Hewlett and Francis Duncan, *Atomic Shield: A History of the United States Atomic Energy Commission* (Berkeley, University of California Press, 1990).

5 John C. Bugher to Brig, Gen. K.B. Fields, "Task Group GABRIEL". 9 March 1953, NARA College Park, AEC, Division of Biology and Medicine, Project Sunshine, RG 326.73, Box 1.

6 John M. Fowler (ed.), *Fallout: A Study of Superbombs, Strontium-90 and Survival* (New York: Basic Books, 1960).

7 Willard Libby, *Worldwide Effects of Nuclear Weapons: Project Sunshine* (Santa Moniva: The Rand Corporation, 1953).

8 'Soviet Hydrogen Bomb', *Atomic Heritage Foundation*, https://www.atomicheritage.org/history/soviet-hydrogen-bomb-program, accessed 12 September 2021.

9 David Holloway, *Stalin and the Bomb: The Soviet Union and Nuclear Energy, 1939-1956* (New Haven: Yale University Press, 1994).

10 Chris Pocock, *50 Years of the U-2: The Complete Illustrated History of the "Dragon Lady"* (Atgeln: Schiffer Military History, 2005).

11 Curtis Peebles, *Shadow Flights: America's Secret Air War against the Soviet Union* (Novata: Presidio Press, 2000).

12 Gregory W. Pedlow and Donald E. Walzenbach, *The CIA and the U-2 Program, 1954-1974.* (Langley: CIA Center for the Study of Intelligence, 2004).

13 Ira Chernus, *Apocalypse Management: Eisenhower and the Discourse of National Insecurity*, (Stanford: Stanford University Press, 2008).

14 Campbell Craig, *Destroying the Village: Eisenhower and Thermonuclear War*, (New York: Columbia University Press, 1998).

15 Jack Broughton, *Rupert Red Two: A Fighter Pilot's Life From Thunderbolts to Thunderchiefs,* (Minneapolis: Zenith Press, 2007).

16 'Thunderbirds History', *Aerobatic Teams,* https://aerobaticteams.net/en/resources/i225/Thunderbirds-History.html, accessed October 2021.

17 'Llegó ayer la embajada aérea enviada por Estados Unidos', *Diario La Nación*, 29 January 1954.

18 'Deployments of USS Franklin D. Roosevelt', *Unofficial US Navy Site,* https://www.navysite.de/cvn/cv42deploy.htm, accessed 12 September 2021.

19 'Alas para las Américas', *Revista Nacional de Aeronáutica*, 14:143 (1954).

20 'Fue un alarde de audacia y de pericia la exhibición de los aviadores de la Unión', *Diario La Nación*, 29 January 1954.

21 Leandro Ariel Morgenfeld, 'El inicio de la Guerra Fría y el sistema interamericano. Argentina frente a Estados Unidos en la Conferencia de Caracas (1954) Contemporánea, Historia y problemas del Siglo XX*, 1:1 (2010).

22 Theo R. Diltz, *Air Force of Argentina, its strategic value in defense of Western Hemisphere*, (Maxwell AFB: US Air Force Research Agency, 1949).

23 Paul Boyer, *Fallout: A Historian Reflects on America's Half-Century Encounter with Nuclear Weapons*, (Columbus: Ohio State University Press, 1998).

24 Matashichi Oishi, *The fisherman, Grappling with the Bomb, Britain's Pacific H-bomb tests*, (Elmira: MacLellan Press, 2017), pp.55–68.

25 Richard Rhodes, *Dark Sun: The Making of the Hydrogen Bomb*, (New York: Simon & Schuster, 1995).

26 Patricia J. McMillan, *The Ruin of J. Robert Oppenheimer and the Birth of the Modern Arms Race.* (New York: Viking, 2005).

27 David Alan Rosenberg, *Origins of Overkill: Nuclear Weapons and Nuclear Strategy. In The National Security: Its Theory and Practice, 1945-1960*, (New York: Oxford University Press, 1986).

28 Brian Clegg, Armageddon Science: The Science of Mass Destruction, (New York: St. Martins Griffin, 2010).

Chapter 5

1 Michael S. Goodman, *Spying on the Nuclear Bear: Anglo-American Intelligence and the Soviet Bomb*, (Stanford: Stanford University Press, 2007).

2 David A. Fulghum, 'USAF Reconnaissance Comes into Focus', *Aviation Week and Space Technology*, 24 July 2000.

3 Chris Adams, *Inside the Cold War: A Cold Warrior's Reflections*, (Maxwell AFB: Air University, 1999).

4 Charles A. Cabell, *A Man Of Intelligence: Memoirs Of War, Peace, and the CIA: the Memoirs of General Charles P. Cabell*, (Boulder: Impavide Publications, 1997).

5 Charles A. Ziegler and David Jacobson, *Spying without Spies: Origins of America's Secret Nuclear Surveillance System*, (Westport: Praeger, 1995).

6   Richard G. Hewlett and Jack M. Holl, *Atoms for Peace and War, 1953-1961: Eisenhower and the Atomic Energy Commission*, (Berkeley: University of California Press, 1989).

7   US Department of Energy, *Restricted Data Declassification Decisions, 1946 to the Present* (RDD-8) (Germantown, USDOE, Office of Health, Safety and Security, 2002).

8   For details, see Sapienza, Antonio Luis, *Revolución Libertadora, Volume 1: the 1955 Coup d'état in Argentina* (Warwick: Helion & Co., 2022) and Sapienza, Antonio Luis, *Revolución Libertadora, Volume 2: the 1955 Coup that overthrew President Perón* (Warwick: Helion & Co., 2023)

9   Decreto N° 6/56, Boletín Aeronáutico Público N°1257.

10 Decreto N° 3595/56, Boletín Aeronáutico Público N°1353.

11 República Argentina, *Ministerio de Aeronáutica, Boletín Aeronáutico Público N°1368*. (Buenos Aires: 11 June 1957).

12 United States of America Embassy, Buenos Aires, Argentina. Letter N° 28 dirigida por el embajador Willard L. Beaulac al ministro de Relaciones Exteriores y Culto de la República Argentina, Dr. Luis A. Podestá Costa. Buenos Aires, Argentina, 3 de octubre de 1956. Archivo del Ministerio de Relaciones Exteriores y Culto, BILPAI 2115.

13 República Argentina, Ministerio de Relaciones Exteriores y Culto. Nota D.A.N N°187 dirigida por el ministro de Relaciones Exteriores y Culto, Dr. Luis A. Podestá Costa al embajador de los Estados Unidos de América en Buenos Aires, Willard L. Beaulac. Buenos Aires, Argentina, 3 de octubre de 1956. Archivo del Ministerio de Relaciones Exteriores y Culto, BILPAI 2115.

14 United States of America, Department of State, *Press release: For the Press, N° 519*, October 3, 1956, https://tinyurl.com/5yz5zh4b, accessed 17 February 2021.

15 United States of America Embassy, Buenos Aires, Argentina. Letter N°26 dirigida por el embajador Willard L. Beaulac al ministro de Relaciones Exteriores y Culto de la República Argentina, Dr. Luis A. Podestá Costa. Buenos Aires, Argentina, 16 de octubre de 1956. Archivo del Ministerio de Relaciones Exteriores y Culto, BILPAI 2121.

16 República Argentina, Ministerio de Relaciones Exteriores y Culto. Nota D.A.N.C. N°2085 dirigida por el Ministro de Relaciones Exteriores y Culto, Dr. Luis A. Podestá Costa al Embajador de los Estados Unidos de América en Buenos Aires, Willard L. Beaulac. Buenos Aires, Argentina, 16 de octubre de 1956. Archivo del Ministerio de Relaciones Exteriores y Culto, BILPAI 2121.

17 Ministerio de Aeronáutica, *Parte de Prensa*. Buenos Aires, Argentina, 18 October 1956.

18 US Centers for Disease Control and National Cancer Institute, *Report on the Health Consequences to the American Population from Nuclear Weapons Tests Conducted by the United States and Other Nations* (Washington DC: USGPO, 2001). http://www.cdc.gov/nceh/radiation/fallout/, accessed 15 October 2022.

19 US Air Force, Air Force Technical Applications Center. *A Fifty Year History of Long Range Detection, The Creation, Development, and Operation of the United States Atomic Energy Detection System* (Patrick Air Force Base: AFTAC, 19970.

20 National Academies of Science, *Committee to Review the CDC-NCI Feasibility Study of the Health Consequences from Nuclear Weapons Tests, National Research Council. Exposure of the American Population to Radioactive Fallout from Nuclear Weapons Tests: A Review of the CDC-NCI Draft Report on a Feasibility Study of the Health Consequences to the American Population from Nuclear Weapons Tests Conducted by the United States and Other Nations* (Washington DC: The National Academies Press, 2003). http://www.nap.edu/catalog/10621/exposure-of-the-american-population-to- radioactive-fallout-from-nuclear-weapons-tests, accessed 15 October 2022.

21 William B. Scott, 'Debris Collection Reverts to Ground Sites', *Aviation Week & Space Technology*, 3 November 1997.

22 John F. Fuller, *Thor's Legions: Weather Support to the U.S. Air Force and Army, 1937-1987* (Boston: American Meteorological Society,1990).

23 Jeffrey T. Richelson, *American Espionage and the Soviet Target*. (New York: William Morrow, 1987).

24 Walter J. Boyne, 'The Early Overflights', *Air Force*, 84:6 (2001).

25 Bernard Nalty, *The Air Force and Nuclear Testing, 1958-1964* (Washington DC: USAF Historical Division Liaison Office, 1965).

26 Leland Taylor, *History of Air Force Atomic Cloud Sampling* (Kirtland AFB: Historical Division, Office of Information, Air Force Special Weapons Center, 1963).

27 William B. Scott, 'Sampling Mission Unveiled Nuclear Weapon Secrets', *Aviation Week & Space Technology*, 3 November 1997.

28 Ralph Lapp, 'Sunshine and Darkness', *Bulletin of the Atomic Scientist*, 15:27-29 (1959).

29 Warren E. Leary, 'In 1950's U.S. collected human tissue to monitor atomic tests', *New York Times*, 21 June 1995.

Chapter 6

1   Peter W. Merlin, *Unlimited horizons: design and development of the U-2* (Washington DC: National Aeronautics and Space Administration, 2015).

2   Richard M. Bissell, Jr., *Memorandum for Deputy Project director, Arrangements with NACA and Kelly Johnson Release of U-2 Photographs*, SAPC-12313, CIA-RDP33- 02415A000200390023-1, 26 January 1957. Declassified and released by the CIA, Washington, DC, United States of America, 11 April 2000.

3   Thomas L. Coleman and Emilie C. Coe, *Airplane Measurements of Atmospheric Turbulence for Altitudes Between 20,000 and 50,000 Feet Over the Western Part of the United States*, NACA Research Memorandum L57G02 (Washington DC: NACA, 1957).

4   Zaur Eylanbekov, 'Project Acquatone', *Air Force Magazine*, July 2010.

5   David Reade, 'U-2 Spyplanes: What you didn't know about them!', *Roadrunners Internationale*,. http://roadrunnersinternationale.com/u-2/u_2_science_2.html,accessed 14 February 2021.

6   United States Department of Energy, *United States Nuclear Tests: July 1945 through September 1992 (DOE / NV-209 REV15)* (Las Vegas: Department of Energy, 2000).

7   P.S. Harris, C. Lowery, and A. Nelson, *Plumbbob Series, 1957 Final*, Defense Nuclear Agency, DNA6005F. (Washington DC: Defense Nuclear Agency, 1981).

8   Robert Standish Norris and Thomas B, Cochran, *United States nuclear tests, July 1945 to 31 December 1992. Nuclear Weapons Databook Working Paper (NWD 94-1)* (Washington DC: Natural Resources Defense Council, 1994).

9   Chuck Hansen, *The Swords of Armageddon, Vol. 8.* (Sunnyvale: Chukelea Publications, 1995).

10 Bill Gunston, *Illustrated Encyclopedia of the World's Rockets & Missiles* (London: Salamander Books, 1979).

11 James N. Gibson, *Nuclear Weapons of the United States, An Illustrated History* (Atglen: Schiffer Publishing, 1996).

12 Jacob Neufeld, *The development of ballistic missiles in the United States Air Force 1945–1960* (Collingdale: DIANE Publishing, 1990).

13 The Organising Commission of the XII Aeronautical Week was made up of the National Director of Civil Aviation, Brigadier Major Carlos García Cuerva (president); Vice Commodore (RA) Enrique Maranesi (vice president);. Mario Clos (general secretary) and Commander Abel Federico Martínez, Captain Arturo Gustavo Massa, First Lieutenant Antonio Santos Casa and Horacio Julio Prechi (members).

14 'Semana Aeronáutica', *Revista Nacional de Aeronáutica*, October 1957, p.59.

15 Tom Hildreth, 'Chronology of the 4050th Air Refueling Wing (AREFWG). Westover AFB, Massachusetts October 1955-April 1957', *Tom's Picture Pages*, http://www.tomhildrethphotos.com/AIRCRAFT/UNITS/4050ARW/4050_AREFWG_5557.html, accessed 14 August 2022.

16 'En las vísperas. Toda mi vida fui bombardero, pero respeto a los cazas' *Revista Nacional de Aeronáutica*. December 1957, p.25.

17 '93rd Bombardment Wing', *Strategic-Air-Command.com*, http://www.strategic-air-command.com/wings/0093bw.htm, accessed 25 December 2021.

18 United States Air Force, Historical Research Agency, *306 Bombardment (Medium) Wing participated in Operation Long Legs, 1-30 November 1957*. IRISNUM 004547. Maxwell AFB, Alabama, United States of America. Unclassified.

19 'Acrobacia aérea y Mach 1', *Revista Nacional de Aeronáutica*, December 1957, p.34.

20 Speckled Trout Membership Association. *Project Speckled Trout*. http://www.projectspeckledtrout.com/about.htm, accessed 17 January 2021.

21 'Buenos Aires–Washington en 11 horas 7 minutos', *Revista Nacional de Aeronáutica*, December 1957, p.38.

22 J.C. Hopkins, *The Development of Strategic Air Command, 1946-1976* (Washington DC: United States Air Force, Office of the Historian, 1976).

23 Erin McClellan, 'Retired crew chief reminisces about 60 years of KC-135 airpower',McConnell Air Force Base, https://www.mcconnell. af.mil/News/Features/Display/Article/931914/retired-crew-chief-reminisces-about-60-years-of-kc-135-airpower/, accessed 25 December 2021.

24 Melvin N. Ledbetter and Colin Bakse, *Airlift Tanker: History of U.S. Airlift and Tanker Forces* (Paducah: Turner Publishing Company, 1995), p.60.

25 Norman Polmar, *Strategic Air Command: People, Aircraft, and Missiles* (Mount Pleasant: Nautical and Aviation Publishing Company of America, 1979).

26 United States Air Force, Historical Research Agency. 93 *Bombardment (Heavy) KC-135 aircraft supported Operation Long Legs flight of B-52, 1-30 november 1957*. IRISNUM 00452720. Maxwell AFB, Alabama, United States of America. Unclassified.

27 'Acorazados del aire sobre la Ciudad', *Revista Nacional de Aeronáutica* December 1957, p.45.

28 Alberto Pollini, Mail addressed to Grupo Aviación Argentina, April 13, 2006. Pollini refers to having witnessed the passage of Boeing B-52s over Buenos Aires, being refueled in flight by Boeing KC-97 tankers.

29 The transport of active nuclear bombs during training flights would only come to light years later due to two accidents that caused the destruction of two B-52s. The first took place on 23 June 1961 in Goldsboro, North Carolina, and nearly detonated at least one of the two 3-4 megaton Mark 39 bombs on board the plane. The second took place on 17 January 1965 over Palomares (Almería, Spain) when a B-52 collided in flight with the KC-135 tanker that was refueling it. Both aircraft were lost. The four Mark 28 thermonuclear bombs of 1.5 megatons each did not explode and could be recovered.

Chapter 7

1 Lloyd R. Leavitt, *Following the Flag. An Air Force officer provides an eyewitness view of major events and policies during the Cold War* (Maxwell AFB: Air University Press, 2010).

2 Secretaría de Aeronáutica, Parte de Prensa N°204. Buenos Aires, Argentina, 18 July 1958, Dirección de Estudios Históricos de la Fuerza Aérea Argentina (DEF-FAA).

3 Secretaría de Aeronáutica, Parte de Prensa N°205. Buenos Aires, Argentina, 18 July 1958, Dirección de Estudios Históricos de la Fuerza Aérea Argentina (DEF-FAA).

4 United States Air Force, Historical Research Agency, *Strategic Reconnaissance Wing. Operation Crowflight, 1 August 1958-30 September 1959. IRISNUM 00460405*, (Maxwell AFB,).

5 *U-2 Timeline of events, 1950´s*. https://www.blackbirds.net/u2/u2-timeline/u2tl50.html, accessed 24 January 2021.

6 Lloyd R. Leavitt, *Following the Flag. An Air Force officer provides an eyewitness view of major events and policies during the Cold War* (Maxwell AFB: Air University Press, 2010), p.192.

7 Andreas Gehrs-Pahl, 'Corrected and completed list of all U-2 and SR-71 units, their bases, OLs and Dets. (Last update January 11, 1995)', http://www.ais.org/~schnars/aero/ol-det.htm, accessed 14 January 2021.

8 Lloyd R. Leavitt, *Following the Flag. An Air Force officer provides an eyewitness view of major events and policies during the Cold War* (Maxwell AFB: Air University Press, 2010).

9 Defence Atomic Support Agency, *U-2 Operations. Special Report on the High Altitude Sampling Program (HASP)* (Washington DC: Defense Atomic Support Agency, 1959).

10 Richard Gould Woodhull, *Flying High. Memoir of a Thirty Year Adventure* (Bloomington: Xlibris, 2013).

11 Lorna Arnold, and Katherine Pyne, *Britain and the H-bomb* (Basingstoke: Houndmills, 2001).

12 Kenneth Hubbard and Michael Simmons, *Dropping Britain's First H-bomb: The Story of Operation Grapple 1957/58* (Barnsley: Pen and Sword Aviation, 2008).

13 Herman Hoerlin, *United States High-Altitude Test Experiences: A Review Emphasizing the Impact on the Environment* (LA-6405) (Los Álamos Scientific Laboratory: October 1976).

14 *Operation Hardtack Preliminary Report* (ITR-1660- (SAN), ADA369152). Defense Atomic Support Agency, United States of America, September 23, 1959.

15 *Operation HARDTACK, Technical Summary of Military Effects Programs 1 – 9*, Sanitized Version (Technical Report). Defense Atomic Support Agency. United States of America, September 23, 1959.

16 United States Air Force, Historical Research Agency, *4080 Strategic Reconnaissance Wing. Details Project Crow Flight and Operation Hard Tack. Detachment 4 discontinued a Plattsburg AFB NY and Detachment 6 organized at Ezeiza Airport, Buenos Aires, Argentina, 1 June 1958 -30 june 1958*. IRISNUM 00460403. Maxwell AFB, Alabama.

17 *Nuclear explosions in the USSR: The North Test Site reference material, version 4- (Technical report)*. IAEA Deptartment of Nuclear Safety and Security. United Nations, New York, United States of America, 2004.

18 Sarov, *USSR Nuclear Weapons Tests and Peaceful Nuclear Explosions 1949 through 1990*. RFNC-VNIIEF, Russia, 1996.

19 Lisa Mundey, 'The Civilianization of a Nuclear Weapons Effects Test: Operation ARGUS', *Historical Studies in the Natural Sciences*, 42 (2012).

20 US Department of Defense, Defense Nuclear Agency, *Operation ARGUS, 1958. Department of Defense Documents: 1–143, 1958*. SBM-85165-062-1, 1996

21 Nicholas C. Christophilos, 'The Argus Experiment', *Proceedings of the National Academy of Sciences*, 15 August 1959.

22 James A. Van Allen, Carl F. McIlwain and George H. Ludwig, 'Satellite observations of electrons artificially injected into the geomagnetic field', *Proceedings of the National Academy of Sciences*, 15 August 1959.

23 Lloyd R. Leavitt, *Following the Flag. An Air Force officer provides an eyewitness view of major events and policies during the Cold War* (Maxwell AFB: Air University Press, 2010).

24 James P. Friend, Herbert W. Feely , Philip W. Krey, Jerome Spar and Alan Walton, *The High Altitude Sampling Program. Volume 2A, Results of Filter Analyses (Less Table 4.3 and Flight Cross-Sections). The Final Report on Contract DA-29-044-XZ-609 prepared for Defense Atomic Support Agency* (Westwood: Defense Atomic Support Agency, 1961).

25 James P. Friend, Herbert W. Feely , Philip W. Krey, Jerome Spar and Alan Walton, *The High Altitude Sampling Program. Volume 2A, Results of Filter Analyses (Less Table 4.3 and Flight Cross-Sections). The Final Report on Contract DA-29-044-XZ-609 prepared for Defense Atomic Support Agency* (Westwood: Defense Atomic Support Agency, 1961).

26 Jay Miller,. *Lockheed Martin's Skunk Works* (Arlington: Aerofax, 1993), p.88.

27 Morley Naylor, *Spy plane down*. Cottage North magazine. www. cottagenorthmagazine.ca. https://docplayer.net/46185626-Morley-g-naylor-emergency-landing-on-a-lake-near-laronge-50-years-ago-march-15-1960.html, accessed 2 May 2021.

28 'Operación "Crowflight"', *Revista Nacional Aeronáutica y Espacial*, December 1958, pp.23-24.

29 'El establecimiento norteamericano en Ezeiza', *Azul y Blanco*, 17 February 1959. Clipping sent by Pablo Luciano Potenze to Gustavo Marón in an email dated July 12, 2020

30 María Valeria Galván, *Publicaciones periódicas nacionalistas de derecha: Las tres etapas de Azul y Blanco*. Thesis presented for the degree of Doctor of History. Supervisor: Daniel Lvovich. National University of La Plata, Faculty of Humanities and Education Sciences, Academic Report. Buenos Aires, Argentina, February 2012.

31 Juan Carlos Murguizur, 'Derivaciones de la Operación Crowflight. La Corriente de Chorro austral y los problemas que suscita', *Revista Nacional Aeronáutica y Espacial*, May 1959, pp.14-15.

32 'Ezeiza: ¿qué hacen allí los americanos?', *Revista de Aviación*, 2:1 (May 1959).

33 'La Base Aérea de EE.UU. en Ezeiza', *Diario Córdoba*, 18 March 1959.

34 Lloyd R. Leavitt, *Following the Flag. An Air Force officer provides an eyewitness view of major events and policies during the Cold War* (Maxwell AFB: Air University Press, 2010).

35 *Revista Nacional Aeronáutica y Espacial*, March 1959, pp.24-26.

36 Fuerza Aérea Argentina, *Libro Histórico de la VI Brigada Aérea* (Buenos Aires: Tandil, 1959).

37 República Argentina, Ministerio de Aeronáutica. *Boletín Aeronáutico Público N°1459*, 1 September 1959.

38 *Revista Nacional Aeronáutica y Espacial*, August 1959, p.12.

39 Albert K. Stebbins III, *HASP Special Report on the High Altitude Sampling Program* (Washington DC: Defense Atomic Support Agency, 1961).

40 Mary Welch, M *AFTAC celebrates 50 years of Long Range Detection* (Washington DC: Air Force Technical Applications Center, 1997).

41 Pablo Luciano Potenze, 'Batallas aéreas de la Guerra Fría libradas en la Argentina', *Gaceta Aeronáutica*, https://www.gacetaeronautica.com/gaceta/wp-101/?p=2027, accessed 25 December 2021.

ABOUT THE AUTHOR

Gustavo Maron was born in Mendoza, Argentina, in 1971 into a family of Lebanese immigrants. In 1998 he graduated as a lawyer from the Law School of the National University of Cuyo. Since then, he has worked as an adviser to various associations, factories, workshops, companies and aeronautical organisations. In parallel, Gustavo is a professor of Aeronautical Law at four Argentine universities. He has published more than 200 investigations and has given more than 100 conferences on different topics related mainly to the Argentine Civil Aviation. He actively collaborates with the Argentine Association of Space Technology and the Mars Society Argentina. He is founder and partner of the aerospace consultancy MACK Aerospace Consulting SRL.

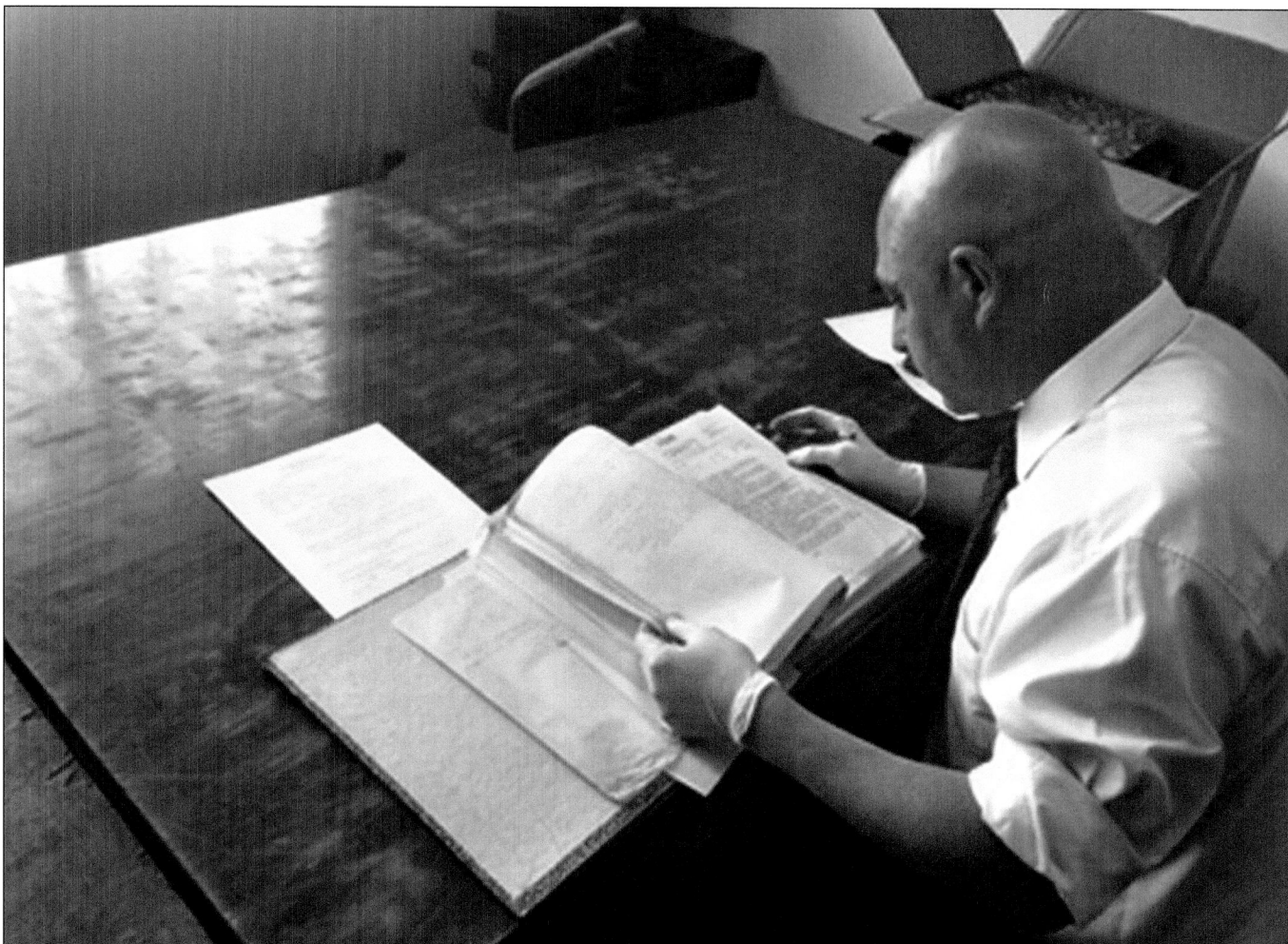